D1325664

Theatrical
LONDON

First published 2006
by Historical Publications Ltd
32 Ellington Street, London N7 8PL
(Tel: 020 7607 1628)

ISBN 1-905286-14-7
British Library Cataloguing-in-Publication Data
A catalogue record for this book is available from the British Library

Reproduction by Liz Morrell and Paddy Donnelly
Printed in Zaragoza, Spain by Edelvives

The Illustrations

The following kindly gave permission to reproduce illustrations:
London Borough of Camden, Local Studies & Archives: 169
Roger Cline: 42, 46, 47, 50, 63, 65, 68, 70, 87, 90, 91, 97, 129, 146, 148, 152
John Haynes: johnhaynesphotography.com: 195, 196
Bridget Jones: 203
Kingston Museum and Heritage Service: 177
Richard Tames: 2, 10, 15, 45, 85, 92, 93, 163, 165, 190, 197, 198, 201, 202, 204, 205, 206, 207
Other illustrations were supplied by the Publisher

Theatrical
LONDON

Richard Tames

HISTORICAL PUBLICATIONS

Contents

Introduction

For the world of English-speaking theatre London has always been 'Headquarters'. To make that claim is not to deny the historical significance of the cycles of 'mystery plays' associated with Coventry, Chester or York, to minimise the vigour of theatrical tradition in such cities as Bristol, Birmingham, Manchester, Liverpool or Glasgow, or to underestimate the role played by touring companies associated with such luminaries as Ben Greet, Sir Frank Benson or Sir Donald Wolfit. Rather it is to recognize that it was in London that the first purpose-built theatres in the English-speaking world were erected and in the capital of England that, as Sir Roy Strong has reminded us, "... something ... occurred which had no parallel in the rest of Europe, the emergence of a popular theatre with a repertory of plays as much in demand at court as they were with the young London apprentices." Shakespeare became the heart of that repertory; and Shakespeare, to our present knowledge, never wrote a line before he came to London or after he left it.

Fittingly, the hand-wrought gates to the reconstructed Globe Theatre proclaim through their emblematic incorporation of such devices as a mask from the Japanese *Noh* drama that Shakespeare was not just, as Ben Jonson finely said, for all time, but for the world. Two centuries after his death Shakespeare could still inspire Verdi to base an opera on one of his most unforgettable characters, move Victor Hugo to write his biography and be translated into Polish (1840), Gujarati (1850) and Hebrew (1874). Three and a half centuries after his death the President of Tanzania was translating him into Swahili – and American actor-director Sam Wanamaker took on his personal crusade to re-establish Shakespeare's own theatre where it had once stood, almost.

That London should have given birth to theatre as a permanent institution, rather than a (literally) passing show, was perhaps the almost inevitable outcome of its being the capital, in terms of both court and commerce, as well as the richest, most populous, most literate and most demographically diverse of all the nation's cities, with the largest concentration of potential playgoers with the taste, time and cash to devote to their diversion. London had, moreover, a quasi-theatrical life before theatre, providing the setting for pageants, processions, fairs and executions on a scale and with a frequency unrivalled elsewhere. Clerkenwell takes its name from the supernumary clerics who enacted plays there on 'holydays'. Had the monarchy chosen to locate its court at some English equivalent of Versailles or had the ancient universities chosen to adopt a less punitive attitude to the drama as an activity, rather than as a source of texts for study, the English theatre might have developed differently. But it didn't. And, *pace* the claims of the birthplace of the Bard – and its undeniable centrality (if not its accessibility) where else but in London could a National Theatre be?

For the first century of their existence in any recognizably modern, secular form, theatres were only to be found in the capital, although English actors were frequently to be seen in the provinces and, already by Shakespeare's day, as far away as Germany where they established a distinctive and lucrative niche market for themselves. Even in London, however, the permanence of theatre was regularly threatened by the hostility of the City Fathers, the capriciousness of courtly patronage and the recurrence of outbreaks of epidemic disease necessitating months, occasionally even years, of closure, not to mention those other recurrent curses of the theatrical profession, fire and financial impropriety. Following almost two decades of closure during and after the civil wars of the mid-seventeenth century London theatre had to be virtually re-invented. Then, after little more than half a century of efflorescence, it succumbed to the deadening hand of a censorship which was to last, technically at least, until 1968 – though circumventing that censorship did give birth to new forms and venues for dramatic experimentation.

London's place in the theatrical history of the English-speaking world derives only in part from its standing as home to the largest concentration of theatrical venues, professional, amateur or educational. It is also, through the voices of Dryden, Addison and Hazlitt, the birthplace of the theatre critic, the reservoir of technical expertise in terms of costumiers, stage-designers, lighting crews and musicians and, since the days of the First Folio, the major centre for the printing, publication and sale of play scripts. For the past century London has also been home to the Royal Academy of Dramatic Art and other distinguished stage-schools, although academies for youthful aspirants to the stage, albeit often short-lived, can be found as far back as the seventeenth century.

Apart from being a breeding-ground for new generations of actors, London has also been a magnet for dramatic talent in all its forms, drawing J.M. Barrie from Scotland, Wilde and Shaw from Ireland, Emlyn Williams and Ivor Novello from Wales and the creators of *Beyond the Fringe* from Oxbridge. Not that the element of symbiosis can be denied, for example with Ireland in the eighteenth century. Congreve was born in Yorkshire but brought up in Ireland and attended Trinity College, Dublin, as did Nahum Tate, born in Dublin and George Farquhar, born in Londonderry. Doggett, Quin and Barton Booth all served their stage apprenticeships in Ireland and Garrick gained his first managerial experience there. For their nineteenth century successors the North American tour would play a similar role and not infrequently provide a much-needed financial lifeline. In the seventeenth century, the 'Golden Age' of Spanish drama, much was pilfered from the Spanish stage to sate a London taste for tales of honour and bloody revenge. In the eighteenth century a peculiarly London genre of 'bourgeois tragedy' made a great impact in Germany and France. In the nineteenth century the reworking of French farces and melodramas became a major source of material for the West End stage.

A further dimension of London's theatrical tradition consists in its representation of itself and its inhabitants on stage, from Falstaff's carousings in the Boar's Head tavern on Eastcheap to the brittle chit-chat of the inter-war drawing-room comedy. For most Restoration dramatists London was virtually the *only* plausible setting for dramatic interaction. Two centuries later the travails of London life would provide the staple fare for the Cockney 'patter songs' of the music-hall stage.

As a city rich in monuments and memorials London cannot be said to have acknowledged its theatrical heritage with particular liberality. Poets' Corner in Westminster Abbey, it is true, has maintained a tradition of tribute, stretching from Jonson and Dryden and Aphra Behn, through Garrick and Siddons, to Olivier, Ashcroft and Coward. Plaques of various types mark the former residences or theatres of over a hundred actors, dramatists, music hall artists and managers. Garrick, Shaw, Wyndham, Gielgud, Olivier, Coward and the drama teacher Jeanette Cochrane have theatres named after them. Shakespeare, Siddons, Irving and Wilde have full-length statues (although Wilde's incorporates his coffin) and Augustus Harris has a bust outside Drury Lane. Streets are named for Betterton, Booth, Kean, Kemble (2), Siddons (2) and Irving. Garrick, with five, shares top billing with Shakespeare, spelled variously, as he did; but that is not much of a haul from over four centuries of thespian endeavour. And, considering that there are some seven thousand pubs in and around the metropolis, the number which have drawn on the drama for their name doesn't even reach double digits. Neither oversight is beyond future remedy.

CHAPTER ONE

The Wooden 'O'

Capital Attraction

Under the rule of the Tudors (1485-1603) London quadrupled the size of its population, from around fifty thousand to over two hundred thousand, despite recurrent outbreaks of plague and other epidemic diseases. The growth of the metropolis rested on its ability to attract a constant annual inflow of migrants, both domestic and foreign. These incomers were predominantly young, optimistic, ambitious, adventurous, often naive, sometimes criminal. Many succumbed to the disease, accidents or casual violence for which the city was notorious. But there were always more to take their place. And they added to the city's restless buzz.

This expansion of population was eased by the dissolution of the religious houses which accompanied the reformation of religion, releasing the assets of more than a dozen great monastic establishments onto the London property market for demolition or conversion to other uses; in the case of the former Dominican house at Blackfriars, for theatrical uses. The City's enterprising commercial elite initiated the expansion of a global commerce with the invention of the joint-stock company, a risk-sharing device to unlock the potential of distant markets in Muscovy, the Levant and the East Indies. Symbolic of the City's new confidence was the construction of the Royal Exchange as a combination of bourse and shopping mall.

London was not only England's biggest port by far, it was also its most cosmopolitan city. Ambassadors and their entourages from France, Spain and the Venetian republic were in semi-permanent attendance on the monarch. Around the fringes of the court were Italian scholars, physicians and artists. Along the Thameside wharves were sailors from the Baltic and the Mediterranean. There were seamen who really had been shipwrecked off the coast of Illyria. An enclave of German merchants still concentrated at the Steelyard, off Cannon Street. There was a disinct community of Irish in Wapping. Some four thousand 'Doche' (i.e. Dutch, Flemish and Germans) were concentrated in the parish of St. Olave, Southwark. From 1550 onwards there was a growing intake of Huguenots, French Protestant refugees, most of them, like the Flemings, skilled and industrious craftsmen such as brewers, carvers, clockmakers, opticians, gunmakers and, especially, printers. It was an irony of English cultural history that the perfection and diffusion of the English language through the discipline of the printed page should owe such a debt to the skills of printers from Continental Europe.

In printing and publishing as in law, politics, medicine, commerce and the manufacture of luxuries London was pre-eminent. London's standing as a 'primate city', dominant over every other urban settlement, became indisputable. Whereas in 1500 it was roughly twice as large as such second rank cities as Bristol or Norwich, by 1600 it was six times bigger – and more than a hundred times bigger than the thriving Midlands market town where William Shakespeare passed his childhood and acquired his education. True, London had no university but in the four Inns of Court and their feeder institutions, the dozen Inns of Chancery, it had a student population to rival either of the ancient English seats of learning. Of these supposed students only a minority seriously intended a career as professional lawyers. Most were the offspring of the expanding gentry class, keen to polish their manners, extend their networks of friendship, enjoy what London had to offer, benefit from the best instructors in the polite arts of fencing, riding, dancing and music – and pick up a smattering of law, perhaps, along the way.

And then there was the Court, a mini-city in its own right, sprawling along Whitehall, housed in a rambling two-thousand room complex with state apartments facing onto the river and a leisure complex of tilt-yards, tennis-courts and cockpits facing onto St. James's Park and its subsidiary palace. Newly built by Henry VIII on the site of a former religious hospital, St. James's Palace was but one of fifty royal residences strung along either side of the Thames, from Greenwich, where the king had established the royal dockyards and armouries, to Richmond, Hampton Court and Windsor, where he could hunt, revel and entertain.

Staging Greatness
Spectacle was an essential servant of monarchy. As Sir John Fortescue argued in *The Governance of England* (1470), " it shall need that the king have such treasure ... for his pleasure and magnificence ... convenient to this estate royal ... for if a king did not so ... he lived then not like his estate...".

Even so cheese-paring a sovereign as Henry VII (reigned 1485-1509) knew not to stint on splendour – or at least the appearance of splendour. If much of the work of Tudor government consisted of unglamorous but essential paper-pushing, at which the king happened to excel, that was essentially a backstage activity of which most outside the administrative elite were but dimly aware. Royal routines for public consumption were, by contrast, occasions for display through costume and ritual. Henry VIII (reigned 1509-47), a huge man with an ego to match, revelled in the role of personifying majesty. Indeed, he was the first English ruler to require his subjects to address him as such. Processions, progresses and tournaments made the monarch the focal point of carefully orchestrated performances. Elaborate 'Disguisings', in which the king

himself might wear a mask and costume, were organised to greet the arrival of distinguished guests. Knightings, betrothals, marriages and coronations called for even more extravagant display, often accompanied by music and dances alluding to the myths and legends of medieval chivalry or classical antiquity. Added to these were the regular feasts and fasts required by the Christian calendar. And for many of these occasions London and its environs, from Greenwich to Hampton Court, provided the setting or back-drop.

In addition to royal pageantry there were, before the Reformation, elaborate religious processions on the occasions of the patron saints' days of the dozens of Livery Companies and, before its suppression by Edward VI in 1548, at Corpus Christi, too. Most splendiferous of all were the junketings which accompanied the swearing-in of a new Lord Mayor each October. The first written description of 'the Lord Mayor's Show' is in the diary for 1553 of undertaker Henry Machyn, who saw "the crafts of London in their best livery with trumpets blowing ..." and after the Lord Mayor himself more "trumpeters blowing, then came a devil and ... the pageant of St. John Baptist gorgeously with goodly speeches and then came all the King's trumpeters...".

Londoners, in other words, grew up knowing a good show when they saw one. Even before the theatre had been invented there was a theatrical dimension to their lives. Major cities like Chester, York, Coventry or Bristol also witnessed occasions of civic and religious pomp and, if they were near enough to the capital - say, Oxford - even the occasional royal visit. But in London the presence of royalty was more continuous, and its attendant apparatus of ritual and display exercised more frequently and on a larger scale.

Royal Revels
Henry VII, even though, unlike his ebullient son, he sought no reputation as scholar, athlete or musician, had his own company of players. As grand titles cost no extra they were known as the *Lusores Regis* (King's Players), although they

probably consisted, if not of the proverbial two men and a dog, then of four men and a boy, the latter, through a piping voice and androgynous appearance, to simulate females when required. A household official to organise royal entertainments, known as the Master of the Revels, was first appointed in 1494, although the office did not become permanent until the appointment of Sir Thomas Cawarden (1545-59), when the duties were formally extended to include censorship.

Under Henry VIII plays were performed in London and at Windsor by choirboys as the Children of the Chapel Royal. These largely took the form of 'morality' dialogues between characters representing good and evil, or embodying their manifestations as virtues or vices. Choristers also took part in disguisings. The choristers of newly-founded (1509) St. Paul's school are recorded as having recited a Latin play by Terence *(see below)* for the king's chief minister, Cardinal Wolsey, in 1528. Under the mid-century Master of the Chapel Children, Richard Edwards, spectators may have been admitted to watch rehearsals of courtly entertainments, for a consideration. These rehearsals were held in the paved hall of the former monastery at Blackfriars under the supervision of the Master of the Revels. From 1553 the Master of St. Paul's, Sebastian Westcott, appears to have systematically recruited boys for their ability to act as well as sing and they are recorded as having made over thirty Court appearances during his period of office (1553-82). In 1567-8 they presented no less than seven plays as part of the Christmas celebrations.

Noble families followed royal precedent to give their patronage and protection to players who would, without notional attachment to some great household, have been regarded as vagabonds, liable to whipping or branding as social parasites, a distinction clarified and confirmed by legislation in 1572. The Statute of Retainers of 1563 had affirmed that any youth not apprenticed was to be considered a vagabond. For this reason when acting companies came to be formally established later in the century the four or five boys attached to each of them was considered to be individually apprenticed to leading members of the company. The Statute of Retainers as re-issued in 1572 introduced restrictions on travelling players and an 'Acte for the Punishment of Vacabondes' of the same year required that actors wear a livery denoting their attachment to the household of distinction. The Tudor obsession with vagabondage ('Hark! Hark! the dogs do bark, The beggars are coming to town') reflected a continuing social panic arising from the impact of two forces both powerful but dimly understood - a surging growth in population and chronic inflation. These in turn were aggravated by the conversion of arable to less labour-intensive sheep-farming and the periodic discharge of soldiers and sailors from foreign wars, setting men on the roads in search of work or, if driven to it, less honest means of living.

Lord Leicester's Men, formed in 1559 under the aegis of Elizabeth I's favourite, Robert Dudley, Earl of Leicester (1532-88), numbered among its ranks both James Burbage (?1530-97), who would build the first true theatre, and Will Kempe (died ca. 1603), who would become the first actor to play Dogberry and Falstaff. Strange's Men, who took their name from Lord Strange, son of the Earl of Derby, were active in the provinces before their eventual appearance at Court in 1582 and also became actively involved in several London theatres over the following decade. Other companies were under the patronage of the Earls of Worcester, Oxford (who united with the Earl of Warwick's men in 1580), Lincoln (known by the family name of Clinton), Sussex and Pembroke. Aristocratic patronage conferred not only a degree of legal protection but might also help to secure an *entrée* to the Great Hall of a great man's residence. In no way, however, was it a guarantee of livelihood and still less did it provide the players with a permanent base. They might be *of* their patron's household but this did not imply they had any right to be *in* it.

Classical Models

The promotion of Greek and the recovery of secular Latin texts which constituted the 'New Learning' of the Renaissance gave educated English readers - including grammar school boys like William Shakespeare (1564-1616) and Ben Jonson (1572/3-1637) – access to the Roman comedies of Plautus (died 184 BC) and Terence (*fl* 184-159 BC). It is therefore no happenstance that the author of the earliest known English comedy *Ralph Roister Doister*, was a schoolmaster, Nicholas Udall (1505-56), who probably intended it to be performed by the boys of Eton or Westminster, at both of which schools he was sometime headmaster. Written some time between 1534 and 1552 the play was only printed *ca.* 1566, a decade after his death. *Gammer Gurton's Needle*, attributed to a Cambridge don, William Stevenson (died 1575) between 1552 and 1563, owes less to Roman models, being set solidly in an English village context. It, too, was probably first performed by schoolboys and was printed in 1575.

Gorboduc (1562), consciously modelled on the five-act tragedies of Seneca (died AD 65), was written for performance at the Inner Temple in the presence of Elizabeth I (reigned 1558-1603) as part of the celebrations of New Year's Day. The collaborative authors were Thomas Norton (1532-84) and Thomas Sackville (1536-1608), both members of that Inn. Like the comedies of Udall and Stevenson this early tragedy, a proto-Lear saga of a divided kingdom and fraternal strife, was written for private rather than public performance.

Seeking a Stage

The existence of public performance as early as the 1520s is, however, implied by the erection in Finsbury Fields of a permanent stage by John Rastell, son-in-law of Sir Thomas More, some time before 1526. It is known to have been still there a decade later. In 1567 what might be considered a proto-theatre, consisting of a ring of scaffolding for galleries, with a separate stage, known as the Red Lion, was put up in the East End suburb of Whitechapel at the expense of grocer John Brayne for the use of his brother-in-law, James Burbage. Its later fate is unknown.

Public performances by itinerant players were, however, usually staged in the yards of major inns, whose patrons would hopefully supply a ready-made audience to be supplemented from the surrounding streets. Landlords benefited from increased sales of drink and food but payment almost certainly depended on a collection taken from the onlookers. Wheedling coins out an impromptu audience was a key thespian skill, known as 'bottling'. Known venues included the Bell and the Cross Keys, both in Gracechurch (then Gracious) Street leading down to London Bridge, the Bull on Bishopsgate and the Belle Sauvage on Ludgate Hill. Outside the City proper were the Boar's Head at Whitechapel and the Saracen's Head in Islington.

In 1574 the City authorities gave permission for regular weekday performances of plays. James Burbage, trained in youth as a master carpenter, saw a business opportunity opening up and borrowed money from his brother-in-law to erect a permanent theatre. The site was just outside the City walls at Shoreditch, on a leased patch of land in the grounds of the former Holywell Priory. England's first purpose-built permanent public playhouse, known simply as The Theatre, opened in 1576. In the same year Richard Farrant (died 1580), Deputy Master of the Children of the Chapel Royal, established an indoor theatre in the royal rehearsals hall at Blackfriars monastery. There were therefore two models for theatrical performance – one outdoor and public, the other indoor and private.

By creating a fixed enclosure Burbage made it possible to achieve two important objects. The first and most essential was the ability to enforce admission charges. Players performing in the yard of an inn or in an open space like a market square could solicit but not compel payment from onlookers who were free to drift away as and when they chose. The second was a bonus in terms of performance, the ability to control or at least minimise extraneous noise from the immediate surroundings and thus greatly to improve audibility. Contemporary usage refers to an audience going to *hear* rather than *see* a play, so this benefit was highly significant and favoured the composition of elaborate speeches to complement stage action. Tudor culture was as much aural as visual. High-flying courtiers vied with their rivals to turn a verse, coin an epigram or make a recondite pun. Common folk got their news from town-criers, listened to open-air sermons at Paul's Cross and patronised street singers of ballads. A third bonus of acquiring a permanent base soon became apparent in the ability to accumulate a much larger wardrobe and collections of props and playbooks (scripts) than could be carted around by an itinerant company. Over time it would also prove possible to install machinery for stage-effects, such as trap-doors and overhead wires, which would likewise have been beyond the use of a travelling company relying on temporary stages.

Tiered galleries around the walls of The Theatre maximised the numbers who could be accommodated and also allowed for the maintenance of social distinctions between those who could afford to pay to be sheltered and seated and those 'groundlings' or 'understanders' who were content to stand in the actual arena. The groundlings paid one penny admission. Another penny was charged for access to the galleries and another for the hire of a stool. It is probable that the stage itself was simply a platform raised on trestles or barrels which could be easily and swiftly disassembled to allow the entire enclosed area within the theatre walls to be used for the baiting of bulls or bears, a brutal pastime initially even more appealing to the average Londoner – not excluding the Court – than attendance at a play. Behind the stage was a 'tiring house' where actors changed costumes and from which they made their entrances through two doors in its facade.

The proximity of actor and audience put a premium on stage presence. Given the absence of scenery and artificial lighting any sense of spectacle had to come largely from the voices and gestures of the actors themselves. The skills of the gymnast, fencer and musician were as valued as those of the rhetorician. In an age and a city obsessed with clothes and finery, costume was the other invaluable accompaniment to action and diction.

Theatres Denounced
By locating The Theatre immediately outside the City's walls Burbage made it readily accessible to the largest and wealthiest concentration of people in the kingdom, but beyond the authority of the City fathers. By the same token the indoor theatre at Blackfriars, being on former ecclesiastical property, enjoyed the protection of the Crown and as an acknowledged 'liberty' was likewise inviolate from other interference. While the Court and nobility and the young gentlemen idling their way through a year or two at the Inns of Court looked kindly on opportunities for being amused, the City's mercantile-administrative elite embodied the emerging Protestant work ethic and regarded playhouses as an unwelcome magnet for "light and lewd disposed persons", plays as a temptation to idleness for their 'prentices and players as potential carriers of the plague. In the same year that weekday plays were authorised the City's Court of Common Council made its hostile attitude to the theatre abundantly clear:

"Sundry great disorders and inconveniences have been found to ensue to this city by the inordinate haunting of great multitudes of people, especially youth, to plays, interludes and shows – namely, occasion of frays and quarrels; evil practices of incontinency in great inns having chambers and secret places adjoining to their open stages and galleries; inveigling and alluring of maids, especially orphans and good citizens' children under age, to privy and unmeet contracts; the publishing of unchaste, uncomely and unshamefast speeches and doings; withdrawing of the Queen's Majesty's subjects from divine service on Sundays and holidays, at which times such plays were chiefly used; unthrifty waste of the money of the poor and fond persons; sundry robberies by picking and cutting of purses; uttering of popular, busy and seditious matters; and many other corruptions of youth and other enormities - besides that also sundry slaughters and mayhemings of the queen's subjects have happened by ruins of scaffolds, frames and stages, and by engines, weapons and powder used in plays."

The year after the opening of The Theatre it had a neighbour and a rival in The Curtain. This doubling of temptation brought down on the theatres a ferocious written assault in John Northbrooke's *Treatise wherein Dicing, Dauncing, vain Playes or Enterludes ... are reproved* (1577). Almost certainly at the behest and with the financial support of the City elite the author laid into plays and players as shameless competitors with true religion:

"It hath stricken such a blind zeal into the hearts of the people that they shame not to say and affirm openly, that plays are as good as sermons and that they learn as much or more at a play than they do at God's word preached ... Many can tarry at a vain play two or three hours, whereas they will not abide scarce one hour at a sermon ...".

And what did the spectators learn? Northbrooke supplied his own comprehensive list:

"... how to be false and deceive your husbands, or husbands their wives, how to play the harlot, to obtain one's love, how to ravish, how to beguile, how to betray, to flatter, lie, swear, forswear, how to allure to whoredom, how to murder, how to poison, how to disobey and rebel against princes, to consume treasures prodigally, to move to lusts, to ransack and spoil cities and towns, to be idle, to blaspheme, to sing filthy songs of love, to speak filthily, to be proud, how to mock, scoff and deride any nation ...".

In 1578 Thomas White, preaching at the City's most prestigious outdoor venue, Paul's Cross, likewise denounced 'theatre houses' as "a continual monument of London's prodigality and folly". In his *Anatomie of Abuses* (1583) Philip Stubbes, having warned actors ("you masking players, you painted sepulchres, you double dealing ambodexters") that their inevitable end was the wrath of God, in warning playgoers likewise, provided unambiguous testimony of the popularity of playgoing:

"For so often as they go to those houses where players frequent, they go to Venus' palace and Satan's synagogue, to worship devils and betray Jesus Christ ... For proof whereof but mark the flocking and running to Theatres and Curtains, daily and hourly, night and day, time and tide, to see Plays and Interludes."

One might speculate that The Curtain's relative lack of success may have discouraged the building of further theatres in the same locality, so that over succeeding decades it was to be Southwark, rather than Shoreditch, which became London's main theatre quarter. There was certainly another theatre out in the village of Newington, beyond the south bank of the Thames, by 1580, although little more is known of it with certainty than the fact of its existence.

Court Patronage

Fortunately for dramatists The Master of the Revels, Sir Edmund Tilney (or Tylney), who served all the way through from 1570 until 1610, was more interested in the profits of his office than in its exercise. Licensing theatres brought him a respectable three pounds a month, reading new plays seven shillings per text. In theory the controller of London's theatrical life, in practice he was content to abdicate his powers of censorship unless gratuitously provoked. As Master of the Revels he was also responsible for the arrangement of court entertainments. The fixed budget he had for this, typically of Tudor bureaucratic practice, took no account of inflation. It was soon realised that the outlay required for the elaborate dance-dramas which would be developed under the succeeding Stuart

1. Lord Howard, patron of the Lord Admiral's Men and Commander of the English fleet that defeated the Spanish Armada in 1588.

2. A plaque in Southwark on the site of Bankside's first theatre. Its vestiges were discovered in 1989.

dynasty as 'masques' *(see p29)* amounted to four times the cost of bringing in a professional company of actors to put on a play. The economics were compelling and effectively guaranteed royal protection for companies capable of meeting court standards, whatever the antagonism of the City. Regular public performances of plays were, moreover, rationalised by interested parties as mere rehearsals of works which might be offered before the Queen. (Contrary to Dame Judi Dench's personal intervention in *Shakespeare in Love* Elizabeth I never entered a public theatre.)

In 1583 a Court company, Queen Elizabeth's Men, was constituted, probably recruiting some of the best of Leicester's Men. Its leading player, Richard Tarleton (died 1588), who had probably been one of them, was generally held to be the outstanding comedian of his time and possibly the model for Shakespeare's Yorick. The known author of several plays, an accomplished musician and 'Master of Fence', Tarleton was mainly celebrated for his extempore clowning and jigs, the clowned playlets performed as an afterpiece to a main work. Robert Wilson (died 1600) was another Leicester turncoat and also an extemporizer and dramatist. The remnants of Leicester's Men dispersed on his death in 1588. The Queen's Men had disbanded by 1594.

The Admiral's Men

In 1585 Lord Howard of Effingham (?1536-1624) was created Lord High Admiral and in the same year a company under his patronage first appeared at Court. The moving spirits were the entrepreneurial and none-too-scrupulous Philip Henslowe (?1550-1616), his future step-son-in-law Edward Alleyn (1566-1626) and a recent Cambridge graduate Christopher Marlowe (1564-93).

In 1587 Henslowe, at a cost of some eight hundred pounds, built the Rose theatre on Bankside in Southwark, another area outside the City's jurisdiction. In that same year Marlowe produced the first part of *Tamburlaine the Great*, whose towering hero Alleyn portrayed on stage. The precise chronology of Marlowe's other major stage works, *The Jew of Malta, Edward II* and *Doctor Faustus*, is uncertain, as is the nature of his work as a government agent and the cause of his murder in an apparent tavern quarrel in Deptford. What is certain, apart from the

3. Christopher Marlowe, a supposed portrait, aged 21, found at his college, Corpus Christi. Marlowe's enigmatic motto (top left) was 'Quod me nutrit me destruit' – 'what nourishes me, destroys me'.

excellence of his classical education and his wayward genius in conjuring fatally flawed protagonists, is that he was criminally violent, a blasphemer and atheist, probably homosexual and greatly admired by other dramatists, even by jobbing wordsmiths like Shakespeare and Jonson, who were despised by the circle of 'University Wits', of which Marlowe was the foremost representative. Three centuries after Marlowe's death, Henry Irving *(see p159)* unveiled a statue of the playwright at Canterbury, where Marlowe had been to school, and declared, " It was Marlowe who first captured the majestic rhythms of our tongue and whose 'mighty line' is the most resounding note in England's literature." Swinburne concurred, hailing Marlowe as "the greatest discoverer, the most daring and intrepid pioneer in all our poetic literature. Before him was neither genuine blank verse nor genuine tragedy in out language. After his arrival the way was prepared, the paths were made straight, for Shakespeare."

Following Marlowe's death Henslowe made much use of the debt-ridden Thomas Dekker (?1570-1632), who in 1598 alone, had at least a hand in some sixteen plays. These still failed to keep him out of prison for debt in 1599, the year in which his undoubted masterpiece, *The Shoemaker's Holiday*, was staged. Crafted by a Londoner for Londoners, its vivid delineations of London tradesmen established a distinctive new genre of citizen comedy.

Henslowe's somewhat chaotic accounts and memoranda, preserved by Alleyn and rather misleadingly known as his 'Diaries', are an invaluable source for understanding the practicalities of contemporary theatrical life. Plays were mounted six afternoons a week and, weather permitting in theatres open to the sky, for up to forty weeks a year. Plague was another recurrent hazard to the playing calendar, forcing closures whenever the number of deaths exceeded forty per week. Even in the new, sturdily Protestant era of Elizabeth plays were also forbidden in Lent.

Travelling companies needed only a limited repertory of as little as two or three plays because, having presented them, they would be moving on to present them to new audiences in the next town or great lord's hall. A company with a permanent base, by contrast, had to keep changing its programme of offerings to maintain its appeal when drawing its audience in a fixed catchment area. Over the course of a year a company might expect to mount between thirty and forty plays, half of them new ones. Actors were expected to play double parts. Given the expected ability to double none of Shakespeare's plays required more than a dozen men and four boys. This meant that London-based actors were expected to carry in their heads at least thirty or forty parts, a leading part consisting of perhaps eight hundred lines and twenty cued entrances and exits. Compared to such metropolitan pressure provincial touring was a holiday.

The going rate for a play seems to have been six pounds, upon payment of which ownership passed from the author to the company. While six pounds might seem a goodly sum when weighed against the penny entrance fee paid by a groundling or the nine pounds which were the average week's takings at the Rose, it does not seem to have been sufficient to keep many dramatists from semi-permanent debt. Henslowe, whose business interests ranged from mining to the manufacture of starch, also developed a useful sideline in money-lending, using his dramatists' and actors' debts to keep them in line. He also imposed fines for arriving late or drunk.

The Lord Chamberlain's Men

Shakespeare's biography from 1585 to 1592, from when he left his birthplace to when he is first recorded as being in London, is virtually a blank. He may have been a schoolmaster. He may have even been a soldier. Most likely he was a travelling actor. But by 1592 he was sufficiently well known in London for fellow-dramatist Robert Greene (died 1592) to berate him in his death-bed confession as "an upstart crow". That year and the following one were particularly difficult as appalling weather caused successive harvest failures, bringing misery to the countryside. London was, additionally, ravaged by plague, forcing the closure of its theatres until 1594. When they did reopen, as a concession to the Lord Mayor and Aldermen, who continued to take a dim view of plays and players, theatrical performances in the inn-yards of the City were banned henceforth. Bereft of a dramatic outlet over this troubled period Shakespeare had turned to poetry, composing *Venus and Adonis* and *The Rape of Lucrece*. Many other actors had headed for plague-free Germany, an expedient first tried in the previous decade. A visitor to Frankfurt's autumn fair in 1592 wrote to his wife – "Here are some English actors whose plays I have seen. They have such splendid good music and are perfect in their dancing and jumping, whose equal I have never seen. There are ten or twelve of them, all richly and magnificently clothed."

In 1594 a new company, the Lord Chamberlain's Men, was constituted under the patronage of a famously-foulmouthed soldier, Henry Carey, Lord Hunsdon (1526-96), first

4. Richard Burbage.

cousin to the Queen and commander of her personal bodyguard. They took possession of The Theatre, recently vacated by the Admiral's Men. The core of the new troupe, most notably its leading player Richard Burbage (?1569-1619), second son of James Burbage, was drawn from Strange's Men, which left London that year. Other founder members included John Heminge, Kempe and Shakespeare. Hunsdon eased 'his' players access to Court so that of the twenty recorded royal commands issued between 1594 and 1597 thirteen went to them and only seven to the rival Admiral's Men. It was the Lord Chamberlain's Company with which Shakespeare was most closely associated and for which he wrote most of his plays. By 1594 he had established his *bona fides* as a dramatist by producing (probably) the three parts of *Henry VI*, *The Comedy of Errors*, *Two Gentlemen of Verona*, *The Taming of the Shrew*, *Titus Andronicus* and *Richard III* – i.e. comedy, tragedy and history, the latter the only safe way to deal, allusively, with politics. It was at The Theatre that the Lord Chamberlain's Men probably staged the first productions of *King John, Love's Labour's Lost, A*

Midsummer Night's Dream, The Merchant of Venice, Richard II, Henry IV parts I and II and *Henry V*. The narrator's apologetic reference to a 'wooden O' (actually a polygon) in *Henry V* implies that The Theatre had by then come to be regarded as out-dated or at least obsolescent.

Swan Song

In 1595 The Swan theatre was opened in Paris Garden, a south bank location notorious for prostitutes, by the parsimonious Francis Langley. In 1596 a visiting Dutchman Johannes de Witt made a sketch of its interior which is the only authenticated depiction of the internal arrangement of an Elizabethan playhouse. Unpublished until 1888, de Witt's sketch shows the stage taking up fully half the floor area of the yard.

In 1597 Ben Jonson's satire *The Isle of Dogs* was performed at the Swan and judged to contain 'very seditious and slandrous matter'. The Lord Mayor and Aldermen wrote to the Privy Council to renew their assault on the theatres as such. In addition to the usual charges of corrupting youth, encouraging vice and idleness, distracting from religious attendance, spreading plague etc. their letter also revealed an awareness of supposed Roman theatrical practice, denouncing contemporary usage as "contrary to the rules and art prescribed for the making of comedies even among the heathen, who used them seldom and at certain set times and not all the year long as our manner is."

In response to the allegedly provocative content of *The Isle of Dogs* the Privy Council banned the performance of all plays in London and ordered the destruction of all theatres, though this draconian step was not pursued and the Lord Chamberlain's Men and Admiral's Men were specifically exempted from the ban. Jonson was consigned to prison, and his co-author Thomas Nashe (1567-?1601) fled abroad. Pembroke's Men, who had performed the play, disbanded and the Swan fell on hard times, being used only occasionally by professional players, more often by amateurs or as an arena for fencing-bouts.

5. *The interior of the Swan Theatre c.1596, drawn by de Witt.*

Jonson was in more trouble in 1598 for killing a fellow actor, Gabriel Spencer, himself a known killer, in a duel at Hoxton. As a first offender and a literate man Jonson managed to get away with being branded on the thumb with a T for Tyburn (so that he couldn't claim to be a first offender a second time). That same year he established himself as a literary celebrity with *Every Man in His Humour*.

The Globe

In 1596, knowing that the lease on The Theatre would soon run out James Burbage leased and converted a room in the Blackfriars monastery for adult theatrical use. The project was, however, frustrated by the objections of local residents who complained of the disruption to their lives that would be caused by both plays and the sort of people they attracted. Hunsdon died that year, passing his patronage to his son and heir, who sided with the objectors. Although the lease on The Theatre had not yet terminated, difficulties with the ground landlord, Giles Alleyn, caused the company to take temporary refuge in the Curtain. Burbage died in 1597, leaving the

6. *Bankside, featured in Wencelaus Hollar's magnificent panorama c.1644. It shows the Globe and the Bear Garden, but their names have erroneously been reversed.*

problem of a future home for the company unresolved. If Alleyn hoped to acquire The Theatre for nothing he was to be disappointed. Richard Burbage and his elder brother Cuthbert instructed carpenter Peter Street to disassemble the timbers, which were then ferried across the river and used in the construction of a new theatre, the Globe, which was significantly larger than its neighbour, the Rose. It was also carefully oriented so that the stage made optimum use of the afternoon light, when plays were actually being performed.

In 1600 yet another new theatre, the Fortune, opened but this time on the north side of London,

7. A first depiction of the Fortune Theatre in Golden Lane.

proved sufficiently remunerative to justify rebuilding in brick following its destruction by fire in 1621.

The year 1600 also marked the parting of the ways between Will Kempe and the Chamberlain's Men. Shakespeare's throwaway line in *Hamlet* about clowns speaking "more than is set down for them" may have revealed the dramatist's irritation at the extempore gags that were Kempe's stock in trade. Following his departure from the company Kempe, for a wager, pledged himself to travel from London to Norwich in nine days doing a Morris dance all the way to the accompaniment of drum and tabor. Carefully timing each section of the route to arrive with maximum publicity at each town or village he passed through, Kempe not only accomplished his feat but published a pamphlet account of his 'Nine Days Wonder'.

End of an Era

In 1603 England's only officially permitted actress, Elizabeth I, supreme player of the varying roles of Virgin Queen, Diana, Gloriana and 'Good Queen Bess', died as she had lived, the centre of all attention. Four and a half decades of unremitting performance laid the foundations of a mythic status which ensured that for two centuries after her death the date of her accession would be celebrated with gratitude. Her passing was inevitably marked by a period of official mourning, which naturally included the closure of all places of entertainment. Scarcely had the theatres re-opened, however, than, as if to underline the withdrawal of her protecting hand, in May 1603 a major outbreak of plague began to carry off some thirty thousand of London's citizens, forcing once more the closure of theatres. When they reopened again in April 1604 it was to be not only under a new sovereign but under a new dispensation.

outside Cripplegate. Its backers were Henslowe and Alleyn, reacting against the competition represented by the new Globe. Indeed the surviving building contract actually specifies that it should follow the proportions of the rival house and "to be in all other contrivations, conveyances, fashions, things and things effected, finished and done, according to the manner and fashion of the said house called the Globe". The galleries were specified at twelve feet high at the bottom storey, which was to be protected from invasion by a fence of "strong iron pikes". The upper galleries were eleven and nine feet high respectively. The cost was set by the contract at £440. The relocation of the Admiral's Men seems to have given them the new audience they needed because the Fortune

Dressing the Part

Little is known with accuracy of stage costuming in Shakespeare's day. Travelling troupes would obviously be limited in the extent of the wardrobe they could carry around with him, though German comments on visiting English players remark on the splendour of their apparel. In plays which had a contemporary setting the ordinary clothes of the day might have served well enough, particularly for subsidiary roles, but this is unlikely to have been the case where heroic, royal or supernatural characters were being represented. Certainly the suspension of disbelief required to accept boys playing women's parts depended on the wearing of appropriate costume. Given the absence of scenery, moreover, costume was virtually the only complementary resource available to the actor otherwise wholly reliant on voice and gesture. The value placed on costumes as a company resource is confirmed by the fact that Philip Henslowe fined his actors for wearing them outside the playhouse.

The court masques devised by Inigo Jones *(see p29)* involved elaborate and incredibly costly purpose-made costumes - wearing them was half the point of the whole enterprise. Commercial acting companies are likely to have relied on the accumulation of opportunistic purchases and the cast-offs of their wealthier patrons, from redundant bits of armour to out-dated items of high fashion.

Players of the Restoration period often took their own stage-wear to the point of style-conscious absurdity and texts of the day are replete with mocking references to details of cuffs, cravats and pockets. In 1711 Addison in *The Spectator* ridiculed the incongruity of actors appearing in historic roles dressed in the most exaggerated contemporary styles. Quite frequently the two modes appear to have been worn simultaneously. The frontispiece to *Henry VIII* in the 1709 collected Shakespeare edition by Nicholas Rowe *(see p48)* shows clearly that while the principal players, Henry VIII and Wolsey, are clothed with a fair approximation to historical accuracy, the supporting actors simply wear the fashion of their day.

As manager of Drury Lane Garrick *(see p61)* accumulated a huge wardrobe, but attempted historical authenticity selectively, for example deliberately choosing not to play Hamlet in period costume. Nor did he always get his effects right when he did try. Hogarth's celebrated depiction of Garrick as Richard III reveals him to be wearing not medieval but Elizabethan costume, complete with such details as slashed sleeves. In 1758 Garrick rationalised his decision to play the part of an ancient Greek in the vestments of a Venetian gondolier on the somewhat conjectural grounds that most gondoliers were said to be of Greek origin.

Individual actors sometimes made their own considered and significant choices in their costuming for various roles. Macklin *(see p61)* famously revolutionised the perception of Shylock from a figure of fun to a personification of manipulative evil by abandoning his traditional red wig in favour of the long black hair and flowing black gown of a contemporary Venetian Jewish merchant. Sarah Siddons *(see p85)* chose to sleep-walk as Lady Macbeth draped in white satin, a traditional signification of insanity.

Kemble's 1823 production of *King John (see p86)* proved a landmark in its concern for historical accuracy. Charles Kean *(see p104)* was almost excessive in his antiquarian purism but was still unable to persuade his own wife, Ellen, to abandon the crinolines or voluminous petticoats which she insisted on wearing underneath whatever historically appropriate costume he had devised for her.

The popularity of dramatised versions of the historical novels of Sir Walter Scott reinforced the revival of interest in authentic dress, boosting a craze for kilts, plaids and tartans which had begun with George IV's state visit to Scotland in 1822 and was sustained by Victoria and Albert's devotion to the Highlands. At the same time as the concern for historical accuracy became generally accepted dramatic improvements in the quality of stage-lighting *(see p75)* made glitter and spangles, liberally used in dim, candle-lit venues, a thing of the past.

Just at the period that the lavish Shakespearean productions put on by Irving *(see p159)* and Tree reached new budgetary heights in the lavishness of their costuming, Edward Gordon Craig *(see p157)* articulated a reaction against uncritical historicism and in favour of more symbolic costuming, aesthetically co-ordinated with lighting and set design. Another novel trend of the early twentieth century was the decision to dress the actors of a play in fashions deliberately different from the one in which it was set. In 1928 the Royal Court presented *Henry V* in the uniforms of World War One but as late as 1960, when a Mermaid production employed World War Two battledress, one critic commented on the production as a "curious experiment". At least there was some self-evident military association involved. In 1937 Edith Evans played *As You Like It* dressed in the courtly costume of Louis XV's France. The 1976 RSC production of *Macbeth*, starring Ian McKellen and Judi Dench, reverted to eighteenth-century usage in dressing players in costumes of differing periods, some pseudo-medieval, others Edwardian. These various tendencies have since been combined in the convention of dressing players in costumes of no precise dating but, through the use of homespun, dull metal or shiny leather, in dress conveying an appropriate emotional feel, thus implying the universality of their roles and of the underlying text.

CHAPTER TWO

Monarchs and Masques

New Companies, New Theatres

Within two months of James VI of Scotland's accession to the English throne as James I of England (reigned 1603-25) he had decreed that henceforth acting companies would be required to have royal, rather than noble, patronage. As a result of this policy of cultural centralisation the Lord Chamberlain's Men henceforth became the King's Men, an acknowledgment of their supremacy over all the other companies.

Oxford and Worcester's Men were assigned to James's consort, Anne of Denmark (1574-1619) as Queen Anne's Men. In 1605 they found a permanent home at the Red Bull, a converted inn on St. John Street in Clerkenwell. This rapidly acquired the reputation of being a 'blood tub' with a notoriously rowdy audience. Thomas Heywood (1573-1641), an industrious hack, was dramatist in residence. Variously an actor, poet and pamphleteer, he also scripted mayoral pageants and claimed to have had a hand - or at least a finger - in the writing of two hundred and twenty plays, as well as defending one of his several professions in *An Apology for Actors* (1612). From 1612 actor Christopher Beeston (?1580-1639) served as the theatre's autocratic manager until the death of Queen Anne, when the Red Bull went even further down market.

James's heir, Prince Henry (1594-1612), became patron of the former Admiral's Men at the Fortune. Other companies were under the patronage of Princess Elizabeth (1611), as Lady Elizabeth's Men and Prince Charles (1612), as the Prince's Men. After Prince Henry's premature death his company was allotted to the husband of Princess Elizabeth, the Elector Palatine, as Palsgrave's Men. The Chapel Children, divided

into the King's Revels and the Queen's Revels, enjoyed a brief come-back and then gradually fell out of royal favour, much to the satisfaction of the adult companies. In 1608 the King's Men were able to take over the venue at the Blackfriars and thus had the option of working all the year round.

In 1613 two cannon, fired during the performance of Shakespeare's *Henry VIII*, set the thatched roof of the Globe theatre alight. Everyone escaped unhurt, except for one man who had "his breeches on fire that would perhaps have broyled him if he had not with the benefit of a provident wit put it out with bottle ale." As the home of the King's Men the Globe benefited from a royal grant towards the cost of reconstruction and it was swiftly reopened in 1614.

In 1613 Lady Elizabeth's Men were merged with the remnants of the Revels company. In 1615 Philip Rosseter, a Revels company actor, with £1,500 from Edward Alleyn, built a playhouse known as Porter's Hall near Puddle Wharf at Blackfriars. It was granted a licence by the authorities and used by Lady Elizabeth's Men and Prince Charles's Men. In 1617, however, the local inhabitants once again pressed successfully for the suppression of a theatre in their midst.

While the Globe was temporarily out of action Henslowe took advantage of his rivals' misfortune to convert a former animal-baiting arena into a theatre, which he called the Hope. The stage remained movable so that the baiting of bulls and bears could be alternated with the presentation of plays. Briefly the home of Lady Elizabeth's Men, the Hope also staged the first performance (1614) of Ben Jonson's *Bartholomew*

8. *The Red Bull at Clerkenwell. An engraving in Kirkman's* Drolls, *published in 1672.*

9. The rebuilt Fortune Theatre in Golden Lane.

Fair. The reopening of the Globe led, however, to a decline in audiences, compounded by the death of Henslowe in 1616. Used by a few minor companies until 1617, the optimistically named Hope then reverted to animal shows and its old name of the Bear Garden.

The Cockpit, as its name proclaims, was built in 1609 in Drury Lane to hold cockfights but in 1616 was roofed over by Christopher Beeston to serve as an indoor theatre for Queen Anne's Men. Burned down by drunken apprentices on Shrove Tuesday 1617, it was, when rebuilt, appropriately renamed the Phoenix, although, confusingly, it was still also frequently referred to by its old name. To confuse matters still

further in 1629-30 the court architect Inigo Jones (1573-1652) rebuilt the Cockpit-in-Court theatre in the Whitehall palace complex. Originally built as a cockpit for Henry VIII, it had been adapted for theatrical purposes in 1604. Remodelled to give a dominating central position to the royal throne, directly opposite the centre of the stage, it seems to have been used for about twenty plays a year.

Although the Fortune was rebuilt in brick after a fire in 1621 the loss of its stock of prompt-books in the blaze proved a severe set-back and its reputation went into decline.

The death of James I in 1625 and the accession of Charles I (reigned 1625-49), coinciding with

10. *A stained-glass window in St Giles Cripplegate church featuring the Fortune Theatre.*

another severe plague epidemic, led to the merger of the King's and former Prince's Men and the formation of a new company under the patronage of his wife, the French Henrietta Maria (1606-69), known as Queen Henrietta's Men or the Queen's Men, led by the ubiquitous Christopher Beeston, with James Shirley (1596-1666) as their resident dramatist. In 1631 another company was formed under the nominal patronage of the infant future Charles II (1630-85) as Prince Charles's Men, the previous troupe of this name having been disbanded in 1625. The reconstituted company took in several players from the Fortune.

In 1637, following another prolonged period of plague-induced closures, Beeston installed a youthful company at the Phoenix called Beeston's Boys. Beeston died, however, the following year, leaving the management to his son, William Beeston (?1606-82). William was arrested in 1639 for presenting an unlicensed play which offended Charles I. He was fined and

imprisoned and replaced by William Davenant *(see pXX)*.

Salisbury Court was the last playhouse to be erected before the outbreak of the civil war in 1642. Built of brick and roofed over, it was located between Fleet Street and the Thames and used by the King's Men from its opening in 1629 until 1631, then (1631-35) by Prince Charles's Men and Queen Henrietta's Men (1637-42).

The biggest outdoor theatres could accommodate some three thousand people. (Fire and safety regulations limit today's reconstructed Globe to half that number.) The indoor theatres were much smaller. The Blackfriars could take less than six hundred. This made higher admission charges essential, which in turn priced out the *hoi-polloi*, effectively making the indoor venues far more socially exclusive. Even the cheapest seats, in the galleries, cost sixpence. To share a bench in the pit, which had the best view, unobstructed by low-hanging candelabra, cost a further shilling.

The excellence of the King's Men as players and of Shakespeare as their house dramatist meant that, of the large, outdoor venues, the Globe alone still continued to attract a fashionable element, though this component would have diminished in high summer with the Inns of Court on vacation and the aristocracy out of town on their country estates.

The Triumvirate of Wit
Of the dozens of dramatists active in this period only three – Shakespeare, Fletcher and Jonson – achieved the dignity of having their works brought together and published as a collected edition and of those only Jonson's were so honoured in his own lifetime.

Born in London, Ben Jonson was instructed in the classics at Westminster School by the eminent topographer William Camden (1551-1623), reviver of the name Britannia for the British Isles. After a short spell in his step-father's trade as a bricklayer, Jonson fought with the Protestant rebels against Catholic Spanish rule in the Low Countries, where he claimed to have killed an enemy soldier in single combat. He then drifted

11. Ben Jonson.

into acting but was no good. After his participation in *The Isle of Dogs* fiasco landed him in gaol, Jonson, perhaps, for lack of alternatives - he wasn't much good as a bricklayer, either – was willing to try his literary hand at anything. *Cynthia's Revels* (1600) was written for the Chapel Children of Blackfriars, who also played *The Poetaster* (1601) in which he began to display his accustomed contempt for other dramatists, dismissing John Marston (?1575-1634) and Thomas Dekker (?1570-1632) as uneducated hacks. Jonson nevertheless collaborated with Marston and George Chapman (?1559-1634) on *Eastward Ho!,* whose injudicious gibes at the Scots earned the instant displeasure of the new Scottish monarch. Once again Jonson found himself in prison but by the following year was sufficiently forgiven to be set to writing masques for the court *(see p29)*. Jonson's modern reputation rests substantially, however, on the comedies of the following decade, *Volpone* (1606), *Epicoene; or, The Silent Woman* (1609), *The Alchemist*

(1610) and *Bartholomew Fair* (1614). *The Alchemist* satirises cupidity and credulity. *Bartholomew Fair* is an episodic portrayal of Londoners in holiday mood. A Folio edition of Jonson's dramatic and poetic works was published in 1616. This raised drama to a new level of respectability, earning him an honorary M.A. from Oxford and appointment as lecturer in rhetoric at Gresham College in the City. Jonson's deep knowledge of the metropolis was belatedly acknowledged by his appointment as City Chronologer in 1628, the year in which he suffered a severe stroke. Dogged by invalidism and increasing destitution, Jonson wrote on until he dropped. Despite his arrogant and quarrelsome character he was a clubbable man, renowned as the unofficial president of a literary circle which met at the Mermaid Tavern in Bread Street. Although he teased Shakespeare Jonson had the highest respect for him and also numbered among his other friends the poet and Dean of St. Paul's John Donne (1572-1631) and the lawyer and philosopher Francis Bacon (1561-1626). A younger generation of well-educated and aristocratic writers were proud to style themselves 'of the tribe of Ben'. Jonson's gravestone in Westminster Abbey bears the inscription "O rare Ben Jonson". Recall Jonson's pride in his classical education. "Orare!" is the Latin imperative demanding praise!

John Fletcher (1579-1625) is famed for his collaborative writings, initially with Francis Beaumont (1584-1616). Both were of gentlemanly status, Fletcher the son of a bishop, Beaumont from Oxfordshire gentry. Beaumont left Oxford without a degree, studied at the Inner Temple without qualifying for the bar and first wrote *The Woman Hater* (1605) for the Boys of St. Paul's and *The Knight of the Burning Pestle* (1607) a witty send-up of the bourgeois weakness for chivalric romance, for the Children of the Chapel Royal. Around 1609 they jointly succeeded Shakespeare as the most prolific suppliers of plays for the King's Men, enjoying major successes with *The Maid's Tragedy* (1610) and *A King and No King* (1611). These were enjoyed by the refined audiences of the Blackfriars rather than the

12. *Francis Beaumont.*

13. *John Fletcher.*

Globe. Beaumont made an advantageous marriage in 1613 and dropped writing soon afterwards. Fletcher then found his collaborator in Philip Massinger (1583-1640), who matched his prolific and facile pen until Fletcher died in the London plague epidemic of 1625. Another Oxford drop-out, possibly an ex-actor, Massinger wrote at least fifteen plays with Fletcher which were long attributed to Beaumont and Fletcher and remained associated with the King's Men until his death. Massinger's most celebrated solo effort *A New Way to Pay Old Debts* (1621) created the role of Sir Giles Overreach, which was to be brilliantly played two centuries later by Edmund Kean *(see p86)*.

Henslowe's Henchmen

Thomas Middleton (?1580-1627) is first identified as a working playwright in Henslowe's papers in 1602, although his earliest known play, *The Phoenix*, written after that date, was for the Boys of St. Paul's, for whom he also wrote three 'citizen comedies', most notably *A Mad World, My Masters*. After leaving Oxford

Middleton may have spent some time at Gray's Inn, then the most pre-eminent of the four Inns of Court and the one from which Elizabeth I had drawn several of her most trusted advisers. By 1600 he was "daylie accompaninge the players", one of whose sisters he married. For Henslowe Middleton collaborated with Dekker to produce *The Honest Whore* (1604) and *The Roaring Girl* (*ca.* 1610). Like Middleton's own single-handed masterpiece, *A Chaste Maid in Cheapside* (1611), these comedies rely on ingeniously interwoven plots and superbly observed dialogue. Middleton's serious side is represented by *A Game at Chess* (1624), a daringly anti-Spanish satire aimed at the court at a time when a royal marriage with Spain was being actively pursued. In it the hated Spanish ambassador Gondomar was "counterfeited to the life". It certainly hit the mark with the audience, running for nine performances until the author was summoned before the Privy Council to explain himself. Middleton also collaborated on several plays with the versatile actor, dramatist and manager William Rowley (?1585-1626), notably a tragedy

The Changeling (1622). His work on pageants and masques for the City of London brought him the appointment of City Chronologer (1620-7). T.S. Eliot took the opportunity of the tercentenary of Middleton's death to publish an influential essay in his praise.

John Webster (*ca.*1580-1634) is also recorded in Henslowe's papers in 1602, as receiving payment for contributions to a lost play. Like Middleton he wrote for the boys' companies, composed Lord Mayor's pageants and collaborated with Dekker and Rowley but his fame rests on two tragedies which were his alone *The White Devil* (*ca.* 1612) and *The Duchess of Malfi* (*ca.* 1613), both incredibly violent tales of family vengeance, mixing bloody horrors with sublime poetry. In the Cold War atmosphere of post-Reformation Europe their Italianate setting appealed to an audience which saw Italy as simultaneously seductive and subversive, the crucible of the *avant garde* in art, architecture and music, the style-setter in fashion and manners, but also the homeland of Machiavelli and the headquarters of the Pope and his dedicated instruments, the hated Inquisition and the indefatigable Jesuits. Webster's surviving commonplace book reveals the extent to which collaboration was paralleled by the routine appropriation and adaptation of lines and passages from the work of others. Webster's two great tragedies were revived more frequently in the twentieth century than the work of any other of Shakespeare's contemporaries.

Actor into Gentleman?

Given what they were usually paid, had Shakespeare remained just an actor, or even a dramatist, he would not have died a rich man as he did. In 1594 he was able to buy a share in the newly-established Lord Chamberlain's Men, perhaps with a loan from the Earl of Southampton, to whom he had dedicated the two long poems he had written during the closure of the theatres in 1592-4. In 1596 Shakespeare made a successful application to the College of Arms for an heraldic coat of arms for his father, exonerating the shame of his fall from financial grace as ex-Bailiff (mayor) of Stratford. Already by 1597 Shakespeare was able to buy New Place, the most prestigious residence in his birthplace. The scare about the future of theatres which induced Alleyn's temporary retirement then *(see below)* may also have motivated Shakespeare to invest in malting, a major Stratford business, at that time. The building of the Globe led the playwright to relocate his London base from St. Helen's, Bishopsgate, where the period of his residence is commemorated by a stained-glass window in the parish church, to the decidedly less salubrious, but considerably more convenient, Liberty of the Clink, on Bankside, where he is likewise commemorated in an even more splendid window in Southwark Cathedral. In Shakespeare's day this was the local parish church, known as St. Mary Overie. The playwright's younger brother, Edmund, came to join him there, probably as an apprentice actor, but within a few months fell victim to the plague of 1603 and was buried in St. Mary's, although his grave is lost. By 1604 Shakespeare was back on the north side of the river, lodging at Cripplegate in the house of a Huguenot family called Mountjoy. It is tempting to believe that he had known them for years since Mountjoy is the name of the French herald in *Henry V,* a play which also contains two scenes of comic relief about learning and speaking French. Although Shakespeare made further purchases of land around Stratford, as late as 1613 he was investing in part of a gatehouse in Blackfriars, as though to keep a foothold in the capital. In that same year he appears to have decided to retire to his birthplace, never to write another line but to be buried in the parish church in the most prominent position of honour, before the altar.

Shakespeare's plays, designed for a vanished playhouse and penned in haste, were printed, both in his lifetime and afterwards, without the author's supervision. Inevitably their textual integrity would be problematic. Companies guarded the texts of their plays jealously in an attempt to protect them from piracy. Resident dramatists were normally under a contractual injunction *not* to publish their work. By the time of Shakespeare's death sixteen of his plays had been printed, but only in workaday quarto-sized editions. The collation of these and a further twenty plays into the famed lavish First Folio of 1623 was the work of two fellow-actors John Heminge (died 1630) and Henry Condell (died 1627). In part the enterprise was a tribute to Shakespeare's standing as the only prominent playwright to have had so stable a relationship with a single, leading company. Perhaps it may also be considered as something of a retirement project. Heminge acted on stage little after 1611 but acted rather as the business manager of the King's Men. Condell is not recorded as acting after 1619 and was wealthy enough to have a country house at Fulham. Both men were churchwardens of St. Mary, Aldermanbury. The Folio was prefaced by a lengthy laudatory poem by Jonson, who famously proclaimed that Shakespeare was "not of an age but for all time". Three further editions of the Folio appeared in the seventeenth century, the fourth being used by Nicholas Rowe *(see p48)* to produce a definitive version.

Edward Alleyn was ranked by contemporaries, such as Jonson, alongside Richard Burbage at the head of the acting

14. Edward Alleyn.

profession. Born the son of a Bishopsgate inn-keeper, Alleyn is known to have been with Worcester's Men by the age of seventeen and to have played at the Rose in 1587, when he was still only twenty-one. By 1589 he was already displaying an entrepreneurial streak, buying "playing apparel, playbooks, instruments and other commodities." By 1592, the year in which he married Philip Henslowe's step-daughter, Joan Woodward, he was certainly with the Admiral's Men and two years later he was their acknowledged star, specialising in the larger-than-life roles which suited his height and booming voice. From 1597 until 1600 Alleyn retired from acting to concentrate on his portfolio of business interests. He returned to the stage with the opening of the Fortune in 1600 and retired permanently in 1603 after welcoming James I to London in a pageant in which he rather appropriately represented The Genius of the City of London. In 1604 Alleyn and Henslowe received a long-coveted joint patent to

15. Edward Alleyn, depicted in a stained-glass window at St Giles Cripplegate church.

act as Masters of the 'sport' of animal-baiting. This gave them control of the Bear Garden at Bankside, the right to supervise baiting at the royal palaces of Greenwich and Whitehall and the highly profitable subsidiary right to breed and sell the mastiffs used in baiting, a must-have fashion-accessory for the nuisance-about-town.

By 1605 Alleyn was in negotiations to buy the manor of Dulwich, which cost him five thousand pounds – enough to build half a dozen theatres. When the previous owner, Sir Francis Calton, let it be known that he was ashamed of selling his inheritance to a self-made man, Alleyn breezily brushed the slight aside:

" ... you tell me of my poor original and of my quality as a player. What is that? If I am richer than my ancestors I hope I may be able to do more good with my riches than ever your ancestors did ...".

For seven years, however, Alleyn continued to reside in Southwark where he had become a person of great parochial consequence, serving as churchwarden and magistrate. In 1613 Alleyn began building the College of God's Gift, the same year as Sir Thomas Sutton, reputedly the richest commoner in England, began to convert the Charterhouse into an almshouse and school. The chapel of Alleyn's College was consecrated in 1616 by the Archbishop of Canterbury in person. The formalities of incorporation were completed in 1619 in the presence of Francis Bacon and Inigo Jones. Alleyn's wife died in 1623 and in confirmation of his elevated social status Alleyn within the year took as his second wife the teenage daughter of John Donne, Dean of St. Paul's.

In his *History of the Worthies of England* Thomas Fuller (1608-61) paid a highly qualified tribute to Alleyn, the undertones of which reveal much about contemporary attitudes towards both actors and the theatre:

"He was bred a stage-player: a calling which many have condemned, more have questioned, some few have excused, and far fewer conscientious people have commended. He was

the Roscius of our age, so acting to the life, that he made any part (especially a majestick one) to become him. He got a very great estate, and in his old age, following Christ's counsel (on what forcible motive belongs not to me to inquire) 'he made friends of his unrighteous Mammon', building therewith a fair college at Dulwich ... for the relief of poor people. Some I confess thought it built on a foundered foundation, seeing in a spiritual sense none is good and lawful money, save what is honestly and industriously gotten ... Sure I am no hospital is tied with better or stricter laws ... Thus he, who out-acted others in his life, out-did himself before his death."

Alleyn's theatrical connections live on in the names of roads in the Dulwich area commemorating Henslowe, Burbage, Shakespeare, Dekker and the Master of the Revels, Tylney. As Dulwich College his foundation has had a long and educationally distinguished history.

The Masque

The masque, combining mime, music, dance, verse, spectacular scenery and elaborate costumes was the court entertainment *par excellence*, not least because the performers were themselves courtiers. It evolved out of the royal and aristocratic 'disguisings' which ritualised the welcoming of eminent guests with dance, gifts and flowery, flattering speeches and the wearing of outlandish costumes, visors - and masks. As an artistic form the masque was to be seminal in introducing the proscenium arch, the front curtain and numerous scenic and lighting effects to English theatre. At a time when public theatres operated with minimal or no scenery and without the benefit of artificial lighting effects the masque represented an altogether more dazzling and sumptuous theatrical experience.

In its developed form the high priests of the masque were Inigo Jones and Ben Jonson, who himself first introduced the term 'masque' to describe this form of entertainment. Jones had travelled in Italy to familiarise himself with its

16. Inigo Jones.

face, collectively representing the Daughters of Niger. A curtain painted with a landscape fell to reveal a vast ocean with the masquers in the foreground "placed in a great concave shell like mother of pearl, curiously made to move upon those waters and rise with the billow." The 'Ethiopian' ladies then disembarked and presented the king with fans symbolising his divinely-ordained and morally unassailable authority, his uniting of England and Scotland to create the new empire of Great Britain and his bestowal of the gift of peace in having ended decades of war with Spain. These themes were to be constantly reiterated throughout the subsequent masques of James's reign.

In *The Masque of Queens* (1609) Jonson introduced a new element of 'anti-masque'. This preceded the masque itself and deliberately used grotesque or bizarre elements to serve as a foil to what followed. Representing chaos, disorder or evil in its various forms the pygmies, beggars or satyrs of the anti-masque stood in opposition to the masque as a symbolic incarnation of harmony, order, virtue and purity. In this first instance Jonson explained that "twelve women in the habits of hags or witches, sustaining the persons of Ignorance, Suspicion, Credulity etc., the opposites to good Fame ... fill that part, not as a masque, but a spectacle of strangeness." The prefatory anti-masque was also distinctive in favouring the verbal over the visual and therefore being played by professional actors, it being beneath the dignity (and probably beyond the capacity) of courtiers to engage in quick-fire cross-talk fizzing with puns and *double entendre*.

architecture but was also aware of the role of design, lighting and costume in Italian theatre, both from personal experience and through the books he brought back or was able later to obtain. He also had the advantage of having worked in Denmark, the home of James I's consort, Queen Anne. In 1604 Jones was appointed to the household of the heir to the throne, Prince Henry, and given control of the artistic side of organising court masques. Jonson, who had been appointed Court Poet in 1603, was deputed with the literary aspect. The partnership was not invariable and became increasingly acrimonious, ending in Jonson's final withdrawal in 1631, after writing at least eight masques.

Their first collaboration, *The Masque of Blackness*, was presented on Twelfth Night 1605. In arranging the stage Inigo used his mastery of the newly-understood science of perspective to ensure that the sight lines converged on the royal throne in the centre of the auditorium, giving the king the perfect view. The blond queen herself played the leading role, surrounded by eleven court ladies, all in black

The masque devised for the 1610 investiture of Prince Henry as Prince of Wales had an appropriately Arthurian theme, Arthur being both an embodiment of chivalric valour and supposedly of Welsh origin. It also marked Henry's performance debut before the court. This was followed in summer by *Tethys' Festival*, which had a naval theme. Queen Anne herself played the sea-goddess and fourteen-year-old Princess Elizabeth (as the River Thames) and nine-year-old Prince Charles (as the wind Zephyrus) also took part.

In aesthetic terms *Oberon the Fairy Prince* (1611) appears to have been a most successful collaboration, with Prince Henry as Oberon. The costumes alone cost over £1,400, of which Jones got just £16 for designing them. *Love Freed from Ignorance and Folly*, produced the following month, netted Jones and Jonson a fee of £40 each, which, combined, represented just over ten per cent of the total budget. The dancing master who rehearsed the court ladies got £50.

In 1617 *The Vision of Delight* evoked a magical transformation of spring out of winter. In 1618 the theme was *Pleasure Reconciled to Virtue* which proved too slow for the king, who lost his temper. In 1619 the wooden banqueting house at Whitehall, built in 1608, burned down and was replaced by Inigo Jones with a stone building, the first neo-Classical structure to be built in central London. Completed in 1622, it cost over £15,000. *The Masque of Augurs*, performed there on Twelfth Night of that year, was written by Jonson to support the proposed (and subsequently abortive) Spanish marriage project. In the antimasque he took the opportunity to poke fun at his collaborator in the *persona* of Vangoose, a deviser of spectacles. In the January masque of 1623 Jones reasserted himself by devising a perspective view of Whitehall, prominently featuring the Banqueting House. Jonson later riposted by lampooning Jones none too subtly in the figure of a cook (Banqueting House - Cook - geddit?) in the antimasque of the last year of James's reign. The title of the masque reiterated the proclaimed objective of the entire Stuart Anglo-Scottish project – *The Fortunate Isles and their Union.*

Masques were incredibly expensive to mount, even by the standards of the spendthrift Stuart court. *The Masque of Queens* of 1609 cost over three thousand pounds, enough to build a warship. Mounted only once or at most twice, masques yet demanded complex stage machinery and lighting effects, costumes of silk and taffeta shot through with silver and gold, orchestras of fifty musicians or more and five hundred plus torches or fine wax candles, not to mention a small army of carpenters, seamstresses and stage-hands, which could run into hundreds. For *Tethys' Festival* the silk merchant's bill alone was just short of two thousand pounds. It was, moreover, a routine custom for the cold collation served after the performance to be trashed all over the floor to make way for the serving of the next, hot course. Such frivolous waste appalled the Puritan element in London which further deplored the frequent incorporation into the masques of non-Christian motifs from myth or classical antiquity, not to mention displays of bare breasts.

In 1626, a year after his accession and following a bruising clash with Parliament over finance, Charles I decided to dispense with the annual masque as an economy measure. Once he had decided to rule without Parliament and had begun to exploit (or abuse) extra-Parliamentary sources of revenue, the king reinstated them in 1631 but capped the budget for each one at £1,400 and ordered courtiers to pay for their own costumes. As these may have cost one hundred pounds or more each (twice the annual rental for a posh London house) this threw the largest single item of costs onto the participants. It also meant that henceforth scenery and costumes were kept to be recycled into later productions.

Under Charles I the spectacular element, especially the dance component, in which the king and queen themselves took part, came to overshadow the literary content, leading to Jonson's disgusted withdrawal in 1631. Jonson's successors as *litterateur* were required to draw up only a few conventional speeches around which the visual effects might be arranged. As the Stuart monarchy edged unknowingly towards its nemesis the themes of its self-congratulatory celebrations ironically became ever more assertive of the perfection of its rule – viz. *Albion's Triumph* (1632) *Coelum Britannicum* (*British Heaven* 1634), *Britannnia Triumphans* (*Victorious Britain* 1638).

The Catholic French queen, who would have been familiar with the notion of actresses in her native country, undertook speaking parts (in English), thus prefiguring by decades the appearance of actresses on the public stage after the civil wars and Restoration. To Puritans this was another proof of the immorality of court life. A few months after the Queen's speaking appearance on stage in 1632 the Puritan pamphleteer William Prynne (1600-69) published a long indictment against the theatre, *Historiomatrix*, including a condemnation of masques, which he stigmatised as an indirect representation of the Mass. Worse still, in his eyes, masques were sometimes staged on a Sunday, when even the iniquitous public playhouses were closed to observe the Sabbath. Prynne's index reference to "Women actors, Notorious whores" was taken as a not-so-veiled attack on the queen herself – although in fact it seems that this may have been a back reference to a visiting French company of 1629, which had included actresses. The author was, therefore, sentenced to be fined £500, pilloried, have both his ears cut off and be imprisoned for life in the Tower. (He was released after Parliament finally reassembled in 1640.) As Prynne was a member of Lincoln's Inn the Inns of Court, fearing royal opprobrium, collectively paid for a masque, *The Triumph of Peace*, to be mounted in the Banqueting House at their expense "as an expression of their love and duty to their majesties." Preceded by a huge parade from Holborn, headed by a hundred mounted lawyers, the whole affair set the Inns back a remarkable £21,000. At the Queen's request it was repeated a week later in the City at Merchant Taylors' Hall.

In 1635 the masque, *The Temple of Love*, was written for the first time by William Davenant, who so pleased the Queen with it that in 1638 he succeeded Jonson as Poet Laureate. It was the last masque to be performed in the Banqueting House because the installation of Rubens' magnificent painted ceiling made it henceforth

impossible to use smoky flambeaux and oil lamps for fear of damaging it. In 1637 therefore the Queen persuaded the king to pay for a wooden 'masquing house' to be erected beside the Banqueting House, of the same dimensions and with a tiled roof. Jones was able to make it, in theatrical terms, state-of-the-art, with built-in provision for scenery to slide in from the wings and scope for the latest lighting and special effects. The last three masques ever staged, all written by Davenant, were to be presented in this venue. The first, *Luminalia: the Queen's Festival of Light*, starring Her Majesty, featured a full-blown aerial ballet. The courtly masque represented the *ne plus ultra* in dynastic wish-fulfilment and political self-deception, bearing about as much relation to the real state of the nation as representations of the countryside as a rustic idyll did to the starvation-edged realities of British village life. So great were the gaps of sympathy and understanding between Court, City and Country that during the 1630s even the theatres, conventionally seen as axiomatically anti-Puritan, carried coded critiques of royal policy in presenting plays which lauded Protestant heroes of the Thirty Years War (1618-48), then raging on the mainland of Europe.

The last masque, performed as the crisis of the reign began to loom with the recall of Parliament, was in effect a plea for reconciliation but wrapped up in obscurely allegorical references to incidents in ancient Greek history. Artistically it was good – but as a political gesture it entirely missed the point. Their majesties were assured in the final song that:

"All that are harsh, all that are rude,
Are by your harmony subdued..."

Alas, not so.

Interregnum

In September 1642 Parliament suppressed the staging of plays "while these ... sad times of humiliation do continue." Given that the closure of theatres was routine in times of plague and had most recently occurred for an extended period between May 1636 and November 1637, and given that no one could have foreseen how long the conflict between king and Parliament would drag on and how radicalized the struggle would become, it is entirely probable that this measure was initially conceived as a purely temporary provision rather than as the successful culmination of a seventy-year campaign by the Puritan interest and the magistracy of the City of London. Within a year, however, surreptitious attempts appear to have been made to put on truncated performances, in the form of skits and puppet-shows. These were, quite possibly, less an attempt to assert some sort of notion of artistic freedom - players had always lived within a constrictive regulatory framework – than attempts to earn a modest crust by responding to the demands of a London population reeling under the onslaught of an avalanche of apocalyptic pamphlets and hell-fire sermons . Thirty years later the bookseller Francis Kirkman published an account of the days when

> "all that we could divert ourselves with were these humours and pieces of plays ... and that but by stealth too and under pretence of Rope-dancing or the like; and these being all that was permitted us, great was the confluence of the Auditors: I have seen the Red Bull play-House, which was a large one, so full that as many went back for want of room as entered."

Kirkman especially praised "the incomparable" Robert Cox (died 1655) "who was not only the principal Actor, but also the Contriver and Author of most of these Farces." One of Beeston's Boys, Cox devised what were known as 'drolls', short farcical pieces abstracted from longer plays, like '*Bottom the Weaver*' taken from *A Midsummer Night's Dream* or 'The Gravemakers' from *Hamlet*. Cox was eventually to be arrested at the Red Bull in 1653 and imprisoned.

The continuing closure of the theatres provoked the publication in 1643 of *An Actor's Remonstrance*, setting out the grievances of unemployed thespians. Playwrights were similarly placed, or rather displaced. James Shirley, author of at least thirty-six plays, was very lucky, as an ex-Royalist and a Catholic convert, to find a post as a schoolmaster. Comedian Andrew Cane (died 1644) of Prince Charles's Men reverted to his first trade of goldsmith and, fleeing to the Royalist capital at Oxford, engraved dies for the king's improvised coinage.

Some found alternative employment, or at least distraction, in preparing play texts for publication, some of them decades after their first performance. A collection of Fletcher's works appeared in 1647. Middleton and Rowley's *The Changeling* of 1622 was not published until 1653, Middleton's *Women beware Women* not until 1657, thirty years after his death. Dekker's *The Witch of Edmonton*, written with Rowley and John Ford (1586-?1639) in 1621, was first published in 1658.

The Globe was pulled down in 1644, when the Burbages' lease ran out. In 1645 the Queen's Masquing House at Whitehall was disassembled plank by plank. In 1647 Parliament decreed that

17. James Shirley, a drawing by J. Thurston.

Rather surprisingly the Red Bull was allowed to survive.

Oliver Cromwell, Lord Protector from 1653 until his death in 1658, did permit the performance of plays in schools and even in private houses. William Davenant, despite having been imprisoned in the Tower (and knighted) for fighting on the Royalist side, was allowed in 1656 to stage, at Rutland House in Clerkenwell, what he disingenuously described as an "Entertainment after the manner of the ancients". The performance began with a dialogue between actors personating Diogenes and Aristophanes on the value of public amusements, followed by another between a Londoner and a Parisian on the excellencies of their respective cities, to the accompaniment of vocal and instrumental music. The climax of the evening was Davenant's own heroic account of *The Siege of Rhodes*, the story being "sung in recitative music" and presented with movable scenery devised by John Webb (1611-72), Inigo Jones's assistant and nephew by marriage. Retrospectively this has been categorised as the first performance of an opera in England. Davenant was also given permission in 1658 to present *The Cruelty of the Spaniards in Peru* and in 1659 *Sir Francis Drake*, whose anti-Catholic themes were doubtless acceptable to the Puritan mentality.

the staging of plays was incompatible with the profession of Christianity. In the same year soldiers broke up a performance of Beaumont and Fletcher's *A King and No King* while it was being played by Beeston at Salisbury Court. In 1649, following the execution of Charles I, the interior of the Fortune was dismantled by soldiers and the same treatment was meted out to the Salisbury Court.

CHAPTER THREE

Restoration

> "... a banisht Court, with Lewdness fraught,
> The seeds of open Vice returning brought.
> Thus Lodg'd, (as Vice by great example thrives)
> It first debauch'd the daughters and the Wives.
> London, a fruitful soil, yet never bore
> So plentiful a Crop of Horns before.
> The Poets, who must live by courts or starve,
> Were proud so good a Government to serve;
> Admixing with Buffoons and Pimps profain,
> Tainted the Stage, for some small snip of Gain."
> John Dryden   Epilogue to *The Pilgrim* (1700)

Restoring What?

When Charles II was invited to reclaim the throne in 1660 it amounted not so much to the restoration of the monarchy as its re-invention. Much the same might be said of the theatre. And, like the monarchy, the theatre derived much of its new guise from the French model, owing more to Molière than to Shakespeare. The closure of London theatres in 1642 had killed off the tradition of attendance by all classes. Re-establishing the habit would face such challenges as the Great Plague, which closed the theatres from June 1665 for sixteen months, and the Great Fire of 1666, which would make at least a hundred thousand Londoners homeless.

The new theatre audience would consist, at least initially, of courtiers and their hangers-on, ladies of pleasure, upper-class idlers and a few of the *nouveaux riches* with the newest fashions to show off. The popularity of specially-written prologues and epilogues, directly addressed to the audience, emphasise the significance of the theatre as an arena of social rendezvous in which the audience was flatteringly conscious of itself as well as of its relationship with the players.

Theatre therefore, as reconstituted under the reconstituted monarchy, owed all to court patronage and, to no little extent, to the tastes and concerns of the monarch himself. On the one hand Charles, a connoisseur of amusement, favoured entertainment in all its forms. On the other, he was keenly aware of the subversive potential of the drama. Determined never to "go on his travels" again, the king was concerned to protect from any challenge the throne that he had waited so long to regain. What the king wanted, and largely got, was a court theatre without the nuisance of having to pay for it himself.

Patently Secure

In 1662 Letters Patent were issued by the king, granting a monopoly of dramatic presentation to two proven and trusted courtiers in the persons of Thomas Killigrew (1612-83) and William Davenant (1606-68). The language employed in this royal decree was suitably high-minded but, read retrospectively from the standpoint of what the Restoration drama notoriously became, somewhat ironic:

"Forasmuch as many plays formerly acted do contain certain profane, obscene and scurrilous passages and the women's parts therein have been acted by men in the habit of women ...

18. Sir William Davenant.

19. Thomas Killigrew.

henceforth no new play shall be acted ... containing any passage offensive to piety and good manners ... And we do likewise permit and give leave that all the women's parts ... may be performed by women so long as these recreations ... be esteemed not only harmless delights but useful and instructive representations of human life ..."

Killigrew's company would concentrate on the classic plays of the period before the closures of 1642 (initially including Davenant's!), while Davenant's would perform new works. Primarily intended as a political safeguard for a shaky regime, the 'patent system' institutionalised a framework which, though variously contested, constrained the development of English theatre until the passage of the Theatres Act in 1843.

Thomas Killigrew had acted as a child, playing devils at the Red Bull Theatre in return for seeing the plays for free. Despite his lack of formal education he became a page to Charles I and Groom of the Bedchamber to Charles II, whom he had accompanied into exile and from

which he had managed to accompany the monarch on the same ship. Killigrew had also, before the civil wars, written several plays, including a successful, bawdy farce *The Parson's Wedding*. Although "a merry droll" according to the diarist Samuel Pepys (1633-1703), Killigrew was to prove less adept as a man of business than Davenant, although he boasted to Pepys that he had greatly raised standards from what had been usual in his youth - wax candles instead of smoky tallow ones, ten violinists instead of two or three, a prostitute for the recreation of the company's younger actors, "now, all things civil, no rudeness anywhere; then, as in a bear-garden." Notwithstanding his pride "that the stage is now by his pains a thousand times better and more glorious than ever heretofore" by 1671 Killigrew had begun to hand over management to his son Charles and by 1677 had done so completely.

Davenant claimed to be Shakespeare's illegitimate son and may well have been his godson. Like the king, Davenant was an

20. The Duke's Theatre, Lincoln's Inn Fields.

enthusiastic philanderer, famously losing his nose to syphilis or, as John Aubrey put it in his *Brief Lives* from "a terrible clap of a black handsome wench that lay in Axe-yard, Westminster".

The New Theatres
Under the direction of these chosen guardians the theatre as a physical entity changed fundamentally. No longer the 'wooden O', open to the sky, it became enclosed from the elements and, highly symbolic of the new dispensation, was to be dominated by a 'Royal Box'. As

Killigrew pointed out to Pepys, under Charles I "the Queen seldom and the King never would come" but under Charles II "now, not the King only for state, but all civil people do think they may come as well as any."

Both Killigrew and Davenant were initially obliged to share the Cockpit and then to accommodate their acting companies in converted tennis courts, which is how many early French theatres had been created. Davenant's, at Lisle's Tennis Court, Portugal Street, off Lincoln's Inn Fields, was the first to incorporate a proscenium arch in a public place of performance. Killigrew's was initially in Gibbon's Tennis Court in Vere Street, off Clare Market. In 1663 Killigrew established his company, the King's Men, in a converted riding-school at Bridges Street, later known as the Theatre Royal, Drury Lane. When this was destroyed by fire in 1672 it was rebuilt, probably to designs by Sir Christopher Wren (1632-1723), on a much larger scale, capable of accommodating an audience of a thousand.

Davenant in 1671 moved his company, known as the Duke's Men from the patronage of the king's brother, James, Duke of York, to the Dorset Gardens Theatre, also known as the Duke's. Built to designs by Wren at a cost of £9,000, the building fronted onto the Thames at Salisbury Court, just off Fleet Street. This location enabled it to draw audiences from the City. The destruction of Killigrew's Theatre Royal ensured a brief popularity, boosted by the attractions of splendid scenery and sophisticated stage machinery imported from France. Attendances declined rapidly, however, following the reconstruction of Drury Lane. Poor acoustics ultimately condemned Dorset Gardens for use as a venue for strong-man acts, fencing displays, animal shows etc. until its demolition in 1709.

Apart from the all-important proscenium arch, framing the on-stage action, the purpose-built theatre of the Restoration period featured other innovations, such as doors for exits and entrances flanking the raked proscenium on which the actors actually performed. Behind the arch was the scenic section of the stage where wing and border scenery, defining the setting of the action, could be moved in and out of position on grooves. Beyond that was a vista section, to give the option of an even greater depth of view. This was flanked by 'tiring' (dressing) rooms. Lighting was provided by chandeliers, more concentrated together than those in the auditorium. The audience sat in the pit, also raked, on rows of backless benches, or in tiered galleries. There was no standing. Sight lines were therefore much improved.

Seating patterns reflected social status, as

21. *The Dorset Gardens Theatre, south of Fleet Street.*

was made clear in *The Country Gentleman's Vade Mecum* (1699). The upper gallery was the domain of servants. Boxes included "one peculiar to the King and Royal Family and the rest for the Persons of Quality". The middle gallery was "where the Citizens Wives and Daughters ... Serving-men, Journey-men and Apprentices commonly take their Places and now and then some disponding Mistresses and superannuated Poets". Lastly came the Pit, the realm of would-be "Judges, Wits and Censurers ... in common with these sit the Squires, Sharpers, Beaus, Bullies and Whores and here and there an extravagant Male and Female Cit." The better class of whore often sported a mask, which supposedly served to preserve her modesty while actually advertising her availability. The poet and dramatist John Dryden (1631-1700) was thoroughly familiar with the phenomenon:

" The play-house is their place of traffic, where
Nightly they sit to sell their rotten ware ...
For while he nibbles at her amorous trap

She gets the money but he gets the clap.
Entrenched in vizor masks they giggling sit
And throw designing looks about the pit.
Neglecting wholly what the actors say.
'Tis their least business there to see the play."

The backstage area remained an unprobed mystery to most. When Pepys took advantage of building works at Drury Lane to penetrate this unknown kingdom he was prompted to discomforting philosophical reflection –

" my business here was to see the inside of the stage and all the tiring rooms and machines; and indeed it was a sight worthy seeing. But to see their clothes ... and what a mixture of things there was, here a wooden leg, there a ruff, here a hobby-horse, there a crown, would make a man split himself to see with laughing – But then again to think how fine they show on the stage by candlelight and how poor things they are to look now too nearhand, is not pleasant at all."

Performances normally began at 3.00 p.m., although the doors were open hours before to allow a lengthy prelude of socializing. The better-off sent their servants in advance to reserve the best places. Half the point of going to the theatre was to be seen and to see others - the theatre was an arena of social display, with the play as an additional mode of self-recognition. Audience and players were very much reflections of each other, both dressed as far as possible in the height of contemporary fashion. The acting style was elocutionary, with diction accompanied and accentuated by flourishes of fans, handkerchiefs, hats and walking canes. Fashion extended to the imperative of seeing new plays early. Runs of more than a few days were in any case a rarity, a dozen or more denoting an exceptional success. Coupled with the possibility of a royal presence this created the phenomenon of the 'First Night' and fostered the emergence of the critic.

The Last of the Red Bull

Before the Patent rights of Killigrew and Davenant were definitively established an attempt was made to revive the Red Bull Theatre in Clerkenwell. Led by a former royalist soldier Michael Mohun (1620-84), its company initially included Killigrew, who soon defected, taking much of the best acting talent with him. The Red Bull thereupon reverted to its tradition of setting low standards and failing to reach even those. On 23rd March 1661 Pepys recorded that he had been "To the Red Bull, where I had not been since plays came up again." It had not been an auspicious foray – "the clothes are very poor and the actors but common fellows ... At last into the pit, where I believe there was not above ten more than myself, and not a hundred in the whole house." The play, Rowley's *All Lost for Lust*, was "poorly done and with so much disorder." When a boy missed his note in a song a senior member of the cast cuffed him round the ear on the spot and the whole place dissolved in uproar. Nevertheless Pepys returned in May to see an attempt at *Doctor Faustus* which proved :"so wretchedly and poorly done that we were sick of it." By 1663 the Bull was reduced to staging fencing and fisticuffs. By 1665 it had been demolished.

The Human Comedy

The distinctive contribution of the Restoration period (although it reached its apogee under William and Mary) was the "comedy of manners" which superseded Jonson's comedy of morals. The most characteristic preoccupation of the principal characters depicted on stage was to appear witty, both in the sense of swift in repartee and in being sharp-witted. Sincerity was at a discount compared to cynical self-advancement through coquetry, flattery and seduction. The world depicted was not so much immoral as amoral, one in which characters were ruled by their appetites and aversions, not moral absolutes. The principal characters were, moreover, free agents in the sense that none of them actually worked and therefore had many empty hours to fill with diversion and intrigue. The stage was populated by recognisable social types - the fop, the rake, the cuckold, the country boor from the shires and his City counterpart, the pompous alderman or scheming merchant. The latter, heirs to the despised and defeated Puritan supporters of Parliament in the civil wars, could be ridiculed with relative impunity as in Edward Ravenscroft's *The London Cuckolds* (1681) which, oddly enough, remained a great favourite on Lord Mayor's Day for a century. The social apex represented by the Court was, however, to be mocked at peril. Edward Howard's *The Change of Crowns* (1667), which ridiculed court manners, was swiftly suppressed on the direct command of the king himself. *Lucius Junius Brutus* (1680) by Nathaniel Lee (?1649-92), which had the temerity to treat with the overthrow of tyrants, met the same fate, even though its author, by presenting it as a story of ancient Rome, sought to distance it from the contemporary crisis around the attempts to exclude the king's Catholic brother from the throne.

There might be little tolerance for political subversion on the stage, but sexual subversion was another matter. And the limits of taste were soon under severe test. When Killigrew's *The Parson's Wedding* was revived in 1664 with an all-female cast, it made even the philandering Pepys blush. In a world of inverted moral values ribaldry and invective held sway, snobbery was taken for granted and topicality of reference served as a guarantor of dramatic authenticity. London provided not only the location of the theatres but the setting for many of the plays. The country, in literary terms, represented the antithesis of polite society, a place of exile and dullness. The metropolitan elite, as reflected on stage, was both self-knowing and self-satisfied. In the words of one of Wycherley's characters "Tis a pleasant, well-bred, complaisant, free, frolic, good-natured, pretty age; and if you do not like it, leave it to us that do."

The comedy of manners was pioneered by Sir George Etherege (?1634-91), himself a man about town who had lived in France and was familiar with both Molière's farces and Italian mime. His first play *The Comical Revenge, or Love in a Tub* (1664), composed in a mixture of rhymed heroics and prose, featured what became, in various combinations, standard elements of the genre –

rivalry in love, a duel, attempted suicide, an impudent servant, a debonair libertine, a wealthy widow, a stupid country knight and a couple of con-men, all of whose various sins and shortcomings result in exposure to ridicule and/or marriage to more or less appropriate partners. In Etherege's *She wou'd if she cou'd* (1668) the archly named Sir Oliver and Lady Cockwood come up from the country to divert themselves in the capital, with dissipation and flirtatious intrigue respectively, precipitating a series of encounters which involve the conventional farcical elements of mistaken identity, drunkenness, being locked in a cupboard, hidden under a table etc. *The Man of Mode* (1676), Etherege's greatest success, intertwines two marriage plots and satirises the empty dandy Sir Fopling Flutter who gives the play its name. Etherege wrote whereof he knew, himself marrying a wealthy widow, attaining a knighthood and serving, somewhat insouciantly, as a diplomat in Turkey and France, where ironically he died, a victim of the political wheel of fortune, as a Jacobite exile.

The Advent of the Actress

The prominent role allocated to feisty females in the comedy of manners reflects another fundamental innovation of the period – the debut of the professional actress. In January 1661 Pepys recorded seeing Fletcher and Massinger's *Beggars Bush* at Vere Street, " it being very well done; and here the first time that ever I saw women come upon the stage." Pepys would later include the actress Elizabeth Knepp among the objects of his roving affections – and hands.

Almost inevitably the sexuality exploited by actresses on stage could only with difficulty be confined there. The first great English actress, Elizabeth Barry (1658-1713), in a career lasting thirty-five years, created more than a hundred roles and excelled in playing the tragic, tear-jerking heroines created by Thomas Otway (1652-85) - whose advances she repulsed in favour of becoming the mistress of her patron, the dissolute Earl of Rochester (1647-80), himself probably the model for Dorimant, the amoral 'hero' of *The*

22. Anne Bracegirdle.

23. Nell Gwyn

Man of Mode. Anne Bracegirdle, (1673-1748) by contrast, despite being Congreve's mistress, maintained an unblemished public reputation and achieved the unique distinction, for a theatrical, of a lying-in-state in the Jerusalem Chamber at Westminster Abbey before her burial there. Writing a century after her death, itself no mean tribute to her fascination, Macaulay had cause to mention her in his monumental *History of England,* characterising her as "a cold, vain and interested coquette, who perfectly understood how much the influence of her charms was increased by the fame of a severity which cost her nothing."

Further proof of the standing achieved by these two early superstars is their inclusion in Sir Godfrey Kneller's equestrian portrait of a triumphant William III as the personifications of Flora and Britannia.

The best-known actress of the age, Nell Gwyn (1650-87) famously became the mistress of Charles II himself. On stage she singularly failed to impress Samuel Pepys when he saw her in serious or tragic parts but was a revelation in

Dryden's *The Maiden Queen* in March 1667 – "so great a performance of a comical part was never, I believe in the world as Nell do this ... It makes me, I confess, admire her." Pepys's peep behind the scenes with Mrs. Knepp produced, however, a rather opposite reaction – " she took us up into the tiring rooms and to the women's shift where Nell was dressing herself and was all unready and is very pretty, prettier than I thought ... But Lord! to see how they both were painted would made a man mad and did make me loath them; and what base company of men come among them" - (he appears to have been forgetting himself) – "and how lewdly they talk!"

Despite the supposed prohibition on males playing female parts some actors defied the ban – and to dramatic effect. When Pepys saw Edward Kynaston (1640-1706) in a revival of Fletcher's *The Loyal Subject* he thought him "the loveliest lady that ever I saw in my life". An enthusiastic cross-dresser in his youth, Kynaston later aged graciously into heroic and dignified roles such as the ageing king in *Henry IV.*

Betterton

The outstanding dramatic talent of the era was Thomas Betterton (1635-1710). Born in Westminster the son of a royal cook, Betterton was initially apprenticed, along with Edward Kynaston, to the bookseller John Rhodes (?1606-?) who may have been a prompter at the Blackfriars Theatre and had become Keeper of the Cockpit which he re-opened in 1660 until the Patent-Holders shut him down and took over his actors.

As a member of Davenant's Duke's Company Betterton quickly became one of its stars. Pepys praises him with superlatives as early as March 1661 and he remained the diarist's favourite actor, warmly commended as "a very sober, serious man, and studious and humble". Under Davenant's firm tuition Betterton learned the value of a thorough understanding of the text and how "to enter thoroughly into the Nature of the Part". Such professionalism was not to be taken for granted. In March 1662 Pepys took his wife to Lincoln's Inn Fields "and there saw *Romeo and Juliet,* the first time it was ever acted. But it is the play of itself the worst that ever I heard in my life, and the worst acted that ever I saw these people do; and I am resolved to go no more to see the first time of acting, for they were all of them out more or less."

The small size of Davenant's company obliged Betterton to undertake a wide range of roles, in total at least two hundred, though never farce. He could neither sing nor dance. Nor was he gifted with athleticism or good looks. According to a fellow actor, Anthony Aston,

"Mr. Betterton, though a superlative good actor, laboured under an ill figure, being clumsily made, having a great head, short, thick neck, stooped in the shoulders and had fat short arms which he rarely lifted higher than his stomach ... He had little eyes and a broad face, a little pock-bitten, a corpulent body, with thick legs and large feet ...".

But he could act. As Aston further noted, "His voice was low and grumbling; yet he could time

24. Thomas Betterton.

it by an artful climax which enforced universal attention even from the fops and orange-girls."

Following Davenant's death in 1668, Betterton became *de facto* co-manager of the company with Henry Harris on behalf of Davenant's heir Charles, then still a child. Betterton was instrumental in the project to build the Dorset Gardens Theatre and travelled to Paris to consult experts and observe current theatrical practice there. He then lived on the premises as rent-free building superintendent, with his actress wife, Mary Saunderson and their two informally adopted daughters, Anne Bracegirdle and Elizabeth Watson, both of whom were trained for the stage. In 1681 the King's Company and the Duke's Company merged to become the United Company, based at Drury Lane, which they clearly thought to be the superior building in theatrical terms. Following financial difficulties which led to quarrels between the patent-holders and the actors, in 1695 Betterton got royal permission to establish a new company. Eight of the 'rebels', including Elizabeth Barry

25. Aphra Behn, drawn by T. Unwins.

stage. Before turning to the drama Aphra Behn (1640-89) was employed to spy on the Dutch. (Unfortunately no one believed her warning of an impending raid on British shipping in the Medway, which turned out to be true.) Of Behn's sixteen plays most were comedies of intrigue, many adapted from Spanish models. The most popular, however, was *The Rover* which appeared in two parts and recounted the exile exploits of a band of cavaliers led by the aptly named Wilmore, another barely-disguised clone of the rakish Rochester. It contained the memorable line "Come away; poverty's catching", which says much for the outlook of a greed-is-good generation. As the widow of a City merchant she was also well qualified to compose *The City Heiress* (1682), a satire on London life. Her best remembered work, which drew on a youthful visit to Surinam, was *Oroonoko, or the History of the Royal Slave*, which contained one of the first sympathetic depictions of a 'noble savage' and deplored the slave trade. Initially (*ca.*1688) a novel, it was adapted for the stage in 1695. In her landmark essay *A Room of One's Own* Virginia Woolf hailed Behn as the first English woman to earn her living by writing. She also achieved the distinction of burial in the cloisters of Westminster Abbey.

Dryden and his rivals

Educated at Westminster, John Dryden settled in London in 1657 and worked as a professional writer. Now best remembered as a poet, he also wrote or collaborated on some thirty plays, many in the style of Corneille and Racine, others attempting to fuse heroic tragedy and contemporary comedy. Appointed Poet Laureate in 1668, in the same year he also published *An Essay of Dramatic Poesy*, contrasting French and English drama with a view to enunciating principles of literary judgment, a task to which he returned frequently in numerous prologues and epilogues, provoking Harley Granville-Barker *(see p157)* to remark tartly two centuries later that "if Dryden's plays had been as good as their prefaces he would have been a dramatist indeed." Dr. Johnson (1709-84) hailed him as

and Anne Bracegirdle, took over the tiny, disused theatre in Lincoln's Inn Fields but the venture proved a struggle, plagued by lawsuits, deaths and desertions, so that by 1705 Betterton was happy to give up management altogether, though he continued to act and had a profitable sideline in teaching voice production to clergymen. On one occasion Archbishop Tillotson asked Betterton why "he could never move people in the Church nearly as much" as the actor did on stage. Betterton replied that it was "easy to be accounted for: 'tis because you are only telling them a story, and I am showing them facts." Respected and respectable, both Betterton and his wife, to whom he was married for forty-eight years "in perfect amity", were honoured with burial in Westminster Abbey. A biography by Charles Gildon was rushed out in the year of his death.

A Feminist Icon

Not only were there females on the Restoration stage, there were also females writing for the

"the father of English criticism". Jonathan Swift (1667-1745) paid flippant tribute in verse:

" Read all the prefaces of Dryden,
For these our critics much confide in,
(Tho' merely writ at first for filling
To raise the volume's price a shilling)."

Much of Dryden's output represented the other major mode of contemporary drama, the so-called heroic tragedy, featuring exotic settings, stylised violence and hyperbolic ranting in rhymed couplets or blank verse. Dryden's *The Conquest of Granada* (1670) and *Aurang-Zebe* (1675), were matched by Elkanah Settle's *The Empress of Morocco* (1673), John Crowne's *The Destruction of Jerusalem* (1677) and Thomas Otway's *Venice Preserv'd* (1682). These heroic plays were modelled on the works of Corneille, which the king and his courtiers had seen in exile. Typically they explored the tensions between the private personality of a prince and his desires and his public *persona* and its duties. Distanced in time and space, they offered a way of referring to contemporary events without actually referring to them. Thus Otway's *Venice Preserv'd,* staged in the aftermath of an alleged 'Popish Plot' to subvert the Anglican monarchy, by showing how a threat to the Venetian republic is thwarted, implicitly argues that stability is so fundamental a political necessity that corruption in government may be tolerated to ensure it.

Allegedly "a moralist at heart", William Wycherley (1640-1716) is described as having employed indecency to flagellate vice. Macaulay was moved to make this point forcefully in his essay *On the Comic Dramatists of the Restoration*: "Wycherley's indecency is protected against the critics as a skunk is protected against the hunters. It is safe because it is too filthy to handle and too noisome even to approach." Even the Anglophile Voltaire (1694-1778) thought Wycherley "very ingenious ... but too bold for French manners." Wycherley's first play *Love in a Wood* (1671) was set in St. James's Park and brought him the favour (and favours) of the king's mistress, the Duchess of Cleveland. His best, and best known,

26. *John Dryden.*

play *The Country Wife* (1675) depicts a jealous husband's attempts to curb the wantonness of a rustic spouse exposed to the temptations of the capital. Wycherley lost favour at court by secretly marrying the widowed Countess of Drogheda contrary to the king's wishes. In a case of life imitating art Wycherley then discovered that she was nowhere near as rich as he had supposed and after her death he was imprisoned for debt. Following a court performance of his last work *The Plain Dealer* (1676) (in which the characters have been to see *The Country Wife*), he was released and given a pension by James II (reigned 1685-88).

The Sullen Lovers (1668), the first play by Thomas Shadwell (1642-92), was a straightforward adaptation of a play by Molière, though he later tried to revive Jonson's comedy of humours. In *The Virtuoso* (1676) Shadwell mocked the scientific pretensions of the recently-established Royal Society and in *The Squire of Alsatia* (1688) he displayed an impressive grasp of the cant of London's criminal underworld. *Bury Fair* (1689) guyed provincials aping metropolitan manners. Viciously satirised by Dryden, the Whig Protestant Shadwell had the last laugh by displacing the recent Catholic convert as Poet Laureate and Historiographer Royal when the Revolution of 1688 transformed the landscape of political patronage.

Thomas D'Urfey (1653-1723), of Huguenot descent, combined Spanish plots with English manners in a prolific output which ranged from ballads to a three-part adaptation of Don Quixote with music by Purcell. A personal friend of Charles II and James II, in 1698 D'Urfey managed so far to outrage contemporary sensibilities that he was prosecuted for profanity.

D'Urfey's contemporary Nathaniel Lee (1653-92), another alumnus of Westminster School and a failed actor, specialised in blood-soaked re-tellings of ancient history, full of scenes of torture and plots which left the stage strewn with corpses. Aptly for one whose works often featured lunatics, Lee died in Bedlam after a drinking bout.

William Congreve (1670-1729) benefited from the mentoring of Dryden and was well served in *The Old Bachelor* (1693), *The Double Dealer* (1694) and *Love for Love* (1695) by the superb acting skills of Thomas Betterton and Anne Bracegirdle. The poor reception of his masterpiece *The Way of the World* (1700), compounded by ill health, failing eyesight and idleness, finished Congreve with the theatre by the time he was thirty. He had moreover the consolation of numerous government sinecures and the distraction of a long-standing affair with the Duchess of Marlborough. Dying as a result of a coach smash, Congreve was buried in Westminster Abbey.

Briefly an actor but hampered by stage fright, limited by a weak voice and periodically crippled by recurrent bouts of rheumatism, George Farquhar (1678-1707) quit the stage after unintentionally injuring a fellow actor when he forgot to exchange his sword for a blunted foil. Farquhar found fame with his second effort *The Constant Couple: or, a trip to the Jubilee*, which ran for an unprecedented fifty-three nights, a record

27. William Congreve, from the painting by Sir Godfrey Kneller.

unbroken until the staging of *The Beggar's Opera* *(see p53)* almost three decades later. In the course of the eighteenth century it would be performed more than four hundred times. Handsome and amorous, Farquhar is supposed to have had affairs with the playwright Susannah Centlivre *(see p55)* and Anne Oldfield but he outdid Wycherley in self-deception by marrying a widow and supposed heiress, who already had three children and turned out to be quite penniless. Her genuine devotion to him ensured an unexpectedly successful relationship. In 1706 Farquhar turned his own experiences as a lieutenant in the Earl of Orrery's regiment to comic account in *The Recruiting Officer*. It ran ten nights on its first production and by the following year was being put on at both London's theatres. Over the course of the century it would be played 512 times in London alone and published in over fifty editions. In 1789, performed by convicts, it reputedly became the first play ever put on in Australia.

In 1707 in six weeks, while lying ill and destitute in sordid lodgings, Farquhar penned his masterpiece *The Beaux Stratagem*. Ironically in view of his own marriage, it recommended divorce as the best remedy for a loveless union. Farquhar lived just long enough to learn of its success. Over the course of the rest of the century actors paid it the compliment of choosing it as their benefit piece on at least 192 occasions, so confident were they of it as a guarantor of good takings.

The son of a London merchant, Sir John Vanbrugh (1664-1726) in his twenties became a soldier and was imprisoned in the Bastille for spying. His first play *The Relapse or Virtue in Danger* (1696) was a huge success. Following the familiar formula of country folk at risk in the wicked city, it works in the usual stock characters denoted by such names as Loveless, Worthy, Sir Novelty Fashion, Sir Tunbelley Clumsey and his daughter Miss Hoyden. *The Provok'd Wife* (1697) likewise features Sir John Brute, Constant, Heartfree and the affected Lady Fancyfull. Vanbrugh subsequently turned to architecture, designing majestic Castle Howard, monumental Blenheim Palace and The Queen's Theatre (1705) in the Haymarket, to whose company he invited Betterton as leader. Vanbrugh also became Clarenceux king-of-arms and in 1714 was the first man knighted by the new sovereign George I.

The excesses of the Restoration stage found their nemesis in Jeremy Collier (1650-1726) whose *Short View of the Immorality and Profaneness of the English Stage* (1698) – which was by no means short – excoriated Dryden, Wycherley, Congreve, D'Urfey and Otway by name, denouncing their output as "faulty to a scandalous degree of nauseousness and aggravation ... viz. their smuttiness of expression;

their swearing, profaneness and lewd application of Scripture; their abuse of clergy; their making their top characters libertines and giving them success in their debauchery." Collier, an Anglican clergyman, took it upon himself to serve as the mouthpiece of an increasingly pietistic bourgeoisie. The monarchy of William and Mary (reigned 1688-1702) was largely indifferent to the theatre and opposition to it was therefore no longer equated with political disloyalty. Collier created a great impact. Congreve and D'Urfey were both subjected to prosecution. Thomas Betterton and Mrs. Bracegirdle were both fined. Several of Collier's targets replied in pamphlet or poetic form, though none to great effect. There was a deeper contemporary significance to the sense of outrage, which was theological as well as moral and therefore perhaps less readily comprehensible to the modern secular sensibility. As Professor John Brewer has emphasised:

"Hostility to the stage was deeply embedded in the English Protestant consciousness. The stage was viewed as a place of trickery and deceit, full of illusions and magic similar to those which the Roman Catholic church had used to bamboozle ignorant observers into becoming credulous believers. For many Protestants, especially clerics, it was a cardinal principle that play-going and going to mass were both forms of idolatry."

Collier returned his energies to his multi-volume *Ecclesiastical History of Great Britain*, having helped to provoke the establishment of several Societies for the Reformation of Manners and thus to create the climate which would demand the production of a 'reformed' and more decorous form of the drama.

Saving Shakespeare

Despite the constant outpouring of new works on the Restoration stage there was still an appetite for Shakespeare. As early as 1660 Killigrew had staged a version of *Othello* as *The Moor of Venice*. But the Bard had to be cut and moulded to fit a changed public taste. Pepys, for instance, dismissed *A Midsummer Night's Dream* as " the most insipid ridiculous play that ever I saw in my life", redeemed only by "some good dancing and some handsome women." More fundamental was the critique derived from French dramatic theory as set forth, for example, in Thomas Rymer's *The Tragedies of the Last Age Consider'd and Examin'd by the Practice of the Ancients, and by the Common Sense of All Ages* (1677), which treated stage characters as representative social types, who behave according to the rules of a classically conceived world order of universal modes of thinking, feeling and acting.

Dryden reworked *Antony and Cleopatra* in blank verse as *All for Love*, in which the original play is barely recognisable, as well as producing a 'corrected' *Troilus and Cressida* (1679), of which he said that he had stripped away "that heap of rubbish under which many excellent thoughts lay wholly buried. Accordingly I new-modelled the plot, threw out many unnecessary persons, improved those characters which were begun and left unfinished...". Dryden also collaborated with Davenant to produce a rendering of *The Tempest*, with an extra sub-plot and additional characters, which Shadwell then modified into an opera, *The Enchanted Island* (1674). Edward Ravenscroft managed to produce a version (1678) of *Titus Andronicus* even more gore-soaked than the original. Nahum Tate (1652-1715) had his *Richard III* banned on political grounds in the

28. *William Shakespeare, from the frontispiece of the First Folio edition of 1623.*

politically jittery year of 1680, so re-presented it as *The Sicilian Usurper*. Tate's 1681 version of *King Lear* cut out the Fool, restored Lear (played by Betterton) to his throne and married off Cordelia to Edgar. An outrage to modern purists, it was hugely successful and kept the Bard's original version off the stage until 1838. In 1681 Tate also reworked *Coriolanus* as *The Ingratitude of a Commonwealth*, adding in a comedy section. Some Shakespeare plays simply dropped out of the repertoire altogether. When *Twelfth Night, As You Like It, The Winter's Tale* and *All's Well That Ends Well* were produced in the 1740s it was for the first time in the eighteenth century.

29. *Scene from* The Taming of the Shrew, *from the first illustrated edition of Shakespeare, edited by Nicholas Rowe, 1709.*

Educated at Westminster and admitted to the bar at Middle Temple, Nicholas Rowe (1674-1718) gave up the law on inheriting an estate and produced seven tragedies, notable for their strong female roles portraying the plight of a virtuous woman, as in the *Fair Penitent* (1703) and *The Tragedy of Jane Shore* (1714), explicitly written "in imitation of Shakespeare's style". Of far more lasting significance, however, was Rowe's six-volume edition (1709) of Shakespeare's plays. Rowe battled to remove textual corruptions and attempted to regularize the divisions of scenes and acts and to add scene and stage directions. Rowe's efforts were recognised by his appointment as Poet Laureate in 1715 and interment in Westminster Abbey.

In 1725 Alexander Pope published an edition of Shakespeare which provoked Lewis Theobald (1688-1744) to issue a pamphlet *Shakespeare Restored* (1726), exposing Pope's many errors.

Pope retaliated by making Theobald the 'hero' of his *Dunciad* (1728), a satire on Dullness. Pope did, however, incorporate many of Theobald's corrections into his second edition. Theobald's own edition (1733-4) far surpassed Pope's revised effort. Over three hundred emendations made by Theobald are still accepted by most modern editors. He was also the first editor to direct attention to the issue of Shakespeare's sources. The edition published by Dr. Johnson in 1765 was noteworthy for a *Preface* which is ranked as one of his finest works of critical prose. The ten-volume edition published by Edward Capel (1713-81) in 1768 established the arrangement of lines usually followed since. In his posthumously published *Commentary, Notes and Various Readings to Shakespeare* (1783) Capel offered the first full scholarly discussion of Shakespeare's sources and attempted to untangle the relationship between the quarto and Folio editions.

In 1778 Edmund Malone (1741-1812) published *An attempt to ascertain the order in which the plays attributed to Shakespeare were written*. His twenty-one volume edition of Shakespeare appeared posthumously in 1821.

Shakespeare's iconic status was reaffirmed artistically as well as through such scholarly devotion. In 1741 an imposing new monument of the Bard, designed by William Kent and executed by Peter Scheemakers, was unveiled in Poet's Corner. At the end of the century the City of London Alderman and print publisher John Boydell (1720-1804) proposed to publish a lavish illustrated edition of Shakespeare. Further to this end he commissioned leading artists of the day to produce paintings of famous scenes and characters which would then be displayed in a public gallery and engraved for reproduction. Boydell's Shakespeare Gallery opened in Pall Mall in 1789. By 1805 thirty-three artists, including such stars as Fuseli and Romney, had contributed 167 paintings. Boydell, however, had run into financial difficulties and with his death the project foundered. The building was disposed of and Christie's auctioned off the paintings.

CHAPTER FOUR

Marking Time

By the opening of the eighteenth century London's population had passed the half million mark. In the newly-founded (1694) Bank of England, an emerging stock market and a developing insurance industry it was forging new instruments to improve the efficiency of its global commerce. In *The Daily Courant* (1702) it acquired the first English newspaper to achieve continuous publication. In the columns of *The Tatler* and *The Spectator* the capital's social and cultural elite found a new way of talking to itself and about itself. In 1708 Betterton's prompter Thomas Downes produced a history of the theatre since the Restoration, entitled in honour of the great Roman actor *Roscius Anglicanus*. But London, for all its expanding size, wealth and sophistication still had only two theatres. In 1705 Vanbrugh's new venue, built on what is now the site of Her Majesty's Theatre, Haymarket, opened as the Queen's Theatre but soon proved acoustically inadequate for plays and and by 1708 had become an opera house instead.

A Varied Career
After leaving Westminster School, where he was a contemporary and friend of Barton Booth *(see p51)* and John Gay *(see p54)* Aaron Hill (1685-1702) made a two year tour of Europe and the Middle East. In 1709, although a complete novice, he was appointed manager of Drury Lane where he wrote his first plays, *Elfrid*, and a farce *The Walking Statue; or, The Devil in the Wine Cellar*. After quarrelling with his actors, Hill left in 1710 and wrote the libretto for *Rinaldo*, Handel's first London opera. Occasionally involved in management, Hill experimented with various dramatic innovations. His play *Fatal Vision* (1710)

was the first in England to utilise the new Italian practice of setting scenery at an angle to the audience. *Fatal Extravagance* (1721) anticipates Lillo *(see p55)* in its attempt at bourgeois domestic tragedy. *Athelwold* (1731), a re-working of *Elfrid*, was unconventional in its effort at historical authenticity, based on Hill's own researches into 'old Saxon dress'. Hill also made four translations from Voltaire, founded a bi-weekly theatrical publication, *The Prompter* (1734-6) and composed a poem on *The Art of Acting* (1746) in which he encouraged the actor to experience in his imagination the emotions appropriate to a part and then to reproduce them physically in terms of look and gesture. Hill's many other projects include a not very good history of the Ottoman empire, an uncompleted epic poem, a venture to clear the river Spey of rocks and the manufacture of potash at Plaistow. Hill's letters and journals do, however, constitute a significant source of information about the state of the theatre in his day.

Drury Lane
Drury Lane enjoyed stability and relative success under a triumvirate of actor-managers of whom the most significant was Colley Cibber (1671-1757). The son of a distinguished Danish sculptor who had carved the spectacular relief panel on the Monument to the Great Fire of London, Cibber had been well educated and was intended by his family to enter one of the learned professions. In 1690, however, in the face of their opposition, he joined Betterton's United Company. Refusing to join Betterton's secession in 1695, he remained with the depleted remnant at Drury Lane and thus became able to take on major roles much earlier than he otherwise might have done. In

30. Colley Cibber.

literary quality. Nonetheless he produced a skilful adaptation of *Tartuffe* and completed Vanbrugh's unfinished last play, *A Journey to London*, as *The Provok'd Husband* (1728). He was also a very good teacher of younger actors and a conscientious manager, as his autobiographical account of the many duties of that office makes clear:

"Every manager is obliged ... to attend two or three hours every morning at the rehearsal of plays ... or else every rehearsal would be but a rude meeting of mirth and jollity. The same attendance is as necessary at every play ... (and) ... at reading of every new play ... Besides this, a manager is to order all new clothes ... to limit the expense ... A manager is to direct and oversee the painters, machinists, musicians, singers and dancers, to have an eye upon the door-keepers, under-servants and officers who, without such care, are too often apt to defraud us or neglect their duty."

Chosen as Poet Laureate in 1730, the relentlessly self-promoting Cibber became a target for venomous attacks from the dramatist Henry Fielding (1707-54), who accused him of committing assault on the English language, and the poet Alexander Pope (1688-1744), who cast him as King of the Dunces in *The New Dunciad*. An anonymous squib observed that:

"In merry old England it once was a rule
The King had his Poet and also his Fool,
But now we're so frugal, I'd have you to know it.
That Cibber can serve both for Fool and for Poet."

Cibber blamed Pope for that one. Pope certainly gave freely of his advice:

"Cibber! write all thy Verses upon Glasses,
The only way to save 'em from our A ....s."

Dr. Johnson was equally dismissive – " It is wonderful that a man, who for forty years had lived with the great and witty, should have acquired so ill the talents of conversation; and he

1696 Cibber wrote a superb part for himself in his first play *Love's Last Shift, or The Fool in Fashion*. Congreve was sniffily dismissive – "it has only in it a great many things that were like wit, that in reality were not wit." Vain, tactless, snobbish, sycophantic and a formidable social climber, the shrill-voiced, hatchet-faced Cibber was scarcely ever deterrred by such criticism. Cibber's creation, the arch-fop rake-hero Sir Novelty Fashion, would be successfully appropriated and promoted to the peerage as Lord Foppington by Vanbrugh in *The Relapse* and reprised by Cibber himself in his best original comedy, *The Careless Husband* (1704). In 1699 Cibber made an adaptation of *Richard III* which imported whole passages from other Shakespeare plays and remained the definitive version for the next one hundred and twenty years.

Cibber's chance to take over Drury Lane came in 1710. He proved more than competent in his choice of plays, though his overriding criterion was their theatrical impact rather than their had but half to furnish: for one half of what he said, was oaths." The novelist Tobias Smollett (1721-71) and the aesthete Horace Walpole (1717-97) were, by contrast, warmly appreciative of Cibber's talents. In 1740 Cibber published a typically self-justifying autobiography – *An Apology for the Life of Mr. Colley Cibber, Comedian* – in which he also recorded a generous appreciation for the thespian genius of his mentor, Betterton.

Cibber's colleagues at Drury Lane were Robert Wilks (1665-1732), Thomas Doggett (1670-1721) and, after a clash of personalities, Barton Booth (1681-1733). Wilks was popular, conscientious and hardworking but often inflexible in his dealings with others, although generous in supporting his old friend Farquhar in his last days. Much praised by Dryden, Doggett also impressed Congreve who wrote the part of Fondlewife in *The Old Bachelor* specifically with Doggett in mind. A fervent supporter of the newly-installed Hanoverian dynasty, in 1716 Doggett sponsored a celebratory annual race for Thames watermen which remains one of the oldest fixtures in the English sporting calendar. Winners of 'Doggett's Coat and Badge' received a prize of five pounds and a handsome scarlet coat with a massive silver armlet embellished with the white horse of Hanover.

Barton Booth (1681-1737) demonstrated a precocious thespian talent while still a schoolboy at Westminster. His connection with the school was subsequently maintained by some judicious property speculation still commemorated in the name of nearby Barton Street. Hired by Betterton while still a teenager, Booth was noted for striking attitudes which were generally admitted to be striking. Possessed of a rich, resonant voice he scored a notable triumph in the title role of Joseph Addison's only essay into the drama, *Cato* (1713), which conveyed a timely patriotic message as Britain celebrated a successful conclusion to the War of the Spanish Succession.

The pattern of programming at Drury Lane was demanding. In the course of the 1721-22 season, for example, over the course of 192 nights no less than seventy plays were presented. Utility actor John Mills, admittedly renowned for his prodigious memory, performed fifty main roles, plus a further dozen minor parts, including a run of twelve nights in which he played twelve different characters. Shakespeare continued to be staple fare, but only the great tragedies. Since actors were not paid anything extra for attending rehearsals they had a vested interest in resisting new material and sticking to classics they had long since mastered and polished. A further conservatism was built in by the 1720s when the managements of the two patent theatres came to an informal understanding that neither would poach actors from the other and they would, as far as possible, open on alternate nights.

The outstanding female player of the Drury Lane company was Anne Oldfield (1683-1730). Mrs. Bracegirdle, conceding the newcomer's talent, withdrew into retirement. Anne had grown up in St. James's where she was 'discovered' by Farquhar in a tavern "reading a Play behind the Bar, with so proper emphasis and such agreeable Turns suitable to each character, that he swore the Girl was cut out for the stage". Lovely in face, figure, voice and diction, she was to play the leading female roles in both Farquhar's last plays, though she later excelled in tragedy. Cibber, who was initially unimpressed by her in rehearsal, changed his mind when he saw her perform and later wrote the part of Lady Betty Modish in *The Careless Husband* especially for her. By 1709 Anne Oldfield was able to negotiate a thirteen-year contract at an annual salary of two hundred pounds plus a benefit performance each February and her summers free. By 1711 she was on three-hundred guineas a year, plus a benefit worth double that. She was to be buried near Congreve in Westminster Abbey but anonymously, denied a monument over her grave because she had had two illegitimate sons, one by the Whig MP Arthur Mainwaring, the other by Charles Churchill, a nephew of the Duke of Marlborough. The sale of her effects took five days. Two biographies of her were rushed out within a year.

31. *The first production of* The Beggar's Opera. *Painting by William Hogarth. Note privileged members of the audience sitting on the stage.*

The Beggar's Opera

In 1714 Drury Lane's rival company was moved to Lincoln's Inn Fields by the tyrannical and parsimonious patentee Christopher Rich (1647-1714), a lawyer rather than a man of the theatre, who died that same year before he could make anything of the translation. It fell to his offspring, John Rich (1692-1761) to do so. Quite uneducated, but a superb dancer and mime, Rich, who appeared under the name of John Lun, was a brilliant Harlequin and in 1717 inaugurated an annual season of pantomimes with elaborate scenery and extravagant costumes which proved an enduring success and made him the most celebrated comedic dancer of his age. Pantomime was essentially a masked dumb-show, drawing its story line from myths and legends, interpolated with arias burlesquing Italian opera and delighting in flamboyant transformation scenes. Cibber was cautiously commendatory of

32. John Rich.

the form, describing it as "a connected presentation of dances in character, wherein the passions were so happily expressed and the whole story so intelligibly told by a mute narration of gesture only, that even thinking spectators allowed it both a pleasure and a rational entertainment."

In 1728 Rich put on *The Beggar's Opera* by John Gay (1685-1732) (which Cibber had, with uncharacteristically poor judgment, turned down) and found himself possessed of a theatrical property which, becoming the greatest commercial success of the century, "made Gay rich and Rich gay". Intended to mock the contemporary craze for Italian opera, by incorporating the popular street ballads of the day *The Beggar's Opera* inadvertently inaugurated an English operatic mode of enduring substance. Dr. Johnson paid a lofty, if ponderous tribute, to the achievement – "Much … must be allowed to the author of a new species of composition, though it be not of the highest kind. We owe to Gay, the ballad Opera: a mode of comedy which at first was supposed to delight only by its novelty but has now by the experience of half a century been found so well accommodated to the disposition of a popular audience, that it is likely to keep long possession of the stage."

The hero and heroine of *The Beggar's Opera*, the highwayman Captain Macheath and his lover Polly Peachum, were taken from London's underworld and immortalised in paint and print by William Hogarth (1697-1764). A projected sequel, *Polly*, was banned, which boosted its sales as a printed publication so much that it was reckoned to have brought in four times as much as it would have from performance. *The Beggar's Opera* itself made such massive profits that Rich was able to fund the building of an entirely new theatre at Covent Garden.

Covent Garden
Designed by Edward Shepherd (died 1747), the builder of Mayfair (he of Shepherd's Market), Covent Garden seated an audience of 1,897, variously distributed in a pit, amphitheatre, two galleries and three tiers of side-boxes. It opened

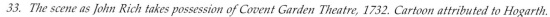

33. *The scene as John Rich takes possession of Covent Garden Theatre, 1732. Cartoon attributed to Hogarth.*

in 1732 with a production of Congreve's *The Way of the World* with James Quin (1693-1766) in the leading part. 'Bellower Quin' was to prove the last great exponent of the old declamatory school, resolutely clinging to original costumes which became increasingly anachronistic with the passage of time.

Rich continued to develop lavish stage effects at Covent Garden but was attacked by Pope and Fielding for pandering to the lowest common denominator of popular taste. Punctilious in paying his actors, Rich also supported numerous theatrical pensioners while himself living in fine style as a country gent at Cowley near Uxbridge – at least until his third wife, Priscilla, an ex-barmaid, former actress in his company and fervent convert to Methodism, imposed a more frugal regimen. Rich could at least find occasional refuge at the meetings of the Sublime Society of Beefsteaks, a patriotic dining club which he had founded in 1735 and whose members included Hogarth, Charles Churchill, Cibber's wayward son, Theophilus (1703-58) and the controversial radical John Wilkes (1727-97). Handel (1685-1759) was another close personal friend. Covent Garden, sold on after Rich's death, fetched sixty thousand pounds.

New Directions in Drama

Of the dramatists of the early eighteenth century Sir Richard Steele (1672-1729), editor of *The Tatler* and *The Spectator*, was the most consistently concerned to respond to the moral strictures enunciated by Bishop Collier. Educated at Charterhouse, where he numbered Addison among his friends, Steele was variously a soldier, bureaucrat, politician, essayist and pamphleteer. Only incidentally a playwright, he nevertheless produced four sentimental and moralizing comedies in an attempt to set a new tone for the English theatre. As its title implies *The Christian Hero* (1701) recommended the positive practice of virtue rather than the detached and world-weary contemplation of vice. It was witty but eschewed satire. Instead of taking depravity as a norm it predicated benevolence as the basis of human behaviour.

34. Sir Richard Steele. Engraving after Kneller.

Steele's last play *The Conscious Lovers* (1722), an adaptation of Terence's *Andria*, was produced by Cibber and excellently served by a cast which included Booth, Wilks and Oldfield. Its immense success led to immediate translation into French and German, inaugurating a Continental rage for *comedie larmoyante* ('tearful comedy') in which tears are freely shed over the misfortunes of virtuous characters unjustly harmed or persecuted until a happy ending is finally contrived in the fifth act. Steele also established the first English theatrical periodical, *The Theatre*, which was published twice weekly in 1719-1720.

Mrs. Susannah Centlivre (1667-1723), who took her name from her third husband, Queen Anne's cook, excelled in men's parts, being more than a little butch herself. Her own plays were comedies of intrigue in the mode of Aphra Behn, most notably *The Busie Body* (1709) and *A Bold Stroke for a Wife* (1718). She enjoyed a long collaboration with Anne Oldfield.

Of Flemish descent and a jeweller by trade, George Lillo (1693-1739) was to pioneer a novel genre, the domestic tragedy, which implicitly challenged the Aristotelian axiom that tragic events only happen to posh people. In *The London Merchant* (1731) a weak-willed apprentice, lured on by his passion for an evil woman, steals from his master and comes to a predictably bad end. Lillo was by contemporary account "content with his little state of life" and thought that others should be too. *The London Merchant* is a bourgeois morality tale by a bourgeois writer for a bourgeois audience, a warning to the discontented, the theatrical equivalent of Hogarth's print series *Industry and Idleness*. Despite its apparent localism, however, Lillo's homily had a profound effect on such Continental writers as Lessing, Diderot and Rousseau.

Scandal and Censorship

Lillo's moralizing, however, cut little ice with those clerics who continued to denounce all theatre as such. William Law declared in his diatribe of 1736 *The Absolute Unlawfulness of the Stage Entertainment Fully Demonstrated*" a Player cannot be a living member of Christ, or in a true state of Grace, till he renounces his Profession". Certainly the not so private lives of some of the most prominent London thespians continued to provide abundant ammunition for the moralist. James Quin, quarrelling with fellow actor Thomas Hallam over a wig, stabbed him fatally through the eye with his cane and was fortunate to be convicted only of manslaughter. After Elizabeth Barry quarrelled with Mrs. Boutel over a veil she used a stage dagger to stab her when they played opposite each other in an appropriately titled piece, *The Rival Queens*. Peg Woffington *(see p62)* took advantage of the same play to do the same to her rival Anne Bellamy. Charlotte Charke, rejected daughter of Colly Cibber, tried to blackmail her father into giving her money by offering to suppress her memoirs of a colourful life involving phases as an actress, waitress, grocer, puppeteer, strolling player, novelist, transvestite and lesbian - to no avail, as she died destitute in a Grub Street garret. Boswell took advantage of the temporary misfortunes of Covent Garden actress Louise Lewis to make her

35. Henry Fielding, after the portrait by Hogarth. Not only a dramatist, but one of the first incorruptible magistrates at Bow Street.

his mistress – and got the clap for it. Sophia Baddeley's long list of lovers included *both* sons of Lord Coleraine.

William Law had it in for playhouses as well as players: "our Playhouse is in fact the Sink of Corruption and Debauchery ... it is the present Rendezvous of the most profligate Persons of both Sexes ... it corrupts the Air and turns the adjacent Places into publick Nuisances ...". And it was undeniable that London theatres were indeed within a few paces of numerous brothels, bagnios and 'jelly houses'. In *The Harlot's Progress* Hogarth has Moll Hackabout ply her trade in Drury Lane. It was not, however, the moral pollution of the theatrical world that was to attract the censure of government but its potential for political subversion.

Old Etonian Henry Fielding (1707-54), having failed to elope with an heiress, settled in London at the age of nineteen, determined to succeed as a dramatist. His first effort, *Love in Several Masques,* was successfully performed at Drury Lane when he was just twenty-one. In the course of the following decade Fielding produced a further twenty-five farces, burlesques and satires, including two adaptations of Molière and *The Welsh Opera* (1731), which openly targeted the royal family. In 1736 he took over the management of the New Theatre, a small unlicensed venue in the Haymarket, opening it with his own *Pasquin*, an attack on the electioneering abuses which were widespread at the time. This was followed by *The Historical Register for the Year 1736* (1737), the forerunner of the satirical revue and an attack on the king's first minister, Sir Robert Walpole (1676-1745) so savage that Walpole manoeuvred Parliament into passing a Theatre Licensing Act which both brought Fielding's theatrical career to an end and saddled English theatre with a censorship regime which was to endure until 1968.

The Act of 1737 sought both to consolidate the Patent theatre monopoly and to assert the control of the Lord Chamberlain (indirectly exercised through an Examiner of Plays) over the content of performances. All plays were to be submitted for censorship fourteen days before performance. Plays could be banned at any time, even if they had been granted a licence. Playhouses required either a patent from the monarch or a licence from the Lord Chamberlain and were restricted to Westminster. Actors working outside the legal theatre were still liable for arrest as vagrants. Forbidden from examining matters of political or religious controversy, dramatists were in effect to be obliged to disengage from the most vital and profound questions of their day. Little wonder that for the next two centuries playwrights would have to have routine recourse to innuendo or take refuge in historical parallels while the greatest writers would choose the unrestricted freedom of other literary forms, most notably poetry and the novel.

Goodman's Fields

Laws, however draconian in intent, do not, however, invariably and consistently achieve their objectives and attempts to challenge or circumvent the monopoly of the Patent theatres continued throughout the eighteenth century. Plays, suitably compressed to suit the restricted circumstances of their performance, were routinely presented during the fortnight of the annual Bartholomew Fair in Smithfield. Held in August, when the theatres were closed, the Fair represented no direct competition to them and help to tide over actors while they waited for the next season's employment. In September the same pieces could be given on the other side of the river, at Southwark Fair.

In 1729 Thomas Odell, a theatrical virgin, converted a warehouse in Ayliffe Street, Goodman's Fields, just south of Aldgate, to become a theatre at the opposite end of town from the usual theatrical locations sanctioned by tradition and convenience. Initially approved by royal licence it was, following protests by the Patent-holders, subjected to the withdrawal of official recognition in 1730. Management was then taken over by the more robust and canny Henry Giffard (*ca.*1695-1772) who rebuilt it even more splendidly to designs by Edward Shepherd. Reopened in 1732 Goodman's Fields featured a spectacular ceiling depicting King George II surrounded by Shakespeare, Dryden, Congreve and Betterton. Giffard's dodge for enabling what he disingenuously referred to as "the late theatre" to get round the patent monopoly was to offer patrons a "Concert of Vocal and Instrumental Music, divided in two parts. Tickets at three shillings, two shillings and one shilling" in the interval of which plays would be "performed gratis by persons for their diversion". Giffard got away with this until 1736 when he tried unsuccessfully to put the place up for sale. Goodman's Fields theatre reopened in 1740 and on Monday 19th October 1741 Giffard presented a production of *Richard III* in which the name part, he claimed (not entirely truthfully) would be played by "a Gentleman Who never appeared on any Stage" – David Garrick.

The Wells

Sadler's Wells at Finsbury, on the northern edge of the City proper, had originated in 1683, offering the novel combination of a wooden 'Musick House' and a medicinal spring of 'excellent steel waters'. Initially the clientele was highly respectable, like Pepys's friend, the dilettante diarist John Evelyn (1620-1706), who took the waters there in 1686; but within a couple of decades the 'tone' had gone. The attractions of the spa faded quickly but the hall became a venue for jugglers, rope-dancers and such-like as well as musicians, attracting the patronage of a less than elite clientele of officers on half pay with time to kill, sailors in port, tradesmen "and others that are musically inclined". According to Ned Ward (1677-1731), author of *The London Spy*, the typical patrons were:

"Butchers and bailiffs and such sort of fellows,
Mix'd with a vermin train'd up for the gallows."

By the 1740s Sadler's Wells had become "villainously disreputable", being referred to in a Grand Jury verdict as a place "of great extravagance, luxury, idleness and ill-fame".

36. Sadler's Wells, c.1720.

37. Joey Grimaldi.

King's successor (1799-1819), Charles Dibdin the Younger installed a ninety-foot long aquatic tank, filled from the nearby New River and reaped the benefits of novelty by staging such 'aquatic dramas' as a re-creation of *The Siege of Gibraltar* (1804) and *Naval Triumph; Or, The Tars of Old England*. The novelty soon palled, however, and Dibdin suffered a further serious setback in 1807 when a false alarm of fire caused a panic, leading to eighteen deaths. More and more Dibdin was obliged to rely on the pulling power of the dancing clown Joseph Grimaldi (1778-1837), scion of a dynasty of dancers who practised a little dentistry on the side.

The grandson of the Italian dancer Giovanni Battista ('Iron Legs') Grimaldi, 'Joey' Grimaldi was the (very late) illegitimate son of Giuseppe Grimaldi (?1710-88) and had made his stage debut, as a monkey - at Sadler's Wells in 1781, while still only a toddler. It was to become one of his most regular venues. Routinely playing sprites and fairies as a child, Grimaldi emerged as a figure in his own right in Dibdin's *Peter Wilkins* and as Harlequin in *The Flying World*, staged at the Wells in 1800. He created his own unmistakable visual trademark by making up in white face with a red half-moon on each cheek. Acting a cross between Mr. Punch and a naughty schoolboy, Grimaldi came to personify irreverent defiance of inhibitions and authority, ingeniously assisted with such perennial props as a leg of lamb, a string of sausages, a coal scuttle or a pretended red-hot poker.

Crippled by arthritis and the excesses of his on-stage exuberance by his early forties, Grimaldi made a round of farewell performances in 1828. By a supreme and most cruel irony, the original 'Joey the Clown' died 'Mr. Grim-all-day', heartbroken by the early death from alcoholism of his own son, Joseph (1802-32). The youthful Charles Dickens *(see p100)* made a half-hearted job of editing Grimaldi's chaotic memoirs. Grimaldi was buried at the church of St. James's, Pentonville, having died nearby at 33 Southampton (now Calshot) Street, in a house since demolished. After his death a Clowns' Service was held every February at Holy Trinity, Dalston to honour his memory.

Sadler's Wells thus represented an opportunity for an enterprising and well-heeled local builder, Thomas Rosoman, who bought the lease in 1746, engaged a regular acting company (1753) and in just seven weeks in 1765, at a cost of £4,225, replaced the old wooden hall with a brick-built theatre capable of seating 2,600. Typical presentations included pantomimes, concerts and acrobats. Under ex-actor Tom King's knowing direction (1772-85) Sadler's Wells skilfully exploited a jingoistic appetite for patriotic spectacle, with rousing songs by Charles Dibdin (1745-1814). (Dibdin, who had been sacked by Garrick, eventually found salvation in one-man shows and in 1803 was awarded a civil list pension for his output of 1,400 songs, many of them celebrating the British sailor). For King nothing was off limits, from dancing dogs to a re-enactment of the storming of the Bastille.

38. *Sadler's Wells in 1798, an illustration by R. Andrews.*

39. *The interior of Sadler's Wells, depicted by Rowlandson and Pugin, c.1808.*

CHAPTER FIVE

Garrick

David Garrick (1717-79) was the English theatre's first superstar - and much more – manager, playwright, theatrical innovator, Shakespeare scholar, lyricist (*Hearts of Oak*), bibliophile, art collector, philanthropist, celebrity and ultimately, icon. Of Huguenot descent, the son of an army officer, David Garrick was brought up in Lichfield where, at the age of eleven, he precociously appeared as Sergeant Kite in a school production of Farquhar's *The Recruiting Officer*, perhaps bringing to the role a certain familial knowingness, as his father actually was one. Garrick also briefly attended Dr. Johnson's short-lived academy Edial Hall before, in March 1737, they trekked to London together, sharing a single horse, to seek their respective fortunes. Although only eight years his senior, Johnson would remain Garrick's literary mentor and, while not uncritical, fiercely protective of 'Little Davy' for the rest of his life.

Debuts, Dublin, Drury Lane

Originally intended for the law, Garrick joined his brother Peter in setting up as wine-shippers but, although he was to prove a more than competent man of business, his passion was already for the stage. Making friends with the actors Charles Macklin (1699-1797) and Henry Giffard, Garrick dashed off a slight but passable burlesque, *Lethe, or Esop in the Shades*, for the latter's benefit night at Drury Lane in April 1740. Later that summer Garrick tried to help Giffard get a licence for his theatre in Goodman's Fields. He also began to rehearse the title role for an amateur production of Fielding's *The Mock Doctor*, given in an upstairs room of the St. John's gatehouse in Clerkenwell. where Johnson was working as a parliamentary reporter for Edward

40. David Garrick

Cave's *Gentleman's Magazine*. The epilogue which Garrick composed for the occasion, the first of many such, was published in the September issue of the periodical. Among his social circle Garrick also began to adopt the *persona* of a critic, deftly mimicking the mannerisms of leading players and denouncing "airs, affectation and Cibberisms" in contemporary productions. In February 1741 Garrick saw Macklin's landmark portrayal of Shylock. A revolutionary interpretation, it banished the traditional caricature villain to present an emotionally wracked human being. Macklin had, moreover, prepared himself for the role by spending time

41. Charles Macklin as Shylock.

III was hailed the following day by a critic as "the most extraordinary and great that was ever known upon such an Occasion." Pope himself proclaimed "that young man never had his equal as an actor and he will never have a rival". Quin, London's leading actor since the retirement of Cibber, observed ruefully "If this young man be right, then we have all been wrong." A legend was born overnight. Remote Goodman's Fields became a place of compelling theatrical pilgrimage "in so much that from Temple Bar the whole way was covered with a string of coaches." Five weeks after his debut Garrick wrote exultantly to his brother that "I have the Judgment of the best Judges (Who to a Man are of Opinion) that I shall turn out (nay they Say I am) not only the Best Trajedian but Comedian in England." Garrick capped his triumph with two comic roles and the staging of his own two-act farce *The Lying Valet*, based on a purloined French plot. In his writing, however, as opposed to his acting, Garrick would always produce the serviceable rather than the innovatory, just as when adapting texts he would do so with an actor's eye to giving his cast the best scope for their varying capabilities.

In the summer of 1742 Garrick played a season at the Smock Alley playhouse in Dublin with the Dublin-born actress Margaret – 'Peg' – Woffington (?1720-60). On their return they set up home together.

Garrick's meteoric ascent was confirmed by his ability to secure a five-hundred pound fee for the forthcoming Drury Lane season, where he played alongside Macklin, Woffington and Kitty Clive (1711-85). Although they drew crowds the house manager, Charles Fleetwood, proved a hopeless administrator and the actors ended the season unpaid. Garrick served as spokesman for them in the resulting dispute and petitioned the Lord Chamberlain for a licence to set up an independent company. This was dismissed out of hand and Garrick was compelled to negotiate with Fleetwood, who agreed to take all of them back - except Macklin, who regarded Garrick's capitulation as a personal betrayal.

Garrick extended his range with the heavy

among Jewish businessmen in the City's 'Change Alley'. Macklin's startlingly natural speaking style made the most striking contrast to the self-consciously sonorous cadences of Quin's stilted Antonio. Pope declared aphoristically "this is the Jew, That Shakespeare drew". Garrick marked Macklin's manner and in due course would make it his own.

In March 1741 Garrick stood in anonymously – and masked – for an indisposed player as Harlequin in a Giffard pantomime. He later preferred to claim that he had made his debut with Giffard's summer company in Ipswich in *Oronooko* under the pseudonym of Mr. Lydall. Garrick's sensational London debut as Richard

42. Peg Woffington.

argument by attacking Quin's version of Macbeth. Thirty years later he would explain to Johnson's biographer, James Boswell (1740-95) the primacy of performance:

> "Speeches and mere poetry will no more make a Play, than planks and timbers in the dock Yard can be call'd a ship – It is Fable, passion and Action which constitute a Tragedy".

Garrick also prepared himself to extend into management in the winter season of 1745-6 by sharing the supervision (and profits) of two Dublin playhouses with Thomas Sheridan (1721-88), having made a final break with Peg Woffington, whom he had once contemplated marrying but now suspected of infidelity.

Celebrity

Garrick had by now become a major London celebrity. An expressive portrait of him as Richard III by Hogarth, a personal friend, made Garrick nationally recognisable as well. Others of Garrick's circle of acquaintance included such distinguished artists as Benjamin Wilson (1721-88), Johann Zoffany (1733-1810), Thomas Gainsborough (1727-88) and Joshua Reynolds (1723-92) and the political opposites John Wilkes and Edmund Burke (1729-97). Little wonder then that Garrick would in due course become the most painted man in England, appearing in at least 450 paintings and engravings. Garrick enjoyed being a celebrity and was good at being one, admitting candidly:

> "It is my utmost pride and ambition to deserve the kind thoughts of the great and the good."

He would also accept the responsibilities that should go with fame, serving diligently as a governor of the Lying-in Hospital and in 1766 founding the Theatrical Fund to relieve theatricals rendered indigent by disability, illness or enforced retirement.

duty roles of Macbeth, Othello and King John, which he found demanding. Over the course of his London career Garrick would play Hamlet ninety times and Lear eighty-five but Macbeth only thirty-seven and Othello only three. Othello required him to black his face which deprived him of the hugely expressive play of facial feature which was one of his great assets. When it was remarked that Garrick was beginning to look old Dr. Johnson would leap to his defence with the self-explanatory assertion that "no man's face has more wear and tear". Contemporary critical convention endorsed this view of the actor's central expertise. John Hill in *The Actor: a treatise on the art of playing* (1750) defined thespian excellence in terms of "expressing to the audience such sentiments as are not deliver'd in the play, yet are not only agreeable but necessary to be understood of the character they represent." So much for the sanctity of the text.

In 1744 Garrick anonymously published *An Essay on Acting* sketching out a prospectus for a new manner of performance and illustrating his

Garrick contracted with John Rich at Covent Garden for the season of 1746-7 and for the first time found himself playing opposite Quin. When

43. David Garrick, a portrait by his friend Zoffany.

Manager

In the spring of 1747 Garrick finally negotiated with James Lacy to become joint manager of Drury Lane, putting up twelve thousand pounds which would return him five hundred pounds a year as proprietor on top of the five hundred guineas he would be paid as an actor. Lacy was to manage the property, scenery and wardrobe, Garrick the stage, actors and playwrights, an arrangement which persisted until Lacy's death in 1774. Garrick's term of management was inaugurated with a prologue composed in consultation with his old mentor Dr. Johnson:

"The drama's laws the drama's patrons give,
For we that live to please must please to live."

Johnson's words, Garrick's philosophy.

The first offering was *The Merchant of Venice* with Macklin reprising his celebrated Shylock. Then came a revival of *The Beggar's Opera* and *Hamlet.* Garrick waited a month before making

44. The first Theatre Royal, from a print published in 1794.

they met on stage for the first time in Rowe's *The Fair Penitent* they were discountenanced by bouts of applause anticipatory as of a combat, Quin colouring, Garrick standing embarrassed. Audiences compared the two actors to Quin's disadvantage but, to the credit of both men, this, though mutually acknowledged, did not damage their relationship. As Bayes in Buckingham's *The Rehearsal* Garrick brilliantly mimicked the well-known actors of the day but deferentially exempted Quin and acknowledged - by refusing to play them himself – Quin's excellence as Falstaff and Cato. Garrick further profited from the success of his farce *Miss in her Teens*, which ran for forty nights and was arguably the best of his twenty plays. He also played for the first time his favourite role, which he would reprise a hundred and twenty times, the philandering rake, Ranger, in Benjamin Hoadley's *The Suspicious Husband.* Through Ranger Garrick proved himself every bit as much the charmer on stage as off.

his own first appearance as Archer in *The Beaux'
Stratagem*, another favourite role which he would
play a hundred times. Later in the season he
played Lear (restoring the Fool), which many
considered his finest tragic role - Reynolds was
said to have needed three days to recover from it.
In 1748 he played Romeo in the first production
of *Romeo and Juliet* to be given in London for
eighty years. His own individual take on the text
was to allow the lovers a brief reunion in the
tomb before death. A decade later he would give
Antony and Cleopatra its first performance since
the Restoration. The staging of Johnson's
painfully wrought blank verse tragedy *Irene* was
a matter of personal loyalty but not a success.

In 1749 Garrick married the Viennese-born
dancer Eva Maria Veigel (1724-1822). As she
was a Roman Catholic their Anglican ceremony
was followed by a blessing in the chapel of the
Portuguese embassy in Soho. Mrs. Garrick gave
up her stage career to become Mrs. Garrick.
Garrick was by now wealthy enough to give her
an immediate settlement of ten thousand pounds.
The only blight on their union was to be
childlessness. Garrick took great delight in
children. Indeed, he claimed that his distracted
Lear was based on the case of a wretched man
who had killed his two-year-old by dropping it
from a window.

In July Garrick bought 27 Southampton Street,
Covent Garden for five hundred guineas and
spent three months having it refurbished (the
house still exists). The four-storey building
afforded ample space for Garrick to indulge his
bibliomania. He also built up an impressive art
collection of two hundred paintings including
works by Hals, Lely, Poussin, Watteau as well as
those of such friends as Hogarth and
Gainsborough. By 1754 Garrick was able to buy
a country home, Fuller House in Hampton-on-
Thames where Robert Adam (1728-92) was
employed to alter the house and Lancelot
'Capability' Brown (1715-83) to lay out the
garden. Adam also designed a temple in honour
of Shakespeare for the grounds. Inside was a
bust of Shakespeare, for which Garrick had
himself posed to the finest sculptor of the day,

*45. 27 Southampton Street, Garrick's old house.
Appropriately, in the 1970s it was used as a
headquarters by the theatrical publishers, Samuel
French.*

Louis-Francois Roubiliac (?1705-62). Garrick
could also afford to invest thirteen thousand
pounds in an Essex estate and purchase shares
in four newspapers. The latter may, of course,
have been less a matter of investment than a way
of ensuring sympathetic reviews and positive
exposure.

While working as a theatre manager Garrick
still made an average of ninety stage appearances
a year, far more than most leading players,
although still only on half the playing nights.
Unlike Irving's Lyceum *(see p160)* Garrick did
not create a one-man show or surround himself
with mediocrities to look better in contrast. Kitty
Clive's acute appreciation, however, emphasises
his contribution to the emergence of the notion of
a director:

"I have seen you with you magic hammer in your hand, endeavouring to beat your ideas into the heads of creatures who had none of their own. I have seen you, with lamb-like patience, endeavouring to make them comprehend you, and I have seen you when that could not be done – I have seen your lamb turned into a lion; by this your great labour and pains the public was entertained; they thought they all acted very fine; they did not see you pull the wires."

Kitty Clive also made another revealing, more personal and petulant, observation – "Damn him, he could act a gridiron!".

Routines and Reforms
The Drury Lane company employed about a hundred and fifty people, just over half of them actors. Outgoings of £40,000 a year turned a net profit varying between £3,000 and £6,000. Unlike their continental counterparts, cushioned by royal subsidies, London theatres had to succeed commercially or go under, with self-evident consequences in terms of what they chose to put on. Garrick, however hard-headed, was also principled enough to exclude a celebrated rope-dancer – Anthony Maddox, the Surprising English Posture Master – "I cannot possibly agree to such a prostitution on any account: and nothing but downright starving would induce me to bring such defilement and abomination to the house of *William Shakespeare*."

A normal evening performance of three to four hours began with an orchestral overture followed by the main piece, an interlude of music or dance and an afterpiece, usually comic or farcical and often featuring stage-tricks or special effects. They especially appealed to half-price late admissions, many of whom had spent the earlier part of the evening drinking heavily and provided a correspondingly boisterous infusion to the audience. It was the incidental or subsidiary elements of the programme which continued to excite the wrathful condemnation of contemporary moralists like the Scottish teacher James Burgh who fulminated against "the scandalous Farces they commonly tag the

46. Kitty Clive.

gravest plays with, or above all … the inhumanly impudent Dances and Songs, with which they lard them between the Acts."

The yearly routine at Drury Lane began with revivals until Christmas, then pantomime, followed by premieres in February and March, then benefit performances to end the season when the Garricks decamped to Hampton.

By following a judicious balance of the old and the new Drury Lane became beyond doubt or dispute Britain's leading theatre. To promote a more disciplined professionalism Garrick ended the custom of allowing social *prominenti* to sit at the side of the stage and restricted their admission to the green room. To cut down the constant haemorrhaging of profits through the loss or theft of items used on stage Garrick had them marked as the property of the management – hence 'props'. Economic realities favoured conservatism in the selection of material for presentation and militated against new plays as Thomas Davies, Garrick's first (1780) biographer noted:

"The time bestowed in rehearsing the piece and the expense of new scenes, dresses, music and other decorations, make it often very ineligible to a director of a theatre to accept a new play; especially when it is considered that the reviving of a good play will answer his end of profit and reputation too perhaps."

Experiments could, moreover, backfire. In 1755 Garrick promoted a new ballet *The Chinese Festival*. Unfortunately for Garrick most of the dancers were French – on the eve of the outbreak of a major war with France. Xenophobic rioters inflicted much damage on Drury Lane. In 1762 Garrick decided to abolish half-price admission after the third act of the main item. The outcome was prolonged and repeated barracking to which he was eventually obliged to defer and which prompted him to take a long foreign holiday stretching over eighteen months. On his return he cut down his personal appearances to some thirty a year, being increasingly troubled by gout, arthritis and kidney problems. Garrick compensated for acting less by writing more. Apart from being able to craft pieces best suited to his theatre and company this also had the advantage of relieving him of the necessity of giving the third night's takings to an author, as was customary.

Jubilee

In 1769 Garrick was flattered by the corporation of Stratford upon Avon into organising a Shakespeare jubilee to mark the opening of its new town hall. Garrick presented the town with a statue of Shakespeare plus a portrait of himself with a bust of Shakespeare. The Jubilee itself was quite literally a wash-out, with Garrick's elaborate preparations drowned by torrential downpours, and not a line of the Bard's words uttered. But Garrick turned frustration and disappointment to brilliant effect in a processional entertainment *The Jubilee*, his most acclaimed creation. The idea seems to have been dreamed up on a coach-ride between Stratford and London with Benjamin Wilson, who brought a painterly eye to the possibilities of a scenic

panorama orchestrated in the less unpredictable environment of a theatre. A triumph of sheer showmanship, it paraded a procession of nineteen splendidly costumed Shakespearean characters, Garrick himself portraying his favourite, Benedick in *Much Ado About Nothing*. The 'plot' – a paper-thin wrap-around – supposedly turned on an Irishman coming all the way from Dublin who undergoes all kinds of fatigues and inconveniences to see the Pageant but unluckily goes to sleep as the Pageant passes by. The stage direction for the finale was " Every character, tragic and comic, join in the chorus and go back, during which guns fire, bells ring &c and the Audience applaud - Bravo, Jubilee, Shakespeare forever! " Between October and the end of the season *The Jubilee* was staged ninety-one times.

Garrick wrote gleefully that "the world is mad after it ... more success than any thing I Ever remember ", with the house packed out within fifteen minutes of opening the doors. Drury Lane prompter William Hopkins recorded with ill-punctuated pride in his diary that

"It was received with bursts of Applause the Procession of Shakespeare's Characters &c is the most Superb that ever was Exhibited or I believe ever will be, there never was an Entertainment produc'd that gave so much pleasure to all degrees Boxes pit and Gallery."

The Jubilee confirmed Garrick's status as the guardian of the cult of the Bard, a key element in his strategy to align himself and his profession with what in his own *Jubilee Ode to Shakespeare* he called the "blest genius of the isle", thus rendering both not only respectable but patriotic. Garrick instituted the tradition that English theatre had a peculiar duty and destiny to perpetuate the legacy of its greatest dramatist and that the performance of a repertory of canonical Shakespeare roles was required of any actor or actress aspiring to greatness.

Adieu

Garrick continued to grow even wealthier. In 1771 he acquired another Essex estate and in 1772 moved out of Southampton Street to Adelphi Terrace, the Adam brothers' magnificent riverside development off the Strand. Declining health, however, prompted him to announce his retirement, provoking a clamour for tickets for his nineteen farewell appearances. The magistrate Sir John Fielding (?-1780), half-brother of the playwright Henry Fielding, commended his career as a contribution to the public good – "the Chastity of Mr. Garrick, as a manager of a Public Theatre, and his exemplary life as a Man, have been of great service to the Morals of a dissipated Age." Burke declared that Garrick had raised acting to the level of a liberal art. Johnson concurred – "his profession made him rich and he made his profession respectable."

Much of Garrick's retirement was spent in visiting the homes of the great, such as Chatsworth, Althorp and Wilton House. He was also a member of The Club, the elite literary circle which revolved around Dr. Johnson and included such luminaries as Oliver Goldsmith (1730-74), Reynolds, Burke and Adam Smith (1723-90). Garrick was most certainly what Dr. Johnson called 'clubbable' and it is therefore appropriate that he has not only a London theatre (there were others in the East End and New York) but also a London club named after him. Founded over half a century after his death the Garrick Club was established in 1831 as a place where "actors and men of education and refinement might meet on equal terms". Garrick's endorsement can readily be imagined.

David Garrick died at Adelphi Terrace of kidney failure. His funeral procession, including a cortege of fifty carriages, took over an hour to pass from Adelphi Terrace to Westminster Abbey where he was buried in Poets' Corner. Johnson would later be laid beside him. The chief mourner was the playwright Richard Brinsley Sheridan (1751-1816), the son of Garrick's old partner Thomas Sheridan and the leading member of the consortium which had bought out Garrick's

share in Drury Lane for £35,000. The pallbearers included a duke, an earl and a viscount, all friends. A biography appeared within a year. Sir Joshua Reynolds was moved to publish *Notes on Garrick*. Those who knew him well knew him well. Goldsmith observed that:

"On the stage he was natural, simple, affecting,
'Twas only that, when he was off, he was acting ".

Reynolds recorded that "Garrick ... made himself a slave to his reputation. Amongst the variety of arts observed by his friends to preserve that reputation, one of them was to make himself rare. It was difficult to get him, and when you had him, as difficult to keep him. He never came into company but with a plot how to get out of it. He was forever receiving messages of his being wanted in another place. It was a rule with him never to leave any company saturated. Being used to exhibit himself at a theatre or a large table, he did not consider an individual as worth powder and shot."

Garrick's wealth at death has been estimated at around £100,000. He bequeathed his large collection of English plays to the British Museum. Garrick was brilliant in the force of his stage presence and the range of his versatility but he was not unique. He revolutionised acting, but he was inspirational, not inimitable. If he had been, his revolution would have died with him.

Lesser Planets

Garrick's own inspiration, Charles Macklin, although eighteen years his senior, also outlived him by a further eighteen years. A touring apprenticeship had enabled him to lay the groundwork for the massive repertory of roles that he would accumulate. His first major success came as Peachum in a 1736 production of *The Beggar's Opera*. His career might, however, have ended three years later when he was fortunate to be convicted only of manslaughter after a fatal quarrel with a fellow actor over a wig. In 1753 Macklin's reputation as a teacher encouraged him to retire to run a drama school and coffee-house, until bankruptcy forced him back to the boards. His first success as a playwright, *Love A-la-mode*, came only at the age of sixty and the seventh attempt. Revolving around the amatory rivalry of an English, an Irishman, a Scotsman and a Jew, Macklin (himself Irish) drew shamelessly on contemporary prejudices in such creations as Sir Callaghan O'Brallaghan and Sir Archy MacSarcasm. Macklin was still acting and writing in his eighties, playing Sir Pertinax Macsycophant in his own play *The Man of the World*, a reworked version of his unpublished *The True Born Scotchman*. Failing memory finally induced retirement at the age of ninety.

Of Garrick's contemporaries Samuel Foote (1721-77) emulated him in achieving an extended career as actor, critic, playwright and manager. He began unpropitiously by using three years at Oxford to squander a fortune and being imprisoned for debt. After training briefly under Macklin, he played at the reopened Little Theatre in the Haymarket and at Smock Alley in Dublin. In 1747 he published a pamphlet on stage practice and dramatic theory *A Treatise on the Passions* and another on *The Roman and English Comedy Considered*. He also began writing his own plays, holding that the function of comedy was to educate as well as entertain, defining it as "a faithful imitation of singular absurdities, particular follies, which are openly produced as criminals are publicly punished, for the correction of individuals, and as an example to the whole community." That at least was what he claimed. The editor of his collected *Works* thought otherwise – "his public feeling we may safely ascribe to the prospect of private emolument and consider that his philanthropy was solely swayed by the probable receipts of his theatrical treasury." Johnson affirmed Foote's cupidity with an anecdote – " He had a small bust of Garrick placed upon his bureau. 'You may be surprised that I allow him to be so near my gold – but you will observe, he has no hands.'"

To evade the restrictions of the 1737 Licensing Act Foote's satirical revue *The Diversions of the Morning* was staged as a noon matinee with the audience invited to take tea. Another briefly successful dodge was a pseudo-auction of

47. *The mimic, Samuel Foote, as Mrs Cole in 1777.*

pictures. A spell (1749-51) in the French capital provided him with the material for *The Englishman in Paris* (1753). He was incensed to find that in his absence Garrick had permitted one of his company to mimic him on stage. This was a case of the biter bit. Foote's own speciality was superb, often savage, mimicry of fellow actors and prominent personalities of the day. Foote's *Taste* (1752) was a first attempt to capitalise an topical allusions but proved unsuccessful, forcing Foote to turn to puppet-plays, theatre management in Dublin and even fortune-telling. Success came at last in 1760 with a satire on Methodists, *The Minor*, in which Foote guyed the charismatic, self-promoting preacher George Whitefield (1714-70) in the persona of Dr. Squintum - an unmistakably unsubtle clue, Whitefield, indeed, having an unnervingly

in the management of Drury Lane while Garrick was on tour. In 1766 the two collaborated to write *The Clandestine Marriage*. Colman was, however, angered by Garrick's decision not to act one of the leading roles and the two then argued for years afterwards about who had contributed what to the play itself. Neither disagreement blighted its success. In 1767 Colman became principal manager of Covent Garden and thus Garrick's main professional competitor. In 1769, adding a note of personal edge, Colman pre-empted Garrick's *Jubilee* by himself putting on a piece about Garrick's Stratford fiasco. In 1773 he stole another march on Garrick when, at Goldsmith's persuasion, he took on Sheridan's *The School for Scandal*, which Garrick had turned down. Retiring from Covent Garden in 1774, Colman failed in a bid to succeed Garrick at Drury Lane and instead took over the

Haymarket from Samuel Foote and turned it round both financially and artistically. A severe stroke in 1789, however, condemned Colman to pass his management responsibilities over to his son, also George (1762-1836) and sadly led to him spending his last years in an asylum.

Fringe Benefits

While the Patent theatres continued to assert their monopoly of 'legitimate' drama in the fashionable West End, new entertainment venues began to appear on the then periphery of the metropolis.

Honourably discharged from the cavalry in 1768, Sergeant-Major Philip Astley (1742-1814), a man of Herculean build and booming voice, was permitted to take his mount with him. He began his show-business career by giving unlicensed displays of his riding skills in the

51. Interior of Astley's Amphitheatre, a print published in 1815.

then open fields around Southwark, south of London Bridge. A chance incident during which he helped George III bring a horse back under control resulted in Astley being granted a licence. In 1769 he therefore erected a canvas-covered ring near the southern end of Westminster Bridge, where the incident had happened and dubbed it with the magniloquent title of Royal Grove. After running shows successfully in Dublin and Paris, Astley returned to London. Destroyed by fire in 1794, his establishment was rebuilt as Astley's Amphitheatre and its repertoire extended beyond equestrianism to include clowns, conjurors, acrobats and swordsmen so that it constituted London's first circus. Another fire in 1803 led to the building of a splendid tiered house with seating for 2,500. Astley passed this over to his son John Philip Conway (1767-1821) who proved a spendthrift. Charles Dickens adored Astley's and immortalized it in *Sketches by Boz* and in *The Old Curiosity Shop.* At the cost of £800 hundred in 1805 Astley recycled the timbers of an old French frigate, *Ville de Paris*, to create the tent-shaped Olympic Pavilion in Wych Street, off Drury Lane – which lost him £10,000 in its first season. Astley senior then returned to Paris to try his luck again but died soon after. After another fire in 1830 Astley's was taken over by the renowned trick-rider Andrew Ducrow (1793-1848) who was a skilled producer but virtually incapable of playing any speaking part - which did not discourage him from designing, at the cost of a phenomenal £3,000, a tomb in Kensal Green cemetery "erected by genius for the reception of its remains". Rebuilt again in 1842 after yet another fire, in 1862 and in 1872-3, after a period under Dion Boucicault *(see p97)* as the pretentiously named New Westminster Theatre Royal and the under the circus-owner George Sanger, Astley's was finally torn down in 1893.

52. The Olympic Theatre, 1831.

53. The Surrey Theatre in 1812.

What became the Surrey Theatre, in Blackfriars Road, was opened in 1782 as the Royal Circus and Equestrian Philharmonic Academy by Charles Hughes and Charles Dibdin, doubtless seeking to exploit the market niche vacated by Astley who had that very year opened up in Paris. Burned down in 1803 (coincidence?) it was rebuilt by Rudolph Cabanel, future architect of the Old Vic. Converted into a theatre in 1809, it was renamed the Surrey, thus incidentally affirming its location outside London and the legal limitations on theatre applicable there.

The affluent Thames-side retreat of Richmond had its own unlicensed theatre by the 1760s. Supposedly modelled on Drury Lane, it styled itself as the Theatre Royal but was also known from its situation as the Theatre on the Green. It opened with a prologue written by Garrick himself and did, according to James Wilson's aquatint of 1804, have a Pit, Gallery and Boxes with separate entrances for each. Boswell described it as "very handsome ... having everything in miniature." It was finally pulled down in 1884. The Victorian architectural extravaganza at Little Green nearby dates from 1899.

In 1787 actor John Palmer opened a new theatre, the Royalty, at Wellclose Square, just east of the Tower and within the jurisdiction of its Governor, who had given the project the go-ahead. But the managers of the licensed theatres were vehement in the defence of their monopoly, threatening to have Palmer and his company arrested as vagabonds. The Royalty's first night was also its last. Palmer complained bitterly to his audience "Tumblers and dancing dogs might appear unmolested before you but the other performers and myself standing forward to exhibit a moral play is deemed a crime."

Let There be Lighting

Techniques of stage lighting were sufficiently advanced in Italy to account for Niccolo Sabbatini to include a substantial discussion of its problems in his 1638 *Manual for Theatrical Scene and Machines*. In this he described concealed lights, methods of dimming and the possible difficulties and dangers arising from excessive smells, smoke and heat. Inigo Jones brought knowledge of advanced Italian lighting techniques to London and in his masques used translucencies and multi-coloured effects. Restoration theatres had tin lanterns, candlesticks with reflectors, footlights and chandeliers. Richard Fleckner's *Discourse of the English Stage* (1660), however, conceded that, compared to the French, the English were still "not knowing how to place our lights for the more advantage and illuminating of the scenes."

Garrick's continental tour of 1763-5 determined him to raise English lighting practice nearer to French standards. He accordingly imported French equipment and a technical expert, Philppe De Loutherbourg (1740-1812) who achieved painterly effects with the use of colour-changing silks.

In 1803 the Lyceum witnessed an historic demonstration of the possibilities of gas lighting but it was not until 1817 that the stage of the same theatre became the first to be lit by gas permanently. Drury Lane followed suit a month later.

That inquisitive German visitor, Prince Puckler-Muskau, was impressed by the lighting effects which accompanied the opening of *Mother Goose* at Covent Garden in the 1820s:

"At the rising of the curtain a thick mist covers the stage and gradually rolls off. This is remarkably well managed by means of fine gauze. In the dim light you distinguish a little cottage, the dwelling of a sorceress; in the background a lake surrounded by mountains, some of whose peaks are clothed with snow. All as yet is misty and indistinct; - the sun then rises triumphantly, chases the morning dews, and the hut, with the village in the distance, now appear in prefect outline. And now you behold upon the roof a large cock, who flaps his wings, plumes himself, stretches his neck, and greets the sun ...".

The great benefit of gaslight was in allowing gradations of brightness, its minor disadvantage, smell, its great danger the possibility of an explosion and an enhanced risk of major fires. Nor could gaslight, for all its superior brightness and flexibility, provide a better beam or shaft of light than any previous mode. The potential of limelight, invented in 1826, was tested by Macready *(see p87)* in his 1837 pantomime *Peeping Tom*. The impact of improved lighting was pervasive. Make-up, costumes, scenery and styles of acting that passed muster under smoky candles or murky oil lamps could seem garish, crude and overblown the more distinctly they were exposed to the gaze of the audience. Irving *(see p159)*, who declared that "stage lighting and groupings are of more consequence than the scenery" introduced the practice of completely darkening the auditorium. Augustin Daly described in a letter to his brother how Irving orchestrated lighting effects to enhance the impact of his own performance:

54. Electric lighting in the foyer of the Savoy Theatre.

"One of his stage-tricks is very effective but quite unworthy of a great artist. He is fond, whenever the scene permits, of shutting down every light - leaving the stage in utter darkness" and having a closely focussed light "which shines only and solely upon his face and head; so that you can only see a lot of spectral figures without expression moving about the scene - and one ghostly lighted face shining out of the darkness...".

Bram Stoker, best known as the author of *Dracula*, served as Irving's specialist lighting director, co-ordinating a team of thirty gasmen and eight limelight operators. Irving's emphasis on this aspect of his staging was underlined by his practice of requiring extensive lighting rehearsals without the distracting presence of other actors.

In 1881 Richard D'Oyly Carte's new-built Savoy Theatre opened with electric lighting, employing 1,158 incandescent lamps, 824 of them on stage. Ever the showman, Carte himself reassured the audience of the safety of the new technology by standing in front of the curtain and smashing a lit lamp wrapped in muslin. Electricity proved to be not only much safer than gas but also a third brighter; it had, moreover, no smell and was much more tolerable, in terms of the heat it threw out, for crews working up in the overhead lighting grid.

By the twentieth century major advances in lighting technique were consistently emanating from the USA and Germany, whose electrical industries were substantially ahead of Britain's. In 1917 the baby spotlights developed in the States by David Belasco's lighting expert, Louis Hartmann, were brought to England by Basil Dean *(see p180)*. Frederick Bentham, however, achieved a significant domestic breakthrough in controlling the intensity of electric lighting by a system of dimmers, transformers and auto-resistances co-ordinated from a single console, ingeniously derived from the mechanism of a cinema organ. In this respect the West End was a decade ahead of Broadway, A generation later Richard Librow, consultant to the National Theatre, would advance Bentham's system still further by the application of computers.

CHAPTER SIX

The Passing of the Patent

Sheridan

The leading domestic talent to fill the immediate void left by Garrick was Richard Brinsley Sheridan, the son of his old collaborator. Born in Dublin and briefly and unhappily educated at Harrow, Sheridan matured in Bath, where his father ran a school of elocution for the socially aspirant residents of a resort then at the height of its popularity. Sheridan's own first literary effort was a skit on the opening of Bath's New Assembly Rooms. Initially written for the local paper, it later bore publication as a pamphlet. Sheridan then became involved in the sort of romantic episode which formed the stuff of much stage nonsense – elopement to France with a beautiful and talented young singer, Elizabeth Linley, an invalid marriage, not one but ultimately three duels with a pompous, bullying rival, paternal intervention, exile to London to study law, paternal forgiveness - marital bliss (1773). Soon after the wedding at St. Marylebone parish church reality obtruded on the newly-weds in the inconvenient fact of near-poverty. Sheridan's solution was to dash off a play in weeks. The result was *The Rivals*. Set in Bath, the plot blends the usual ingredients of parental demands, expected inheritance, blighted love, disguise, deception, duel, misleading love letters etc. and introduces to enduring effect the wonderfully pretentious and absurd Mrs. Malaprop, whose mangling of the English language was to add her name to it as an eponym. The play, produced at Covent Garden in 1775, not only proved a great success but also enabled Sheridan to penetrate the social circles to which he had long aspired. In the same year he also turned out a farce, *St. Patrick's Day*, and a comic opera, *The*

55. *Richard Brinsley Sheridan; pastel by John Russell, 1788.*

Duenna. It was this instant track record which enabled him to find the partners to finance the buy-out of Garrick's share in the management of Drury Lane, where in 1777 he presented *A Trip to Scarborough*, a cleaned-up musical reworking of Vanbrugh's *The Relapse*. Sheridan's arrival among the capital's literary elite was marked by his election to The Club, on the proposal of Dr. Johnson himself. In May of this personal *annus mirabilis* appeared Sheridan's best play *The School for Scandal*, produced with Garrick's assistance from retirement and with a superb

56. A contemporary engraving of a scene from A School for Scandal, *at Drury Lane, 8 May 1777.*

cast, revelling in the aptly-named roles of Surface, Candour, Backbite, Premium and Sneerwell. *The Critic* (1779) vivaciously burlesques the traumas of rehearsing and staging a ludicrous tragedy about the Spanish Armada, pillorying two savage but inept theatrical critics, Dangle and Sneer, and the dramatist Sir Fretful Plagiary, a thinly disguised version of the versatile and in fact accomplished Richard Cumberland (1732-1811). In the same year Sheridan assumed sole responsibility for the management of Drury Lane.

Universally acclaimed, Sheridan's successes enabled him and his wife to rub shoulders with the aristocracy – and raised their living expenses accordingly. In due course he would acquire a bank account at Coutts' the royal banker and a succession of increasingly prestigious addresses in Orchard Street, Bruton Street. and Hertford Street, culminating in a fine house at No. 14 Savile Row and a succession of country residences at Harrow, Barnes, Isleworth and Wanstead. The personal friendship of the Prince of Wales (who became obsessed with Mary Robinson, one of Sheridan's company) enabled Sheridan finally to achieve membership of exclusive Brooks's club after being black-balled three times because his father had been on the stage. While the fourth ballot was being held the Prince used his rank purposely to delay Sheridan's antagonist in inconsequential conversation until the voting was over. *The School for Scandal* would enjoy seventy-three performances over the following dozen years and bring in profits of £15,000. But Sheridan had acquired political ambitions. Unable entirely to cast off the public school prejudice that the theatre was not only a precarious but an ungentlemanly mode of livelihood, Sheridan not unsurprisingly proved a less efficient business manager than Garrick. Money worries, professional and personal, would dog the rest of his days.

Sheridan became a friend and political ally of the charismatic Charles James Fox (1749-1806). The invariably dishevelled and unshaven Fox, a self-destructive libertine, drunk and gambler was capable of exerting a mesmeric power over the

House of Commons when he spoke. Sheridan yearned to do likewise. In 1780 he became MP for Stafford and only two years later became under-secretary for foreign affairs, an office he came to perform as desultorily as he did that of manager of Drury Lane. Fortunately his father had secured the services of Mrs. Siddons *(see p85)* and J.P. Kemble *(see p84)*, who kept attendances up. Appointed secretary to the Treasury in 1783 Sheridan did indeed shine as a Commons orator. In 1787 he became the leading light for the prosecution of Warren Hastings for alleged misgovernment in India, a cause in which he delivered a speech lasting five hours. Thanks to his friendship with Fox he gained access to the sparkling opposition *salons* at Holland House and Devonshire House.

1792 proved to be Sheridan's *annus horribilis*. Eliza died and Drury Lane was declared so unsafe that it had to be demolished. Although he was able to raise the £150,000 required for rebuilding with apparent ease, this was only at the cost of greater indebtedness and a hit-and-miss payroll policy which did not endear him to his company. In 1795 he remarried. His literary gifts did not desert him. It was Sheridan, during the Bank of England crisis of 1797 who referred to "an elderly lady in the City of great credit and long standing", dubbing her thereafter as 'The Old Lady of Threadneedle Street'. A decade later

57. The fire which destroyed Covent Garden Theatre on 12 September 1808.

58. The new Theatre Royal, Drury Lane, rebuilt in 1812.

it was Sheridan who composed the epitaph for Lord Nelson's memorial in Guildhall.

Sheridan's adaptation of Kotzebue's *Die Spanier in Peru* as *Pizarro* in 1799 bought a brief, welcome but transitory respite in terms of regard and cash but in 1802 the bankers were put in charge of the theatre's finances. The formation of a new 'ministry of all the talents' in 1806 pointedly found no place in the Cabinet for Sheridan. Fox, from whom he had in any case grown apart, died that same year. The income from a Duchy of Cornwall sinecure was soon squandered. In 1809 the rebuilt Drury Lane was destroyed by fire while Sheridan was speaking in the Commons. He stayed to finish his remarks then repaired to the Piazza coffee house opposite the blaze, which he watched calmly while demolishing fortified wine in copious quantities. When this *sang-froid* provoked wondering comment Sheridan, surely with an eye to posterity, delivered himself of the immortal line " may not a man take a glass or two by his own fireside." As a consequence of this catastrophe

the burden of debt became insupportable. He was entirely excluded from management and in 1811 lost his seat at Stafford after thirty years. In 1813 he was arrested for debt and carried off to Sloman's sponging house. Friends rallied but both Sheridan and his wife became ill and were reduced to living in squalid grandeur. He died in the front room of his Savile Row house. At his splendid funeral four lords acted as pall-bearers. Significantly he wished to lie near Fox at the western end of the Abbey in what was to become Radicals' Corner; instead he was buried by Garrick in the north transept, in Poets' Corner.

Bigger, Not Better

The reconstruction of both Covent Garden and Drury Lane on a far grander scale at the end of the first decade of the nineteenth century prompted theatrical veteran Richard Cumberland to ponder the implications for the relationship between actor, audience, playwright and producer:

" Since the stages ... had been so enlarged in their dimensions as to be henceforward theatres for spectators rather than playhouses for hearers, it is hardly to be wondered at if managers and directors encourage those representations to which their structure is best adapted. The splendour of the scene, the ingenuity of the machinist and the rich display of dresses, aided by the captivating charms of the music, now in great degree supersede the labours of the poet. There can be nothing very gratifying in watching the movement of an actor's lips when we cannot hear the words that proceed from them, but when the animating march strikes up and the stage lays open its recesses to the depth of a hundred feet for the procession to advance, even the most distant spectator can enjoy his shilling's worth of show."

Such cavernous venues favoured not only major spectacles and the exploitation of special effects but also a more declamatory and stylised mode of acting. Even the formidable Mrs. Siddons found Drury Lane a challenge, referring to it feelingly as "the Wilderness".

Elaborate pantomime proved reliable fare. Prince Puckler-Muskau commented on a Christmas pantomime at Covent Garden that "the web of the story is ... spun on through a thousand transformations and extravagances, without any particular connexion but with occasional good hits at the incidents of the day; and above all, with admirable decoration and great wit on the part of the machinist."

The more than half century between the death of David Garrick and the final repeal of the Patent Act in 1843 was an era of eminent actors and mediocre theatre, with melodrama, thinly derived from German inspiration and French imports, to fill the creative vacuum. *Menschenhass und Reue* (*Misanthropy and Repentance*) by the prolific August von Kotzebue (1761-1819), suitably disguised by Benjamin Thompson as *The Stranger* (1798) enjoyed a lasting popularity, while Mrs.Inchbald (1753-1821) transformed *Das Kind der Liebe* (*The Love Child*) into *Lovers' Vows* (1798), which was still sufficiently shocking to feature as a daring project for genteel amateur

59. Mrs Inchbald; a print published in 1821.

dramatics in Jane Austen's *Mansfield Park* (1814).

The first (1802) self-proclaimed 'melodrama' on the London stage was *A Tale of Mystery* by Thomas Holcroft (1745-1809), whose own life would have supplied the material for a dozen. The self-educated son of a shoe-maker, Holcroft was successively a pedlar, stable-boy, shoe-maker, schoolteacher and strolling player. His first wife left him, his second and third died, his only son committed suicide, he was himself partially paralysed by a stroke and tried for treason - none of which prevented him from learning French, German and Italian, writing a comic opera, novels, plays and the earliest London stage adaptations of *The Marriage of Figaro* and *Les Liaisons Dangereuses*.

Melodrama would remain a dominant theatrical mode for three-quarters of a century, appealing to an audience which lacked the classical education or acquaintance with the conventions of high society which previous dramatists often took for granted. Holcroft's French inspiration, Pixerecourt (1773-1844), had

60. Douglas Jerrold.

61. Clarkson Stanfield.

explicitly stated that he was writing for people who couldn't even read. Melodrama offered varying combinations of spectacle, glamour, dashing heroes, black-hearted villains, imperilled heroines, sensational happenings, moral simplicities and happy endings. An early and successful exponent was Dickens' friend, Douglas Jerrold (1803-57), the author of some seventy plays. The son of an actor-manager, Jerrold drew on his own experience as a sailor to create a rollicking nautical melodrama *Black-Ey'd Susan* (1829), based on a century-old song by Gay, which remained a safe bet at the box office for decades. Typical melodramatic predicaments are revealed in other Jerrold titles such as *The Rent Day, The Factory Girl* and *The Prisoner of War*. Despite the reliance on stock, stereotypical characters, melodrama could therefore be socially engaged to the extent of attacking contemporary evils such as exploitative landlords or employers. Jerrold's *The Mutiny of the Nore* (1830) attacked flogging and the same author's *Fifteen Years of a Drunkard's Life* beat the drum for temperance.

Much stage fodder was simply an opportunistic attempt to cash in on the craze of the day. The forgotten productions of W.T. Moncrieff (1794-1857) provide an illustrative example. Lessee at various times of the Queen's, Astley's, the Coburg and the City Theatre, Moncrieff knocked out over a hundred plays over the course of his career. *The Lear of Private Life* (1820), an adaptation of a novel by Mrs. Opie, represented a domestic Regency reincarnation of Shakespeare. In the same year almost fifty thousand Londoners queued up outside the Egyptian Hall on Piccadilly to pay for the privilege of seeing Gericault's sensational canvas *The Shipwreck of the Medusa*. Moncrieff gave them the chance to see a dramatised version of the real-life tragedy which had inspired it. The following year he produced *Tom and Jerry*, the best of numerous stage adaptations of sporting journalist Pierce Egan's documentary sketch of the lads-about-town collectively known as 'the Fancy', *Life in London*. It was the first piece to achieve a recorded run of over a hundred performances. In 1823 Moncrieff exploited the vastness of the Drury Lane stage and the skill of scene-painter Clarkson Stanfield (1793-1867) to present *The Cataract of the Ganges*, with a troupe of horses and real water in the cataract for the finale. In 1831 he cashed in on the nationwide agitation for the ending of parliamentary abuses and the enlargement of the franchise with *Reform; or, John Bull Triumphant*.

The audience for melodrama was the by-product of the breakneck growth of London and other cities fuelled by Britain's ever-growing global commerce, by the novel force of industrialisation and by imperial expansion fed by victories in war. Britain's first census in 1801 revealed that the population of its capital was nearing the million mark; by 1811 it had passed it, by 1851 it would more than double again. By far Europe's largest city when the nineteenth century opened, London would be the world's largest city when it closed. The centre of global trade and finance, London also represented world's largest single concentration of wealth, with a seemingly inexhaustible appetite for consumption and amusement. As Golby and Purdue observe in their synoptic survey of English popular culture:

"Excitement, novelty and spectacle became all important. Commercial forces did not replace either the elite or the popular traditions in popular entertainment; rather, they mixed them up with a magnificent unconcern for past distinctions and niceties ... Shakespeare, melodramas and performing animals did not merely co-exist but intermingled. Patent theatres sought to retain their privileged position behind protective legislation but were forced to ... anglicise and plebeianise their opera, to set Shakespeare amidst spectacular stage sets and follow him with performing dogs. Unlicensed theatres mounted their challenge to the monopoly of drama ... a battle they were not to win until 1843 but in which they were to be successful in skirmish after skirmish."

These developments become all the more comprehensible in the light of contemporary changes in the nature of audiences. Once again Puckler-Muskau supplies valuable testimony of behaviour of the shirt-sleeved, orange-peel throwing occupants of the gallery:

"The most striking thing to a foreigner in English theatre is the unheard-of coarseness and brutality of the audience ... the higher and more civilised classes go only to the Italian Opera and very rarely visit their national theatre ... English freedom here degenerates into the rudest licence and it is not uncommon in the most affecting part of tragedy ... to hear some coarse expression shouted from the galleries ... followed ... either by loud laughter ... or by the castigation and expulsion of the offender ... And such things happen not once but sometimes twenty times in the course of a performance ..."

Mrs. Jordan

Dorothy (Dorothea Bland) Jordan (1761-1816) became as much a social phenomenon as a theatrical one. The illegitimate daughter of an Irish actress, she excelled in breeches parts and playing hoydens until, pregnant and fleeing her employer and seducer, she assumed the name of Mrs. Jordan and was taken up by Sheridan who saw her in York during race week. At Drury Lane she wisely left tragedy to Mrs. Siddons and was painted by Romney in the characteristic role of Priscilla Tomboy. Hazlitt *(see p90)* observed that "her person was large, soft and generous, like her soul." Having had a further three children by barrister Richard Ford, she broke with him in 1791 to become the mistress of the Duke of Clarence, subsequently William IV (reigned 1820-30), by whom she had ten children but still managed to make occasional stage appearances. They parted in 1811 and, following her last appearance in 1814, she was swindled out of her wealth and, fearing arrest for debt, fled to Paris, poverty and an obscure death. Even her grave was swept away by a building project of the 1930s.

62. Mrs Jordan.

63. John Philip Kemble.

The Kembles

Sheridan's eclipse was met by the rise of the remarkable Kemble dynasty. They were not all brilliant but there were a lot of them. Hardworking John Philip Kemble (1757-1823) was born the son of a provincial theatre manager and acted with his father's touring company from childhood. Initially intended for the Catholic priesthood, he quit in his teens to build a self-claimed repertoire of 126 roles before his London debut as Hamlet in 1783, a role in which he was to be much admired by Hazlitt. In 1788 Kemble took over Drury Lane and went on to play a towering Coriolanus, the epitome of a painstakingly studied, stentorian classicism for which he became renowned. Leigh Hunt discerned a studied deliberation in Kemble's method – "it would appear that he never pulls out his handkerchief without a design upon the audience, that he has as much thought in making a step as making a speech, in short that his very finger is eloquent ... He does not present one the idea of a man who grasps with the force of genius but of one who overcomes by the toil of attention."

Disabled by gout and asthma and hindered by altercations with Sheridan, Kemble moved to Covent Garden in 1796. Under-insured when the theatre was destroyed by fire in 1808, he came to the brink of bankruptcy. (Other incidental casualties included the wine stock of the Beefsteak Society and an organ which had belonged to Handel.) Kemble, however, still managed to rebuild and reopen in 1809. Revising the prices of admission in an attempt to recoup his position he was faced with 'Old Price' mobs demonstrating for over sixty successive nights. The rioters were careful not to break up the theatre, only to make performances impossible. Finally Kemble, like Garrick before him, was forced to give way. In 1815 Kemble published his stage adaptations under the portentous title of *British Theatre*. He finally retired, no doubt gratefully, to Lausanne in 1817. Kemble is memorialised in the Kemble's Head pub at the corner of Bow Street and Long Acre.

Kemble's sister, the statuesque and imposing

64. Sarah Siddons; from a sketch by George Romney.

65. Charles Kemble.

Sarah (1755-1831) acted under her married name of Siddons. William Siddons was a young actor whom she married at St. Marylebone, against parental opposition, when she was only eighteen. A child prodigy, Sarah Siddons failed on her London debut as Portia at Drury Lane in 1775, withdrew and undertook a thorough provincial apprenticeship before reappearing in London in 1782 and establishing a dominance that would last for three decades. By 1782 Sir Joshua Reynolds, President of the Royal Academy, was painting her as *The Tragic Muse*. In 1785 her Lady Macbeth confirmed her standing as Britain's greatest tragedienne and inspired another striking portrait, by Sir William Beechey, which fancifully portrays her holding a mask, wearing a turban and grasping a dagger. By 1789 Mrs. Siddons was appearing at St. Paul's Cathedral as the personification of Britannia. Hazlitt thought her "tragedy personified - She had no need of the robes, the sweeping train, the ornaments of the stage; in herself she is as great as any being she ever represented in the ripeness and plenitude of her power." Leaving Drury Lane in 1790 she acted only occasionally until moving to Covent Garden in 1801. Her last

appearance, as Lady Macbeth, took place there in 1812. The ascent of her career, like Sheridan's was matched on the London property-ladder. Initially lodging on the Strand, by 1784 she was in newly-built Gower Street where peaches grew on the back of her house which was then "effectually in the country and delightfully pleasant". In 1790 she moved on to Great Marlborough Street and in 1805 out to Westbourne Farm, on the way to Paddington. The site of her final (1817-31) home at 27 Upper Baker Street is now occupied by the Lost Property Office for items mislaid on London's transport system. The existence of an appropriately larger than life-size statue of Sarah Siddons in Westminster Abbey is testimony to her public standing. In 1897 an outdoor statue of Sarah Siddons was unveiled by Sir Henry Irving in the churchyard at St. Mary's, Paddington Green, where she lies buried.

Charles Kemble (1775-1854) was by twenty years the younger brother of Sarah Siddons and playing leads when he made his London debut in 1794. Unlike his better known siblings, he was effective in comedy as well as tragedy. As manager (1822-32) of Covent Garden, however,

66. Fanny Kemble.

67. Edmund Kean in the role of Richard III.

he was unable to retain his best players but his 1823 production of *King John* (Faulconbridge was a major landmark in its pioneering attempt to present historically accurate costumes). By 1829 Kemble's managerial position was critical and he was obliged to summon the talents of his daughter to a profession he had hoped to spare her. As Juliet, Frances 'Fanny' Kemble (1809-93) made a debut of such force that the production was able to make a highly profitable tour of New York and Philadelphia. On returning home Kemble was pleased to accept the role of last but one Examiner of Plays (1836-40), a position which he passed on to his son. Kemble was a founder member of the Garrick Club. Having hoped to become a writer, Fanny instead successfully exploited many of the roles associated with her aunt Sarah Siddons. After a failed American marriage she reluctantly returned to the stage and found a livelihood into old age (1848-74) by giving celebrated public readings of Shakespeare on both sides of the Atlantic. In retirement she lived at 26 Hereford Square, penning copious volumes of autobiography.

Kean

While the Kembles were eminently respectable - in the case of Mrs. Siddons intimidatingly so - Edmund Kean (1790-1833) was the personification of the self-destructive genius. The illegitimate son of a minor actress who tried to exploit him as an infant prodigy, he rejected her to undertake a gruelling provincial apprenticeship, becoming an accomplished mime and skilled acrobat. Swarthy and athletic, he looked like and sometimes believed himself to be a gypsy. Kean made a sensational London debut, as Shylock, at Drury Lane in 1814 when the theatre was overshadowed by the financial crisis of Sheridan's last years. Defying tradition, he eschewed both caricature and pathos to play the Jew as a monster of demonic and dynamic evil. By the end of his first season he had added Richard III, Hamlet, Othello and Iago to his list of triumphs. Coleridge famously remarked of Kean's stage passion that "to see him act is like reading Shakespeare by flashes of lighting".

Mrs. Siddons, who could quite literally look down on the diminutive newcomer, delivered a verdict of crushing condescension – "You have done well, sir – very well. It is a pity there is too little of you to go far."

Years of struggle, followed by adulation, soon metamorphosed back into further years of struggle, chiefly against the bottle, but additionally against the bounds of sexual propriety. Playing the Theatre Royal, Richmond the increasingly temperamental Kean was incensed when the audience politely applauded the rest of the cast as enthusiastically as they had him and wrote to the manager "I have the greatest respect for you and the best wishes for your professional success; but if I play Richmond again – I'll be damned." In 1831, nevertheless, Kean became Richmond's lessee and moved into the adjoining house. During his last appearance, in 1833, as Othello, he collapsed on stage, dying within weeks. The Kean Street at the rear of Drury Lane is named, not for him, but for his less talented but infinitely more respectable son, Charles *(see p104)*. Alexandre Dumas Senior thought Kean's life so extraordinary that he wrote a play about it. In 1954 this was adapted by Jean-Paul Sartre, presumably as an illustration of how to live the authentic life of personal choice to the point of self-extinction. One of Kean's favoured roles, in Massinger's *A New Way to Pay Old Debts* was, indeed, Sir Giles Overreach.

Elliston

Robert Elliston (1774-1831), a drinking-companion of Kean's, led an equally untidy personal life. Outraging his respectable uncles by running off to take to the stage in Bath, Elliston displayed versatility in tragedy and comedy. In London he would become proficient enough to merit critical essays - and eventually obituaries - from the pens of both Leigh Hunt (1784-1859) and Charles Lamb (1775-1834) and to win the praise of Lord Byron (1788-1824), Macready and Mathews *(see p89)*. Excelling in the mirthful and the gallant on stage, Elliston seemed incapable of repose, ever needful of bustle and void of inner

depth. As Hunt crisply put it "his feelings follow each other like the buckets on a water-wheel, full one instant and empty the next." Elliston proceeded into management to tweak the collective nose of the Patent Theatres by running a series of minor houses. At the Royal Circus and Equestrian Philharmonic Academy (1809-14) in Blackfriars Road, which he converted and renamed the Surrey *(see p74)*, he defied the restrictions of the Patent Act by the ploy of inserting a ballet into every play – including Hamlet and Macbeth. He also shrewdly converted the former stabling to provide front-of-house facilities for refreshment and recreation unrivalled even in the West End. Elliston was, however, quite consciously not seeking to rival the West End but to pioneer a new type of neighbourhood playhouse which would serve the densely-populated burgeoning suburbs on the ever-expanding periphery of the metropolis. At the Olympic (1813-19) in 1815 he became the first manager to install gas-lighting in a theatre auditorium (rather than on stage). The 'Great Lessee', having rebuilt the Olympic, then switched sides to become manager of Drury Lane (1819-26), where Kean was his leading player. By the fairly direct device of raising salaries he successfully lured major talents from Covent Garden, then languishing under the lacklustre direction of Charles Kemble. Lacking a long enough pocket to sustain this policy Elliston's tenure ended in bankruptcy. Ruined in health by two seizures, he returned to the Surrey in 1827 where, thanks to Jerrold's *Black Ey'd Susan*, he finally brought off a box-office triumph. Elliston's efforts to continue on stage, however, shattered his constitution and following a third seizure he died at his home in Great Surrey Street, leaving a wife, nine children and three bastards.

Macready

The career of William Charles Macready (1793-1873), by contrast, began in bankruptcy and ended in respectability. The son of a West Country theatre manager, Macready was intended for the law and sent to Rugby but withdrawn at fifteen when his father was imprisoned for debt. The

68. William Macready delivering an address on his last appearance, at Drury Lane on 26 February 1851.

stage was one of the few fields in which a penurious teenager might just make good and was, in any case, something he knew about. That said, Macready remained an embittered success for forty years, as his candid diaries make abundantly clear.

He made his debut, as Romeo, at Birmingham in 1810. In 1816 he was hired by Covent Garden as a counter-attraction to Kean but made little impact until 1819 when he gambled on challenging his rival in his best known part, Richard III. It paid off splendidly but it was the demonstration of paternal love that was eventually to become Macready's trademark. His mannered style became noted for 'the Macready pause'. In a critique of his Othello Hazlitt remarked that "Mr. Macready's powers are better adapted to the declamation than to the acting of passion – that is, he is a better orator than actor." Leigh Hunt opined that "his grace looks more the effect of study than of habit" and observed with slight unease " you are not sure what sort

of person he will be when he leaves the stage."

Aiming constantly to raise standards of popular taste, Macready worked with a range of playwrights to bring out new material. His collaborators included Sheridan Knowles (1784-1862), Dickens, Robert Browning (1812-89) and most successfully, Edward Bulwer-Lytton (1803-73).

In 1838 Macready succeeded in ditching Nahum Tate's bastardized *Richard III* in favour of something much closer to the original text. He was meticulous about rehearsals, even to extras rehearsing crowd scenes. He endorsed the trend towards more accurate costuming. He introduced limelight to Covent Garden. An ill-tempered snob, Macready made many enemies by constantly disparaging his own profession. Spells as manager of Covent Garden (1837-9) and Drury Lane (1841-3) bankrupted him and forced him back onto the stage to build up a retirement fund. By 1848 he was sufficiently recovered to be living at 5 Clarence Terrace, overlooking Regent's Park. When he did finally retire in 1851 Tennyson wrote a sonnet in his honour. Macready's diary entry was a simple "Thank God!"

Madam Managers

'Madame Vestris' as she was known professionally was born in Soho as Lucy Elizabeth Bartolozzi (1797-1856), a descendant of an Italian immigrant engraver and founder member of the Royal Academy. Married briefly as a teenager to a French ballet-dancer who promoted her debut as a singer in 1815, she was blessed with good looks, a lovely voice and shapely legs and, following his desertion, employed them skilfully to establish her career, alternately singing affecting ballads to middle-brow audiences and playing cross-dressing 'breeches parts' in rougher houses. In 1831 she daringly took over the Olympic Theatre to become London's first female manager. At the Olympic she raised still higher the standards of accuracy applied to historical costuming and props. In this she was invaluably assisted by the playwright, musician and antiquarian James

69. Madame Vestris.

70. Charles Mathews the Younger.

Robinson Planche (1795-1880), who had devised the costumes to Kemble's pioneering 1823 *King John.* Elected a Fellow of the Society of Antiquaries at thirty-four, he would publish a definitive *History of British Costume*, become a founder member of the British Archaeological Association and eventually be appointed Somerset Herald. Planche was, however, anything but a fusty scholar. A practical man of the theatre, he wrote over 150 plays and librettos and left a memoir, *Recollections and Reflections* (1872) which throws unique light on the English theatre practice of his days.

In 1838 Madam Vestris married the urbane but improvident light comedian Charles James Mathews (1803-78). After a successful American tour, they jointly took over the management of Covent Garden (1839-42) where the hit they had with the youthful Dion Boucicault's *London Assurance* (1841) could not save them from being imprisoned for debt. They repeated the same saga subsequently at the Lyceum (1847-55), then known as the Royal Lyceum and English Opera House. In the 1840s they lived at Westbourne Farm, the former home of Sarah Siddons. Madam Vestris, who is credited with inventing the box set, died a few days after her husband's release from a second term of imprisonment for debt. Mathews found personal salvation in a second American tour which brought him a wealthy marriage and enabled him to devote the rest of his days to travelling and writing.

Like Madam Vestris Frances Maria 'Fanny' Kelly (1790-1882) started out as a singer and was a regular member of the Drury Lane company from the age of twenty until she was in her forties. Charles Lamb was so smitten with her that he not only immortalised her in an essay but even proposed marriage. Another rejected suitor actually took a shot at her during a performance. In 1833 she struck out on her own by establishing a Theatre and Dramatic School at the Strand Theatre and kept her personal finances afloat with a one-woman show of

71. Fanny Kelly, c.1819.

Dramatic Recollections. In 1840 Kelly transferred her drama school to a purpose-built theatre tacked onto the back of her house at 73 Dean Street, Soho. The opening evening proved a fiasco thanks to a complex (horse-powered!) scene-changing mechanism which was so noisy it drowned out the actors and made the whole building seem to tremble. Persevering nevertheless she was to number among her pupils the ebullient Dion Boucicault and the *farceuse* Mrs. Keeley (1806-99). Although the threat of bankruptcy drove Fanny Kelly into retirement in 1849, her tiny two-hundred seat house, grandiosely known as the Royalty, was to make an astonishing contribution to theatrical history before being blitzed out and then demolished (1953). The first (1875) Gilbert and Sullivan collaboration, *Trial by Jury*, was played at the Royalty, the first (1891) English public performance of Ibsen's *Ghosts*, the initial (1892) production of George Bernard Shaw's first major play *Widowers' Houses*, the first London production of Brandon Thomas's *Charley's Aunt* (1892) and the premieres of Ibsen's *A Doll's House* (1893) and *The Wild Duck* (1894).

The Critic

In temperamental William Hazlitt (1778-1830) the London stage found one of its earliest professional critics. Young enough to have been awed by Mrs. Siddons, he was most prolific in the years immediately after her retirement, writing for *The Examiner*, the *Morning Chronicle*, *The Champion* and *The Times*. In 1816 he researched and completed the unfinished memoirs of the disaster-prone playwright Thomas Holcroft and in 1817 published a study of *Characters of Shakespeare's Plays* and an essay *On Actors and Acting*. Hazlitt's reviews were sufficiently durable to merit hard-cover publication in 1818 as *A View of the English Stage*. Another barbed sally came in an essay of 1824 *Whether Actors Ought to Sit in the Boxes?* Hazlitt's most original work *The Spirit of the Age* (1825) repeatedly explores the metaphor of public life as a stage. William Hazlitt was the first English writer to make a substantial part of his living from descriptive criticism. Despising critical theory, he trusted himself "to feel what was good"

New Competitors

Out on the fringes of London perhaps dozens of would-be theatres achieved precarious existences. Peckham had a theatre in the 1790s, offering the standard popular fare of farce and melodrama. In 1799 a play in three acts was published under the title *The Peckham Frolic or Nell Gwyn*. John Baldwin Buckstone *(see p107)* made his youthful debut at Peckham in *The Dog of Montargis*. By 1819, however, the venue was being referred to as "half theatre, half barn" and by 1822 "the old theatre" had closed and the building taken over by a Lancasterian School for Boys.

Apart from the Olympic and the rebuilt Surrey, the number of non-Patent theatres continued to proliferate in more central parts of the capital.

First built on the Strand in 1806, by local tradesman John Scott to launch his daughter's projected stage career and initially known as the Sans Pareil, the Adelphi was re-named in 1819 and achieved notoriety in 1821 with *Tom and*

72. The Sans Pareil Theatre. A print published in 1816.

Jerry which inspired a craze embracing the whole paraphernalia of tacky souvenirs, novelty items and memorabilia. The Adelphi then built on this breakthrough by presenting stage adaptations of the novels of Sir Walter Scott. In 1834 by then self-styled as the Theatre Royal, New Adelphi, it installed England's first sinking stage.

The Lyceum, just off the Strand, was built in 1771 by architect James Payne as an intended concert and exhibition hall and first used for entertainment by the opportunistic Dibdin and Astley. Converted into the English Opera House by musician Dr. Samuel Arnold in 1794, it struggled against the power of the Patents by presenting concerts, freak shows and the first (1802) fixed display of Madam Tussaud's waxworks. As manager Samuel Arnold junior managed to gain a licence for summer performances, rebuilt in 1815-16 and managed to recruit such talents as Fanny Kelly before fire (1830) necessitated another rebuilding (1834), west of the original site which is covered by Wellington Street.

What is now the South Bank was until the first decade of the nineteenth century still largely an undeveloped area of market gardens. The construction of three major bridges in the immediate post-war years, at Waterloo, Southwark and Lambeth, initiated a period of frenzied building. What was to become the Old Vic opened in 1818 as the Coburg, just south of Waterloo Bridge within a year of the bridge being opened. Designed by Rudolph Cabanel of Aachen, it was intended as a home for melodrama. Derided for its 'transpontine' location, it nevertheless drew on the burgeoning suburbs around it to play to packed houses. After extensive refurbishment in 1833 it was renamed the Royal Victoria in deference to the teenage heir-apparent to the throne but soon declined to become a rough house, attracting purely local audiences in an area which had soon lost its promise to become a fashionable *faubourg*.

Also south of the river was the Rotunda at Blackfriars, opened as a lecture-theatre-cum-

73. The Royal Coburg Theatre in Waterloo Road, 1820, later to be the Old. Vic.

74. The St James's Theatre in King Street, 1835.

75. The Strand entrance to the first Lyceum Theatre.

museum but converted to a theatre *ca.* 1830 and renamed the Globe.

The St. James's was opened in King Street, St. James's in 1835 for John Braham (1777-1856), whose tenor voice had made him a fortune and whose theatre lost it for him by 1838. In the long run the theatre was to have a more distinguished history than its inauspicious beginnings might suggest.

Built as a bazaar at the eastern end of Oxford Street in 1830, the Princess's was converted into a theatre and named for Princess Victoria but not opened until 1840 and then as a concert hall - which soon failed, reverting to theatrical and operatic presentations in 1842.

In the East End the Royalty Theatre in Wellclose Square burned down in 1826. Rebuilt and reopened in 1828 it collapsed three days later, killing ten people.

The Pavilion, opened at Whitechapel, also in 1828 lasted until 1934. A City Theatre at Cripplegate lasted only a couple of years. The City of London in Bishopsgate, opened in 1837. To its north were the Standard in Shoreditch (1835) and the Britannia, Hoxton (1841).

The Ending of the Patent

The ending of the Patent monopoly was perhaps inevitable in an age which had seen the demolition of the East India Company's trading monopolies with India and China and the abolition of tithes and tariffs. Competition was the watchword of the age. A rage for reform was fuelled by antipathy towards corruption, privilege and inefficiency. Parliamentary committees proliferated to conduct enquiries and recommend legislative remedies for perceived evils. In 1832 a Select Committee was appointed to enquire into the condition of the Theatre. Its leading light was Edward Bulwer-Lytton who that very year had found fame with his novel *Eugene Aram.* The Committee set itself three major objectives. The first was to protect playwrights from plagiarism by establishing an effective copyright law. 'Lytton's Act' effected this to a conditional extent in 1833. The second was to challenge the Lord Chamberlain's role as censor,

76. *The rebuilt Lyceum Theatre*

77. *The Princess Theatre in Oxford Street.*

79. John Braham.

80. Edward Bulwer Lytton in his apartment at
Albany.

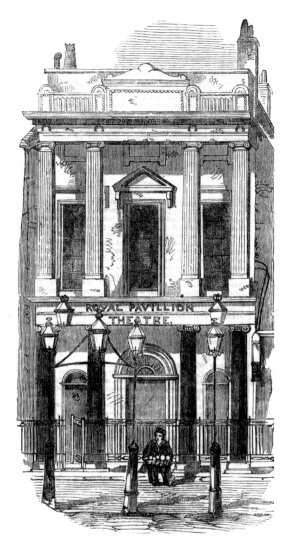

78. The Pavilion Theatre, Whitechapel in 1856.

which came to nothing. The third was to
investigate and challenge the Patent Theatres'
monopoly over legitimate drama. After a delay of
eleven years this bore fruit in abolition in 1843.
Vain, talented, foppish and extravagant, Bulwer
is now best remembered for *The Last Days of
Pompeii*, which inspired early cinematic
extravaganzas but he also wrote plays for
Macready, several of which proved durable, most
notably *Richelieu* (1839), which was frequently
revived.

American Connections

A professional London theatre company played in the colonial capital of Williamsburg as early as 1752. Benjamin Franklin, who spent a good quarter of his long life in London, once remarked sniffily that it had nothing much on American cities - except for its playhouses. Transatlantic theatrical contacts were put on a mutually energising basis once the inauguration of regular 'liner' services began in the 1820s, sailing to regular timetables, regardless of passenger numbers. The advent of steam-powered, screw-driven ships from the 1840s onwards minimised the effects of adverse weather, further diminishing the tyranny of distance. Improved shipping services helped to increase the outflow of English-speaking emigrants, many of whom remained attached to their language and culture, if not to their country. Theatrical stardom on both sides of the Atlantic at last became a possibility.

One of the earliest manifestations of this possibility assumed the ugliest possibly form as a rivalry between William Macready *(see p87)* and Edwin Forrest (1806-72), the first native-born American theatrical superstar. Macready first toured the US in 1826, then again in 1843. Forrest had performed with Kean and appeared in London in 1836 and again in 1845, when he had explicitly challenged Macready to show his superiority. Enmity between the supporters of the two actors erupted in the course of Macready's third American tour when the Astor Palace Opera House riot led to thirty-one deaths. The manager at that time was James Henry Hackett (1800-71), who in 1827 had been the first American actor to appear in London as a proclaimed star – but flopped.

The experience of the gifted African-American Ira Aldridge (1807-67) was also less than encouraging. Arriving in England at seventeen, he was recognised as sufficiently talented to take over from the dying Kean as Othello in 1833 but received a mixed press, much of the hostile reaction clearly racially motivated. After more than a quarter century touring the provinces and Ireland, he set out to conquer Europe and did so, being honoured and even decorated by more than one European monarch. A widely-praised return to the West End in 1865 may have offered some consolation to a man who mastered forty roles and has retrospectively been acknowledged as a pioneer of psychological realism.

Charlotte Cushman (1816-76), the first native-born American actress of the first rank, enjoyed better fortune. Tall and powerfully built (she played Romeo against her sister's Juliet), she played opposite Macready on his second U.S. tour and made her London debut at the then-not-yet-fashionable Princess Theatre. By her return to the USA in 1849 she was considered by many the greatest living English-speaking actress.

Charles Dickens was rapturously received on his first visit to America in 1842 but soon revised his first favourable impressions and subsequently caused much offence with his *American Notes* and the harsh American stereotypes in *Martin Chuzzlewit*. Fervent and doubtless sincere in his denunciation of slavery he had more personal reasons for disliking America viz. its total disregard of European copyrights which meant that while his books sold by the million he received not a penny for them. A quarter of a century later, however, Dickens returned (1867-8) to make a reading-tour which mesmerised audiences and created lock-out crowds *(see p102)*.

81. A Charles Dickens 'Reading'.

82. Dion Boucicault.

While American tours often saved the careers or mended the fortunes of many distressed British actors and actresses the prospect was not universally appealing. Macready recorded with fervour in his diary "Give me a crust in England. God speed me in my labours for my blessed family's sake. Amen! No America."

Ebulllient, energetic Irish-born Dion (Dionysius Lardner) Boucicault (originally Boursiquot) (1820-90) skilfully exploited both his ethnicity and his verbal facility to become famed – and notorious – on both sides of the Atlantic. Early success with *London Assurance (see p89)*, starring Madame Vestris and her husband, Charles Mathews Jr., was followed by fruitful collaboration with Benjamin Webster *(see p83)*, a trip to Paris, an adaptation of *The*

Corsican Brothers from the French (1852) and, for Charles Kean, and a sensational playing of the title-role in his own play *The Vampire* (1852). At this height of his powers Boucicault had his contract terminated by the ultra-respectable Kean on account of his scandalous relationship with actress Agnes Robertson (1833-1916) (*a.k.a.* 'The Pocket Venus'). Unabashed, Boucicault became first Agnes' manager in America, then joint manager with her of theatres in New Orleans, Washington and New York. He also developed actor-training and fire-proof scenery and established better copyright laws and a system of profit-sharing for writers which would eventually lead to royalties. As a dramatist he made a serious impact with *The Poor of New York* (1857), *The Octoroon* (1859) and *The Colleen Bawn* (1860) – which would one day become the first Irish-produced film to be made in Ireland and in 1860 provided the vehicle for a brilliant London come-back for husband and wife. For the next dozen years they dazzled London with such pieces as *Rip Van Winkle* (1865), *The Flying Scud (see p108)* and the titillating courtesan-play *Formosa* (1869). Boucicault's third Irish melodrama, *The Shaughraughan* (1874) was to be one of the best of the genre. In 1885, in the best tradition of the lovable Irish rogues he played on stage with such bravura relish he made a bigamous marriage to an American actress forty-four years his junior, repudiating his liaison of more than thirty years with Agnes as not legally binding. The judgment of the *Dictionary of National Biography* was opaquely phrased but damning – his "brilliant literary and histrionic qualities were not supported by any rigorous moral code."

Edward Askew Sothern (1826-81) made an American debut in 1852 but shot to sudden star status in the 1858 production of Tom Taylor's *Our American Cousin* as Lord Dundreary, a splendid creation immortalised by eponymous drooping side-whiskers of extraordinary dimensions. The play ran for five months straight and by 1861 had achieved four hundred performances. Sothern went on to play the title role in T.W. Robertson's *David Garrick* (1864) and remained a draw in both the UK and the US. Sothern's American-born son, Edward Hugh Sothern (1859-1933) made his debut in New York and became America's foremost Shakespearean player.

The splendidly named American-born Hezekiah Linthicum Bateman (1812-75) first managed his child prodigy daughters before taking over the Lyceum where his decision to feature Irving in *The Bells* (1871) gave the actor his most well-known role. Bateman's wife, Sidney (1823-81) carried on at the Lyceum on his death and later managed Sadler's Wells. Daughters Kate (1843-1917) and Ellen (1844-1936) made their debut in Shakespeare in New York at six and five, then in London two years later. Kate went on to appear with Irving. Ellen played Richard III, Shylock and Macbeth before retiring. Virginia (1853-1940) and Isabel (1854-1934) made their London debuts in 1865 and also went on to join Irving's company. Virginia later gave birth to novelists Fay Compton and Compton Mackenzie. Isabel co-managed

83. Edward Sothern.

Sadler's Wells before becoming a nun.

Daly's Theatre in Cranbourn Street was opened in 1893 for American Augustin Daly (1838-99). A critic turned prolific dramatist, Daly had made himself a dominant feature of the American theatre scene before undertaking his first European tour in 1884. Daly's came to specialise in musicals.

From 1898 until his death the American 'star maker' Charles Frohman (1860-1915) ran the Duke of York's Theatre, enjoying success with J.M. Barrie's *The Admirable Crichton* (1902) and *Peter Pan* (1904) in which the name part was first played by Dion Boucicault's daughter Nina, then in her forties.

Eugene Stratton (1863-1944) was an American 'black-face' impersonator who came to London with the Haverley minstrels in 1880. When the minstrel craze passed he switched to music hall but had no success until he reverted to his negro *persona* as a solo artist. In this guise Stratton was without rivals until his retirement in 1914. Whistling soulfully, soft-shoe shuffling on a darkened stage, he imbued a racial caricature with dignity and elegance and made 'Lily of Laguna' a musical 'standard'.

CHAPTER SEVEN

Mid-Victorian

Railways, Royalty and Respectability

The efforts of exacting professionals like Macready to raise the standard of what was put on the stage and the status of those putting it there were limited by the tastes and understanding of the audiences they could attract. If the views expressed by a Lambeth costermonger to the investigative journalist Henry Mayhew (1812-87) are at all representative they reveal what the profession was up against:

"Love and murder suits us best... Of *Hamlet* we can make neither end nor side; and ... would like it to be confined to the ghost scenes and the funeral and the killing off at the last. *Macbeth* would be better liked if it was only the witches and the fighting. The high words in a tragedy we call jaw-breakers ... We are fond of music ... Flash songs are liked and sailor's songs and patriotic songs."

A decade later Thomas Wright described the 'roughs' sitting up in 'the gods' as coming in

"with unwashed faces and in ragged and dirty attire, who bring bottles of drink with them, who *will* smoke despite the notice that 'smoking is strictly prohibited' and that 'officers will be in attendance'; who favour the bad with a stamping accompaniment and take the most noisy part in applauding or giving 'the call' to the performers. The females of this class are generally accompanied by infants, who are sure to cry and make a disturbance at some interesting part of the performance."

Fortunately for Macready and his disciples technological and social changes would enable them to reach out to sections of society with rather more elevated interests and more restrained habits of public behaviour. London's first railway, from London Bridge to Deptford and Greenwich opened in 1836. By 1850 the capital was connected by rail with all the major provincial cities. Regular, reliable services, travelling at speeds of up to sixty miles an hour, superseded the romantic-looking but uncomfortable, and in adverse weather far less reliable, stage-coaches. Henceforth London managers could send out entire companies with touring versions of West End successes or to try out productions, complete with full wardrobes and bulky sets of scenery. Development of suburban commuting opened up another possibility. As early as 1854 West End theatres were taking advertising space in the timetables of the Eastern Counties Railway in the hope of luring Essex residents to evening performances in town. Lavish Christmas pantomimes could be mounted with a view to drawing in family groups. Whereas a theatre which had to rely on a restricted local community for its audiences would have to keep changing its offerings to maintain their interest this need no longer be the case. As John Hollingshead *(see p109)* explained in 1866 to a House of Commons Select Committee on Theatre Licences and Regulations "the provincial people come up to town and fresh audiences are created every night." Much longer continuous runs became feasible. Cutting down the costs of mounting new productions, long runs became the prime aim of every commercially-driven management. Tom Taylor's *The Ticket of Leave Man* (1863) set a standard in achieving a first run of 407 nights.

If central London theatres could attract respectable audiences from further afield they could increasingly afford to ignore the lower end of the market, for whom the rapidly-proliferating music halls *(see p117)* were better suited. With the rougher elements thus siphoned off, the atmosphere in the theatre could become not only more respectable but, on occasion, respectful even.

The application of steam-power to shipping similarly revolutionised the logistics and economics of international travel, making it feasible not just for theatrical luminaries but even run-of-the-mill music hall artists to work on both sides of the Atlantic and for producers to despatch not merely leading players but whole companies. The refusal of the United States to acknowledge international copyright conventions until 1891 was a significant source of irritation, provoking British managements to tour their own productions to pre-empt or at least rival American pirate versions. By the same token it also became much easier and cheaper for French or German companies to mount productions in London, thus exposing London managers to Continental influences.

In a society in which a new royal family sought consciously to embody domestic perfection the theatre also benefited from renewed royal patronage. Victoria was a youthful fan of Vestris and Mathews. The proximity of the St. James's Theatre to Buckingham Palace encouraged her to sample its exotic French productions in the 1840s. In 1852, at the newly-fashionable Princess's, Victoria saw Dion Boucicault's *The Corsican Brothers* no less than five times. Finding the climactic duel scene, played by Charles Kean and Alfred Wigan "most impressive and creepy", she even made a detailed sketch of it in her personal journal.

Perhaps in unconscious deference to the Victorian cult of domesticity theatres also began to pay attention to comfort, as well as splendour, installing plush, upholstered, tip-up seats, carpeting foyers and aisles and decorating boxes with drapes, potted palms and flock wallpaper *(see p105)*. The introduction of matinees attracted those whom distance or disinclination might have deterred from attending evening performances.

From the 1870s onwards the cult of dining-out in mixed company gave rise to the theatre supper and encouraged a trend towards shorter and later programmes so that eating could be fitted in beforehand or afterwards. This trend was reinforced by the need to take account of the travel times of suburbanites, as Edward Tyrell Smith informed the 1866 Committee "I try to get my theatre over by 11 o'clock; people come up to town on purpose and they can go back by the 11 o'clock train."

The changing nature of the audience was inevitably reflected in what was presented on the stage, less 'thud and blunder' and greater urbanity and a growing focus on domestic issues rather than social problems. As the middle-classes were also the reading classes adaptations of classic authors like Scott and contemporary authors like Dickens were extremely popular. *Uncle Tom's Cabin* inspired at least nine stage versions. Mrs. Henry Wood's tear-jerker *East Lynne* (1866) was adapted at least fourteen times. Even the dramatists became increasingly bourgeois. Tom Taylor (1817-80), author of successes like *Our American Cousin* (1858) and *The Ticket-of-Leave Man* (1863), was also successively editor of *Punch*, Professor of English at the University of London and a civil servant in the Health Department.

Charles Dickens, Theatrical Addict

Making a speech in 1846 Charles Dickens (1812-70) declared that "I tried to recollect ... whether I had ever been in any theatre in my life from which I had not brought away some pleasant association, however poor the theatre and I protest ... I could not remember even one."

Dickens' first, childhood visits to the theatre were in Rochester, where he first saw Grimaldi. In London Dickens claimed that for the three years he worked as a shorthand clerk at Doctors' Commons he went to the theatre almost every night. He patronised Sadler's Wells and the Britannia at Hoxton, as well as such West End houses as Madame Vestris' Olympic and the Adelphi. He was a particular fan of Madame Vestris' father-in-law, Charles Mathews senior

(1776-1835), whose one-man 'At Homes', in which he imitated a succession of characters, would provide a model for Dickens' own public readings of his works. Macready, whom he greatly admired, became a close personal friend and was a fellow member of the Garrick Club, to which Dickens himself was elected in 1837. Dickens' closest friend and first biographer, John Forster, was both an enthusiastic amateur actor and the chief dramatic editor of *The Examiner*. *Pickwick Papers* was dedicated to the dramatist Sir Thomas Noon Talfourd (1795-1854). Dickens' other theatrical friends included Douglas Jerrold, Bulwer-Lytton and the influential French tragedian Charles Fechter (1824-79), who presented him with the miniature Swiss chalet which the author adopted as a refuge for writing in. Dickens also numbered among his theatrical acquaintance such managers as Phelps, Buckstone and Webster *(see below)*. He heartily disliked the snobbish Charles Kean.

Dickens' own knowledge of the drama was both deep and extensive. His writings contain hundreds of references to Shakespeare and he also admired the works of Jonson, Sheridan and Molière. This in no way precluded his enjoyment of simpler theatrical fare. In his preface to his edition of the memoirs of Grimaldi Dickens acknowledged a passion for pantomime.

His own first effort at writing a play was at the age of nine, *Misnar, The Sultan of India*, based on a story from *The Arabian Nights*. As a schoolboy of thirteen he was already staging melodramas. At sixteen he drafted a romance set in a Venetian inn. In 1833 a Shakespearean parody *O'Thello* was performed by members of his family. In 1836 Dickens enjoyed a modest success with a comic burletta, *The Strange Gentleman,* performed as an afterpiece for an entire season at the recently-opened St. James's Theatre. Dickens hoped that his operetta *The Village Coquettes* would "introduce me to the Public, as a dramatic writer" but it closed after sixteen performances. A farce *Is She His Wife?* was staged for only a few nights and another, *The Lamplighter*, went into rehearsal but was withdrawn before performance. Although he later collaborated on plays with

the humourist Mark Lemon (1809-70) and novelist Wilkie Collins (1824-89), these early disappointments convinced Dickens that his own peculiar genius did not favour writing for the stage.

Actors, actresses and the theatre in its many forms do, however, feature in many of Dicken's novels and stories, most notably the Crummles family and their touring company, who take in the fugitive Nicholas and Smike in *Nicholas Nickleby*. Mr. Jingle in *Pickwick Papers* is a strolling player. Punch and Judy men Codlin and Short and Mrs. Jarley's waxworks appear in *The Old Curiosity Shop* and the ballet in *Little Dorritt*. The inept actor Mr. Wopsle provides comic relief in *Great Expectations* while Sleary's circus evokes memories of Astley's in *Hard Times*.

Having dabbled in family productions and produced a comedy for the garrison in Montreal while visiting Canada in 1842, in 1845 Dickens set about organising amateur theatricals on a regular basis, recruiting to his company Forster

84. Amateur theatricals at Tavistock House, the home of Charles Dickens, on 6 January 1857. The cast includes Dickens, Mark Lemon, Augustus Egg and Wilkie Collins, the author of the play.

TAVISTOCK HOUSE THEATRE.

UNDER THE MANAGEMENT OF MR. CHARLES DICKENS.

On *Twelfth Night, Tuesday, January 6th, 1857, at a quarter before 8 o'clock, will be presented*
AN ENTIRELY NEW
ROMANTIC DRAMA, IN THREE ACTS, BY MR. WILKIE COLLINS,
called

THE FROZEN DEEP.

The Machinery and Properties by Mr. Ireland, of the Theatre Royal, Adelphi. The Dresses by Messrs. Nathan, of Titchbourne Street; Haymarket. Perruquier, Mr. Wilson, of the Strand.

THE PROLOGUE WILL BE DELIVERED BY MR. JOHN FORSTER.

CAPTAIN EBSWORTH, *of The Sea Mew*	. . . .	Mr. Edward Pigott.
CAPTAIN HELDING, *of The Wanderer*	. . . .	Mr. Alfred Dickens.
LIEUTENANT CRAYFORD	. . . .	Mr. Mark Lemon.
FRANK ALDERSLEY	. . . .	Mr. Wilkie Collins.
RICHARD WARDOUR	. . . .	Mr. Charles Dickens.
LIEUTENANT STEVENTON	. . . .	Mr. Young Charles.
JOHN WANT, *Ship's Cook*	. . . .	Mr. Augustus Egg, A.R.A.
BATESON } *Two of The Sea Mew's People*		Mr. Edward Hogarth.
DARKER }		Mr. Frederick Evans.
(Officers and Crews of The Sea Mew and Wanderer.)		
MRS. STEVENTON	. . . .	Miss Helen.
ROSE EBSWORTH	. . . .	Miss Kate.
LUCY CRAYFORD	. . . .	Miss Hogarth.
CLARA BURNHAM	. . . .	Miss Mary.
NURSE ESTHER	. . . .	Mrs. Wills.
MAID	. . . .	Miss Martha.

THE SCENERY AND SCENIC EFFECTS OF THE FIRST ACT, BY MR. TELBIN.
THE SCENERY AND SCENIC EFFECTS OF THE SECOND AND THIRD ACTS, BY Mr. STANFIELD, R.A.
ASSISTED BY MR. DANSON.
THE ACT-DROP, ALSO BY Mr. STANFIELD, R.A.

AT THE END OF THE PLAY, HALF-AN-HOUR FOR REFRESHMENT.

and Jerrold, Mark Lemon, *Punch* cartoonist John Leech, playwright Tom Taylor and the investigative journalist Henry Mayhew. Their first play was Ben Jonson's *Every Man In His Humour*. Dickens not only acted but was also director, stage manager and prompter. The play was presented at Miss Kelly's bijou Royalty Theatre in Dean Street, Soho. Although it was a private performance it involved very public people and was reviewed in *The Times* and other papers. Prince Albert himself requested a performance, which was put on at the St. James's before a distinguished audience with the proceedings going to support a sanatorium run by the distinguished Dr. Southwood Smith. Six more performances were given, three of them at Bulwer-Lytton's great mansion, Knebworth House. Fletcher and Massinger's *The Elder Brother* was subsequently presented at the Royalty as a benefit for Miss Kelly.

In 1848 *The Merry Wives of Windsor*, in which Dickens played the part of Shallow, toured to Manchester, Liverpool, Birmingham, Edinburgh and Glasgow. In 1851 Bulwer-Lytton's specially-written comedy *Not So Bad As We Seem*, was presented at Devonshire House on Piccadilly before the Queen herself and repeated shortly afterwards at the request of the Duke of Devonshire. On that occasion Dickens appeared in an accompanying farce in six roles, necessitating lightning changes of costume. Once again the production went on a provincial tour. Pressure of work then limited Dickens' involvement in theatricals to Christmas pieces given for children in the schoolroom at Dickens' grand home, Tavistock House. In 1855 Dickens put on Wilkie Collins' *The Lighthouse* three times at home and then repeated it at Campden House, Kensington in aid of the sanatorium at Bournemouth. In 1857 Dickens put on another Collins drama *The Frozen Deep* and was invited to put on another private performance for the Queen. It was then repeated again for the benefit of Douglas Jerrold's widow.

One significant by-product of Dickens' amateur theatricals was the Guild of Literature and Art, founded at Bulwer-Lytton's suggestion at Knebworth in 1850. Its aims were "to encourage life assurance and other provident habits among authors and artists, to render such assistance to both as shall never compromise their independence and to form a new institution where honourable rest from arduous labour shall still be associated with the discharge of congenial duties" – the last-mentioned requiring the construction of almshouses at Stevenage. Bulwer-Lytton's comedy *Not So Bad As We Seem* was written to raise funds for the Guild. Tickets for the Devonshire House performances were £5 each, with the Queen donating £150. By the end of its tour the play had raised £2,500. The Stevenage houses were completed in 1865. Dickens was also a warm supporter of the Royal General Theatrical Fund which had been founded in 1839 to relieve indigent theatricals. Dickens was both one of the original trustees and a regular speaker at its dinners.

Dickens' interest in amateur theatricals gave way to his own, intensely theatrical, public readings from his own works. He not only revelled in the crowds and the applause but also found that he could earn more, and more quickly, by reading than writing. Distinguished men of letters, such as Thomas Carlyle (1795-1881) and Samuel Taylor Coleridge (1772-1834), had set a precedent by giving public lectures. Fanny Kemble had given successful readings from Shakespeare. Dickens' readings appealed, moreover, to respectable bourgeois who still regarded the theatre as taboo. He began with readings for charity, usually adult education institutions but, after buying his country home at Gad's Hill, outside Rochester, needed cash to refurbish it and began giving weekly readings at St. Martin's Hall, Long Acre. He later moved to St. James's Hall, off Piccadilly, which could hold over two thousand people. At £50 a night and all expenses paid, Dickens earned more than Macready at his height. Eventually Dickens' fee would rise to £80. These London occasions were followed by national and later American tours, both wildly successful but so exhausting that they undoubtedly hastened his death.

Dramatizations of Dickens' works became a staple of the nineteenth century stage. Even before 1840 *Pickwick Papers, Oliver Twist* and *Nicholas Nickleby* had been staged at least sixty times. By the 1840s unauthorized dramatizations of novels were appearing before they were even finished. By 1850 at least 240 productions are known to have been staged, a quarter of them *Nickleby*, with *Oliver Twist* and *The Cricket on the Hearth* the next most popular items. At Christmas 1845 there were no less than a dozen versions of *The Cricket on the Hearth* playing at different London venues. Dickens' own public readings may have accounted for a diminution in the number of dramatizations in the 1850s to 180 - as well as his own efforts to use legal constraints against pirate versions. His death was followed by a decade and a half of the greatest theatrical interest in his works, sustained by the desire of a new generation of actors like Irving, Tree and J.L. Toole to take on Dickens' roles. Dickens himself had prepared a stage version of *Great Expectations* for Toole but it was never used. The first production was actually put on at the Royal Court Theatre in 1871 in a version prepared by W.S. Gilbert.

The most assiduous dramatizer of Dickens' works was Edward Stirling (1809-94), who knew at first hand the world of the Crummles from his own youthful apprenticeship with a fairground tent theatre company. In 1829 he appeared at the London Pavilion Theatre and would eventually play the Adelphi, Covent Garden, Surrey, Olympic, Lyceum and Drury Lane. In 1838 Stirling adapted *Nicholas Nickleby* for the Adelphi where it ran into the following season. Dickens himself gave a cautious approval. Other Stirling adaptations included *The Fortunes of Smike, Pickwick, Martin Chuzzlewit* and *The Cricket on the Hearth*.

Making a Go Of It

While much mid-Victorian theatre remained mediocre and formulaic, there were managers who achieved lengthy periods of sustained success.

Benjamin Webster (1789-1882) began as a

85. The grave of Benjamin Webster in Brompton Cemetery.

provincial dancer and harlequin, worked his way into the Drury Lane company, got a chance to shine in comedy with Madame Vestris at the Olympic, then showed what he could do as a manager (1837-53) at the Haymarket, presenting new plays by Jerrold, Boucicault and Bulwer-Lytton. His 1844 production of *The Taming of the Shrew* was boldly experimental in confining itself to what were then believed to be the dimensions of an Elizabethan stage. Webster also managed the Adelphi from 1853 until his retirement at the age of eighty-five but there was constrained by the low-brow tastes of its habitual audience. Webster's successor at the Haymarket, the veteran low comedian John Baldwin Buckstone (1802-79) used his long period of control (1853-79) to made it the home of comedy.

From his first appearance at the Haymarket as Shylock, Samuel Phelps (1804-78) had set out to challenge the legacy of Kean by replicating his most celebrated roles as Hamlet, Othello,

86. Samuel Phelps.

87. Charles Kean with the young Ellen Terry.

Richard III etc. Phelps took immediate advantage of the abolition of the Patent monopoly to take over the then unfashionable Sadler's Wells, whose typical patrons Dickens had described in 1841 in blood-chilling terms – "As ruffianly an audience as London could shake together. It was a bear-garden, resounding with foul language, oaths, cat-calls, shrieks, yells, blasphemy, obscenity; a truly diabolical clamour. Fights took place any where at any period of the performance." Given this social context Phelps' achievement in staging all but four of Shakespeare's plays between 1844 and 1862 seems truly heroic and, indeed, historic because in 1849 he put on the first serious modern production of *Antony and Cleopatra* and the first *Pericles* since the Restoration. By 1847 Phelps had so far tamed the rowdies that he could put tickets for his productions on sale in New Bond Street. An eyewitness of 1853 recorded Phelps' theatrical revolution:

"There sit the working classes ... as orderly and reverent as if they were in church ... *A Midsummer Night's Dream* abounds in the most

delicate passages of Shakespeare's verse: the Sadler's Wells pit has a keen enjoyment of them and the pit and the gallery were crowded to the furthest wall on Saturday night with a most earnest audience, among whom many a subdued hush arose, not during but just before the delivery of the most charming passages."

Charles Kean (1811-68), son of Edmund, had a very different upbringing from his vagrant father and went to Eton. His celebrated surname bore him through a moderately successful acting career but it was as manager that he showed his true talents. A gentlemanly manner may well have helped him gain the appointment of director of the Queen's private theatricals at Windsor in 1848.

Taking over the struggling Princess' Theatre in 1850, he made it the most fashionable in all London. Kean's special concern was to produce classical plays with the highest degree of historical accuracy. The sets for his 1852 productions were devised with the advice of architectural historian and editor the *The Builder* magazine George Godwin. In the same year in reviving Byron's *Sardanopolous* he required his scene painters to consult the findings of Layard's archaeological excavations, recently published as *Nineveh and its Remains* (1849). Such productions were accompanied by such weighty documentation of the sources consulted that Kean was elected a Fellow of the Society of Antiquaries in 1857. Concerned also to maintain high technical standards, Kean was also the first to develop an effective technique for focusing limelight. As thrifty as his father had been feckless, Kean was able to retire with a fortune in 1859.

Built in 1772 as a concert room, the Prince of Wales's Theatre on Tottenham Street was known by the mid-nineteenth century as 'the Dust Hole'. In 1865 it was bought by Marie Wilton (1839-1921). Acting since childhood, a lengthy (1858-64) spell at the Strand theatre, had made her, much against her wishes, the 'Queen of Burlesque'. Anxious to bury this sobriquet and ambitious to establish a career in legitimate drama, she launched herself into management at the age of twenty-five on a borrowed thousand pounds. The first time she went to inspect her new acquisition she was barracked by the audience and had orange-peel thrown at her. Raising the admission price to a minimum of seven shillings rapidly deterred both the rougher element and their dependants, the sellers of oranges, pies etc. Astutely renaming her acquisition in honour of the recently-married and highly popular Prince Of Wales, Marie Wilton refurbished it like a Victorian parlour, with carpeted aisles, chintz drapes and seats complete with anti-macassars. Admirably suiting this domesticated setting was the staging of a series (1865-70) of annual comedies by T.W. Robertson (1829-71). The eldest of twenty-two offspring of a family of itinerant provincial actors, Robertson had had his first play staged when he was only sixteen but thereafter struggled to survive as a bit-player, prompter, stage manager and prolific journalist, working for both Samuel Phelps and Madame Vestris before giving up on the theatre around 1859. Probably thanks to

88. *Squire Bancroft.*

Robertson's friend and Marie's business partner, the playwright H.J. Byron (1834-84), she agreed to take on his play *Society*, which was remarkable for its ultra-realistic depiction of the superbly-observed minutiae of Victorian domestic behaviour. Credit must be given to the ensemble playing of the company but the otherwise conventional enough piece proved a sensation. Robertson's successor of 1866, *Ours*, featured the making of a roly-poly pudding. Act I of *Caste* featured a comic tea-and-sandwiches *tour de force* which the playwright never surpassed and gave Marie Wilton her best role, as Polly Eccles. This was followed by successful runs for *Play* (1868), *School* (1869) and *M.P.* (1870).

At the end of this run Marie Wilton married her leading man Squire Bancroft (1841-1926),

89. The Bancroft grave in Brompton Cemetery.

The Brompton Set

Peter Cunningham's *Handbook of London* (1850) noted of the Brompton area that "it has long been and still is the favourite residence of actors." One of the earliest was George Colman the Younger (1762-1836), who lived at 22 Brompton Square from 1825 until his death. Colman had benefited from the same elite education as his father – Westminster and Christ Church – and had succeeded him as manager of Covent Garden. Despite a clandestine marriage and a career playing low comic roles, despite personal profligacy and a penchant for costly litigation, Colman was appointed as the Lord Chamberlain's Examiner of Plays in 1824. In this capacity, as the *Cambridge Guide to English Literature* wryly notes "he earned considerable resentment, exercising a prudery in judgment at odds with his own work." Colman's house was subsequently occupied by the actor James Vining (1795-1870) who progressed from Shakespeare to fops to an oft-repeated role as Dr. Manette in stage versions of Dickens' *A Tale of Two Cities.*

90. George Colman the Younger.

at the same time surrendering the reins of management into his hands. Bancroft had made his London debut in *Society*, whose title summarised in a single word his own ambitions. Tall, handsome, monocled and impeccably mannered, he looked every inch the English gentleman he sought to personify. Moving on from the Prince of Wales's in 1879, the Bancrofts then took over and renovated the Haymarket, which they ran until 1885. They then retired, seriously rich, in their mid-forties, with a nest-egg of £120,000. In 1888 Bancroft published *Mr and Mrs Bancroft, On and Off the Stage*, the first of many, rather repetitive, volumes of memoir and autobiography which would fill a retirement considerably longer than his acting career. In the year of Queen Victoria's Diamond Jubilee Bancroft became only the second actor to be honoured with knighthood. He and his wife now lie in Brompton Cemetery beneath a massive and immaculate slab whose opaquely-worded inscription gives only the barest hint of the theatrical life which brought them fame and fortune – *From Shadows and Fancies to the Truth.*

91. John Baldwin Buckstone.

No. 23 Brompton Square was the home of William Farren (1786-1861) in 1824-36 and 1854-61; between those years he lived at No. 30. An accomplished Shakespearean, Farren was in private life unsocial, unintellectual and tight with money. His daughter Nellie (1848-1904) became the queen of burlesque at the Gaiety and was vividly described by the playwright H.J. Byron as a "peal of laughter, ringing its way through life."

Melancholic John Liston (1776-1846) lived at No. 40 Brompton Square. Ironically he was the first comic actor to command a higher fee than a top tragedian.

The success of the prolific farceur and low comedian John Baldwin Buckstone (1802-79) was sufficient by 1835 to enable him to move into recently-built No. 2 Onslow Terrace. Three years later Buckstone tried to place his son in the local grammar school but, even when he offered to buy a share in it to become a proprietor, he was rebuffed "on the ground that I am an actor and that such a person in a public school would incite in the boys a desire to see plays, which would unsettle their minds." Nonetheless by 1840 Buckstone could afford to move into Brompton Square itself, at No. 6.

No. 19 Brompton Square was home to the Keeleys. Robert Keeley (1793-1869) made his breakthrough in *Tom and Jerry*. His wife, Mary Ann Keeley (1806-99) excelled in breeches roles, enjoying a personal triumph in Buckstone's lurid but sympathetic portrayal of the Georgian gaol-breaker *Jack Sheppard* (1839).

Successful manager Benjamin Webster *(see p103)* lived at 3 Brompton Road. A member of his company, Alfred Wigan (1814-78), who specialised in roles requiring fluent French or a convincing rendition of broken English, died at 33 Brompton Square.

The scholarly antiquarian J.R. Planche *(see p89)* was the first occupant of 6 Egerton Terrace. Although he provided texts which Webster, Buckstone and Madame Vestris found entirely acceptable, Planche is dismissed by the *Oxford Companion to the Theatre* with the acerbic observation that "his work for the theatre, which was extremely successful in its day, seems to have had no literary merit whatever and divorced from its music and spectacular effects is quite unreadable." Notwithstanding this magisterial judgment Planche's extravaganzas apparently proved a major source of inspiration to W.S. Gilbert. One of Planche's last projects was to organise the armour collections of the Tower of London into an historically coherent display.

The career of John Reeve (1799-1838) is a classic illustration of the perils of a talent which became the victim of its own facility. Forsaking Gosling's bank for the boards, Reeve discovered in himself a great gift for mimicry. A huge hit as Jerry Hawthorne in *Tom and Jerry*, he became a sore trial to successive managers, being constantly drunk and constantly failing to master his lines.

92. Last curtain. The grave of Tom Foy (1866-1917), 'the Yorkhsire Lad' in Brompton Cemetery.

Buckstone handled him skilfully by drafting parts which consisted of little more than catch-phrases, leaving the performer to fill out the role with his "great flexibility of feature and limb". Reeve, eagerly complicit in his own self-destruction, played shamelessly on the sympathy of his audiences, amending each stumble or over-long pause with a leer or a wink or a hissed reminder that they liked a glass as much as he did. During his final season he gave one of the first theatrical representations of Sam Weller. Having once more conspicuously failed to master his part in another drama, he collapsed on his way home from its second performance and died at his house at 46 Brompton Row.

New Theatres

The opening of the Holborn Theatre Royal at High Holborn in 1866 inaugurated a decade in which a new London theatre came into existence almost every year. Few were destined for long-term viability.

Three theatres were built in the West End for Sefton Parry (1832-87), who also had a hand in the opening of another at Greenwich. Born into a theatrical family, Parry was brought up to do stage carpentry, paint scenery and even make

93. Henry Pettitt (1848-93) was a prolific author, chiefly of melodramas and a collaborator with George Conquest, Augustus Harris and George Sims.

costumes. He also wrote a drama, optimistically entitled *The Bright Future* for the Grand Theatre at Islington. In 1859 he had been to Cape Town and put on the first professional theatricals presented there. He then took a touring company around the world, accumulating enough capital to begin speculating in theatres. Parry's first venture, the Holborn Theatre Royal opened with a safe bet, *Flying Scud; or a Four-Legged Fortune*, a racing drama written by Dion Boucicault and starring a real live horse on stage. The house failed, however, to achieve momentum under a series of rapidly changing managements and when it was destroyed by fire the First Avenue Hotel was built on the site.

The Queen's in Long Acre was built in 1867 to designs by C.J. Phipps for Lionel Lawson, a member of the family which owned the recently-established, rapidly-prospering and then populist *Daily Telegraph*. The Queen's was larger than any other London theatre except Drury

94. *The first Gaiety Theatre and Restaurant in The Strand.*

95. *John Hollingshead.*

Lane and the opera houses. Its first, successful, decade was distinguished by performances by such rising stars as Henry Irving, Ellen Terry *(see p159)* and Charles Wyndham *(see p143)* but it closed in 1878 and was converted for use as storage.

The Globe, opened in 1868 in Newcastle Street, Strand was another Sefton Parry venture. Believing the area was about to be comprehensively redeveloped, he threw up a ramshackle structure, largely with an eye to the compensation he could extract in the event of its demolition – which would not happen for another thirty years. In 1893 the Globe enjoyed unanticipated success with the first of its 1,446 performances of Brandon Thomas's frantic farce

Charley's Aunt, a perennial favourite of repertory and amateur dramatic companies ever since. In 1899 actor-manager Sir John Hare played in Pinero's *The Gay Lord Quex*, in which ladies on stage were shown smoking for the first time; this ran for three hundred performances.

The Gaiety, also opened in the Strand in 1868, was another Lionel Lawson enterprise, with the management entrusted to journalist John Hollingshead. In 1878 it became the first theatre in England to have light bulbs installed on its street frontage. The main fare was burlesque, until George Edwards (1852-1915) switched to musical comedy in the 1890s, inaugurating the era of the celebrated 'Gaiety Girls' who attracted hordes of smitten, supposedly aristocratic, 'Stage Door Johnnies' and dined half price at swanky Romano's in the Strand. Although the Gaiety would also be demolished for the Aldwych redevelopment in 1903 it would arise, phoenix-like nearby, for another generation of existence.

96. The Gaiety Girls.

Toole's opened in William IV Street in 1869 as The Royal Charing Cross Theatre and proved itself sufficiently to be rebuilt by Thomas Verity in 1876. Veteran actor John Toole (1830-1906) staged comedies and farces from 1879 until gout forced his retirement in 1895 and the site was reclaimed to become the outpatients' department of Charing Cross Hospital.

The Opera Comique, opened in 1870, was neighbour to the Globe, although built mostly underground, and was similarly rickety. Despite the primarily financial ambitions behind its creation it was to have a not undistinguished history before its demise in 1899. In 1871 the Comedie Française made it the venue for its first ever appearance outside France and was followed by other visiting foreign companies. In 1877 Richard D'Oyly Carte took over as manager and that year staged the first Gilbert and Sullivan opera *The Sorcerer*, followed by *The Pirates of Penzance* (1880) and *Patience* (1881). A last note of distinction was sounded by the

97. J. L. Toole.

98. Richard D'Oyly Carte, a Spy caricature in Vanity Fair in 1891.

99. The Vaudeville Theatre in the 1950s.

debut of the future Dame Marie Tempest *(see p150)* in 1885.

The Royal Court Theatre also opened in 1870, on the south side of Sloane Square, in what was then a Dissenters' chapel, as the New Chelsea. Rebuilt in 1871, it was renamed the Belgravia and staged a run of Pinero comedies in the 1880s before being relocated to a new (i.e. the present) building on the east side of the square in 1888.

The third theatre opened in 1870, again on the Strand, was the Vaudeville. Built by C.J. Phipps, it was managed by three actors and gave Henry Irving his first, addictive taste of fame in James Albery's comedy *Two Roses*. The Vaudeville then achieved viability with long runs such as H.J. Byron's comedy *Our Boys* (1875-9, 1,362 performances) and Joseph Derrick's farce *Confusion* (1883-4, 437 performances).

The Criterion of 1874, designed by Thomas Verity as an annex to the flagship restaurant of the Spiers and Pond catering empire, was one of the first theatres to be built entirely underground. It opened with *The American Lady*, a comedy by H.J. Byron, who also acted in it and was the theatre manager. From 1875 to 1899 the Criterion was managed by Charles Wyndham and from 1879 until 1919 he was also the lessee.

The Imperial, opened in 1876 in Tothill Street, Westminster, was also part of something else, in this case a rambling entertainment complex incongruously and rather inappropriately called The Royal Aquarium – it did have an aquarium but was rather short on fish - which also included a concert/lecture hall, picture

100. The first Royal Court Theatre in the old Ranelagh Chapel in Chelsea.

gallery and reading-room. The theatre, at the western end of the building, opened with *Jo*, an adaptation of Dickens' *Bleak House*, featuring the pathetic slum boy crossing-sweeper. Marie Litton tried (1878-80) to refocus the house towards its intended theatrical destiny by adopting the separate designation of Imperial Theatre and staging revivals of *Uncle Tom's Cabin* and *She Stoops to Conquer*. It was then briefly managed by royal mistress Lillie Langtry. A total, costly internal make-over was followed by a disastrous re-opening with *The Royal Necklace* and its immediate withdrawal and closure. After an interval of a few years demolition followed to make way for the construction of the Methodist Central Hall.

To Serve the Purpose of the Drama

Designing London's theatres has involved such distinguished architects as Sir Christopher Wren, Robert Adam, Henry Holland and John Nash but not until the nineteenth century did the design of theatres become an architectural specialism, dominated by a handful of practitioners.

The pioneer of specialist theatre designing was Samuel Beazley (1786-1851), who had the significant advantage of also being a prolific playwright and therefore equipped with a trained understanding of the demands of stagecraft. (He once wrote an 'Indian spectacle' specifically to put a performing elephant on stage.) Beazley built or rebuilt seven London theatres, including the Lyceum, where his massive portico of 1834 still survives, the St. James's, Miss Kelly's Royalty and the City of London, at Norton Folgate. Beazley, who was born in Parliament Street, Westminster has been described as a 'Victorian Vanbrugh', not only combining the careers of dramatist and architect but having also been a soldier and an adventurer as well. (In the Peninsular War he is said to have woken up after a battle to find himself laid out for burial. On another occasion he helped the Duchess of Angouleme evade an advancing Napoleonic army.) Beazley wrote at least ten plays in the 1830s alone and was equally prolific as an architect, designing theatres in Dublin, Birmingham, Belgium, India and South America, as well as hotels, mansions and railway stations.

Trained in his native Bath, Charles Phipps (1835-97) reconstructed the city's Theatre Royal and designed another at Nottingham before opening a London office in 1866. His earliest commissions were the Queen's Theatre in Long Acre (1867), with decor in Greek mode and the

101. The architect, C. J. Phipps.

Gaiety (1868), which was Gothic. In 1868 he moved his family to the capital, living and working the rest of his life at 26 Mecklenburgh Square in Bloomsbury. Phipps' standing as the preferred architect of the theatrical establishment can be judged from his list of clients - the Bancrofts, for whom he reconstructed the Theatre Royal, Haymarket (1880); D'Oyly Carte, for whom he built the Savoy (1881); Irving, the Lyceum (1885); and for Tree, Her Majesty's (1897), which was singled out for praise by the hypercritical George Bernard Shaw. What particularly

102. Her Majesty's Theatre was rebuilt in 1897 on half its site, with the Carlton Hotel to its south.

recommended Phipps to such demanding clients was his ability to cram the essential lobbies, dressing-rooms etc. into cramped sites and to put his buildings up at speed, thereby diminishing borrowing costs and loss of revenues while a venue was out of action. Phipps' standard London plan was widely copied by his provincial imitators. His other London theatres also included the Vaudeville, the Prince of Wales and the Lyric. In collaboration with Walter Emden (1847-1913), the son of the lessee of the Olympic Theatre, he also designed the Garrick and the Duke of York's.

Thomas Verity (1837-91) set up his London practice in 1870 and became Surveyor of Theatres to the Lord Chamberlain. His best-known London creations were the Comedy, the Criterion and the Kingsway. His last major project was, however, the celebrated Pavilion at Lord's Cricket Ground, in collaboration with his son Frank, to whom he passed on his practice. Frank maintained the theatrical connection, designing the Carlton Theatre and a bijou dining-room for the Beefsteak Club. The practice is still in business as Verity and Beverley.

The doyen of theatre architects was undoubtedly Frank Matcham (1854-1920) who built a hundred and fifty new houses and was involved in the alteration, refurbishment and rebuilding of over fifty more. Apprenticed to Jethro T. Robinson, who, like Verity, served as Theatre Surveyor to the Lord Chamberlain,

103. *Fire was a frequent enemy of theatres. Pictured above are three stages of the Surrey Theatre in Blackfriars Road. At the top is the old theatre in 1865; the new interior of the same year is in the roundel beneath, and below are the ruins after a fire, again in 1865. The theatre was rebuilt once more by J. Ellis.*

104. Frank Matcham's plan for the Hackney Empire.

Matcham married his boss's daughter and took over the business when his father-in-law died shortly afterwards. Having never completed a formal training Matcham was much derided as 'architecturally illiterate' but proved to be not only prolific but innovative in improving standards of ventilation and acoustics and diminishing fire risks. Matcham theatres are also noteworthy for the exuberance of their internal decor and his trademark use of exotic 'Oriental' motifs. Surviving London examples of Matcham's work include the Hippodrome, Hackney Empire, Coliseum, Palladium and Victoria Palace.

Born in Australia to the actress Dolores Drummond, W.G.R. Sprague (1863-1933) was articled to Matcham. At the height of his productivity, between 1899 and 1907, he designed Wyndhams, the Albery, Aldwych, Strand, Globe (now Gielgud) and Queen's. Other Sprague theatres include the Ambassadors and St. Martin's and the Terriss Theatre, soon renamed the Rotherhithe Hippodrome.

CHAPTER EIGHT

Heyday of the Halls

Origins

The 'Music Hall' emerged from the association of singing with drinking. The public house 'free and easy' was a Regency version of *karaoke*, with customers providing their own songs and recitations. Unlike the theatre proper, patrons were expected to smoke, eat, drink and chatter throughout performances. Audiences were expected to be enthusiastic rather than respectful.

A newspaper editorial of 1837 thundered against the "epidemic of vocal music" which had "spread its contagious and devastating influence amongst the youth of the Metropolis, the London apprentice boys" and denounced "Free and Easies; free as air they are for the advancement of drunkenness and profligacy and easy enough of access to all classes with little regard to appearances or character."

Publicans, concerned on the one hand to create and maintain the momentum of a good time and on the other to guard against excesses of vulgarity or violence which might jeopardise their licence, assumed the role of chairman. More genteel versions of the 'free and easy' could be found in assembly-room entertainments at some hotels, like the Royal Standard Hotel at Victoria, and in suburban London tea-gardens, like Miles's Music House at Sadler's Wells, where singers might appear on a small stage. Smoking was permitted, both sexes were admitted and light refreshments could be bought.

In 1825 the Eagle, at Shepherdess Walk, City Road became the prototype of a new setting for entertainment, subsequently acknowledged by journalist and theatre manager John Hollingshead as "the father and mother, the dry and Wet nurse of the Music Hall". Within little

105. *George Conquest.*

more than a decade it was well enough established as a London landmark for the youthful Dickens to have Jemima Evans and Samuel Wilkins go there in his *Sketches by Boz.* The Eagle subsequently moved up-market to become the Grecian Theatre, offering melodrama, music and acrobatic feats by its manager (1872-8), the dashingly-named George Conquest (1837-1901), who excelled in spectacular aerial combats and playing grotesques like goblins and monkeys. Ironically the house was to be sold in 1884 to the Salvation Army. Demolished in 1901, it was rebuilt as a flamboyant public house.

106. Evans's Music Hall to the rear of 43 King Street, Covent Garden.

A more elevated inspiration for the emerging music hall format was supplied by Evans's Music-and-Supper Rooms at 43 King Street, Covent Garden. Evans's was housed in a seventeenth century mansion which had once been the home of Sir Thomas Killigrew and then, in 1774, had become one of London's earliest hotels, Joy's. In the 1840s ex-comedian W.H. Evans fitted out the dining-room as a venue where late-night suppers could be enjoyed to the accompaniment of singers. Forerunners to this format were the 'Cyder Cellars' in Maiden Lane or the 'Coal Hole' in the Strand, where a rough and ready cabaret of comic songs and monologues was provided as a free accompaniment to the consumption of equally basic fare. Evan's enhanced the quality of the entertainment, the refreshments and the setting.

In 1844 one of the entertainers, 'Paddy' Green (Greenmore), took over the establishment and around 1856 enlarged the premises by building out over its garden. Sam Collins (1826-65), founder of Collins' Music Hall, also made his first appearance there. A former chimney-sweep, born Sam Vagg in London, Collins affected an Irish persona, complete with billycock hat, shamrock and shillelagh. Evans's clientele was initially strictly male allowing for material that was often *risque* and behaviour that verged on the rowdy. As competition from rival venues proliferated the ban on females was lifted in 1854. Evans's closed in 1880 and was later home to the National Sporting Club which staged after-dinner amateur boxing bouts for the appreciation of dinner-jacketed all-male audiences.

107. *Sam Vagg, alias Sam Collins.*

108. *Collins' Music Hall at Islington Green.*

The Pioneers

The short life of Sam Collins had many parallels among the early generation of music hall stars. The son of a Drury Lane Shakespearean actor, Sam Cowell (1820-64) made his debut at nine in the USA. On returning to England he gradually dropped his straight career to exploit the 'coon-songs' he had learned in the States and become a comic vocalist specializing in patter songs such as '*The Ratcatcher's Darter*' (Daughter). Cowell took advantage of the newly-developed railway network to subject himself to a series of exhausting national tours in 1857, 1858 and 1859, then spent 1860-61 touring the USA and Canada. Having turned to the bottle to cope with his punishing schedule he returned to London a virtually destitute drunk. After his death fellow-artistes organised a concert to raise a fund for his widow and children. Frederick Robson (1821-64), who was only five foot tall and known as 'Little Robson', died of liver failure. Singer songwriter Harry Clifton (1832-72) had such success with *Pretty Polly Perkins of Paddington Green* that his music publisher presented him with a diamond ring. He also wrote *A Dark Girl Dress'd in Blue* which was still being sung with gusto by Stanley Holloway almost a century later. The dandified Alfred Vance (1839-88) ('The Great Vance. The Versatile! The Inimitable!'), a great favourite of the Prince of Wales, sang in praise of Veuve Cliquot champagne until he staggered off the stage of the Sun music hall, Knightsbridge to die of a heart attack, leaving an estate of just thirty-nine pounds. Tall, handsome George Leybourne (1842-84), the original 'Champagne Charlie', lived up to his stage *persona* of the free-spending, hard-drinking man-about-town and died as he had lived, still top of the bill but penniless. James Henry Stead (?-1886) had an extraordinary run of popularity with a single song *The Perfect Cure*, which he sang with his arms held tightly by his sides

109. George Leybourne.

tavern concert-rooms. Playhouses were under the jurisdiction of the Lord Chamberlain and forbidden to allow smoking or drinking in the auditorium. Tavern concert-rooms were subject to no such restriction and came, moreover, under the rather less forbidding auspices of local magistrates. Given the average working man's ideas of the essential features of a good night out, it would not be difficult to predict the preference of the mass of ordinary Londoners in pursuit of diversion.

The doyen of the publican-entrepreneurs was Charles Morton (1819-1904), hailed perhaps a little over-generously as 'The Father of the Music Hall'. Starting out as a mere waiter, by the age of twenty-one he was running a small Pimlico tavern which featured 'harmonic meetings'. By 1849 he had graduated to the Old Canterbury Arms in Westminster Bridge Road and in 1852 built over its adjacent skittle-alley to create the Canterbury Music-Hall, a venture which proved so profitable that by 1854 it had been replaced by the New Canterbury, with a large platform stage and accommodation for 1,500. The author F.G. Tomlins applauded this establishment for its contribution to the enrichment of domestic life –

> "I think that the model music hall ... is the Canterbury Hall, where you see artisans and small shopkeepers, with their wives and families, and it is a piece of actual humanity to the wife to take here there; it is quite a godsend to the wife and family to get out of their dull homes and to go occasionally to these places ...".

At the other end of the scale of comfort and respectability was the music hall at Hungerford Market visited by the author of *The Night Side of London*, J. Ewing Ritchie, in 1857:

> " ... there might have been a hundred and fifty persons there; the hall seemed about half full ... The audience consisted chiefly of young persons of both sexes, and while the males had each their yard of clay [pipe], the ladies indulged in bottled stout. One or two awful young swells ... were present but they ... were not in keeping with the

while performing complicated contortions and leaping up and down stiff-legged an estimated 500 times. When the public had had enough of it Stead could find nothing to replace it and died, deranged and in squalor in a Seven Dials attic but leaving over three thousand pounds.

Building the Halls

The earliest music-halls were essentially extensions of particularly enterprising pubs, both physically, as accommodations tacked onto existing premises, as at the Britannia in Hoxton or the Grapes in Southwark Bridge Road, and organisationally as shows managed by publicans, providing and co-ordinating local amateur and professional talents, with the balance of the programme shifting increasingly to the latter. The 1843 Theatres Act made a distinction which, although never consistently applied with rigour, separated playhouses from

110. The Canterbury Music Hall in 1856.

character of the place, which a candid regard to truth compels me to denominate as seedy, to say nothing of the damp, tunnel-like atmosphere which not even the fumes of tobacco and grog and gas could overpower."

In 1861 Morton opened the Oxford Music-Hall at the junction of Oxford Street and Tottenham Court Road. Morton broke new ground in presenting Sunday evening performances and advertising in superior publications like *The Times*. In acknowledgment of his managerial skills, he was at various times involved in reviving the fortunes of the Philharmonic, Islington, the Gaiety, the Palace at Cambridge Circus, the Alhambra and the Tivoli.

Morton's success with the Canterbury inspired numerous imitators over the subsequent decade. In 1852 London had four free-standing music halls and twenty-two integral to pubs; by 1854 the respective figures were seven and ninety-two. The Canterbury's first serious rival was the

111. The Oxford Music Hall, 1861.

Holborn Empire, opened in 1857 as Weston's. Rebuilt in 1887 as the Royal Holborn and again in 1906 as the Holborn Empire, it survived until being blitzed in May 1941. The Bedford was built in 1861 on part of the tea-garden of the Bedford Arms in Camden High Street. In 1862 a small concert room attached to the White Lion Inn on the Edgware Road was replaced by a new building, initially known after its proprietor as Turnham's, renamed the Metropolitan in 1864. Capitalising on the success of a room attached to the Lansdowne Arms at Islington Green, Collins's opened in 1863 in a new building seating 600. Although Collins died within two years, not yet forty, his widow carried on the venture with success. The Swiss-Italian Gatti brothers, Carlo and Giovanni, having laid the foundations of their catering, cafe and ice-cream empire, opened a restaurant in Westminster Bridge Road which in 1865 was licensed as a music-hall. A year latter they acquired tenancy of two of the arches under the newly-built Charing Cross station, to make way for which, ironically, one of their own restaurants had been demolished. Here in 1867 they opened another music-hall, known as Gatti's-Under-the-Arches, to distinguish it from Gatti's-Over-the-Water.

The longevity of any particular music-hall depended on the unpredictable interaction of location, managerial competence, investor optimism, the vagaries of theatrical fashion and popular taste, commercial pressures for alternative site use and the ever-present hazard of fire. In 1856 the Surrey Garden Music-Hall opened in the Surrey Zoological Gardens but burned down in 1861. A building on its site, used by St. Thomas's Hospital until 1872, was remodelled as a music-hall but only survived until 1877, to be demolished the following year. Wilton's opened as a music-hall in 1858. Situated in Grace's Alley, off Cable Street, it had previously been a public house, the Prince of Denmark, dating from 1828, Extended and lavishly fitted-out with mirrors, mahogany and a massive gas-chandelier, its auditorium was claimed to be "the handsomest room in town". Devastated by fire in 1877, it became a Methodist mission in

1885 and then a rag warehouse before a campaign to save it from demolition led to its acquisition by the Greater London Council in 1966. Despite the brevity of its days of glory Wilton's remains the oldest surviving music-hall in the metropolis.

In 1861 the 'Long Room' at the Sir Hugh Myddelton's Head in Clerkenwell was replaced by Deacon's Music Hall, at a cost of £5,000, with seating for eight hundred. Closely integrated with its immediate locality, the 'Glue Pot' as it was affectionately known, in 1883 staged a gala evening to raise funds for the benefit of the Finsbury Dispensary. Top-line artistes from Collins' Music Hall volunteered their services and were complemented by singers drawn from the ranks of the local fire brigade. In 1884 the house was enlarged to hold a thousand but in 1891 it was torn down to make way for the construction of Rosebery Avenue. The great Lottie Collins (1866-1910) graced the last night with a rendition of the hit song for ever after associated with her, which she had first performed that year in the Islington pantomime *Dick Whittington - Ta-Ra-Ra-Boom-De-Ay.*

Bill of Fare

The early music-hall programme was dominated by the traditional fare of the 'harmonic meeting', being a mixture of madrigals and glees interspersed with lengthy burlesque ballads. Sam Collins sang soulfully of *The Rocky Road to Dublin* and warned his audiences that *No Irish Need Apply.*

E.W. Mackney (1825-1909) was the first important English-born blackface performer, accompanying himself on piano, guitar, banjo and bones and performing farmyard imitations on the violin. Tiny but indomitable Jenny Hill (Elizabeth Pasta) (1851-96), 'The Vital Spark', was the first female performer to achieve star status, abandoning duettist faux gentility in favour of racy solo numbers. Doubling as a pub skivvy and entertainer while in her teens, she survived a disastrous early marriage to prove herself as an interpreter of melodramatic song-sketches featuring working-class victims of the privations she had herself known from youth.

The other sure-fire source of a positive audience response was ultra-patriotic material in praise of the armed forces. In 1877, at the height of international tension generated by the Russo-Turkish war, 'The Great Macdermott' (Gilbert Hastings Farrell) (1845-1901) belted out to the audience at the London Pavilion " *We don't want to fight but by jingo if we do, We've got the ships, We've got the men, We've got the money, too.*" The threat of war faded but 'jingoism' passed into the language. Like many successful stars he dashed from one house to another, repeating the same material. On one evening in 1878 he opened at the Royal Aquarium in Westminster at 8.15, was out at the Metropolitan on Edgware Road at 9.10, back at the London Pavilion on Piccadilly Circus at 10.00 and finished out at Collins in Islington at 10.50, a schedule which serves as a handsome testimony to the efficiency of London's horse-drawn cab services.

Local history, too, could be reflected and memorialized on-stage. The East End Match Girls, who fought an extraordinarily effective strike in 1888, which resulted in a surge of unionisation of the unskilled, were celebrated in a music hall song, *The Girls from Bryant and May.* This described them forsaking their usual Bank Holiday resort of " 'appy 'ampstead" in favour of gate-crashing the swanky Henley Regatta, a wildly improbable scenario but a neat reversal of the prevailing convention whereby nobs went 'slumming' to penetrate the mysteries of the East End.

Bigger and Better

The success of the music-halls in attracting ever larger audiences prompted their extension and up-grading. Rebuilding and refurbishment invariably involved the insertion of a proscenium arch stage and the disappearance of separate tables and chairs in favour of rows of upholstered seats, often in two- or even three-tiered galleries as the old-style music-hall metamorphosed to become a 'palace of varieties'. The Mogul Saloon in Drury Lane, retained its nickname of the 'Old Mo' when it had become a music-hall in 1851; in the course of successive rebuildings in 1872, 1891 and 1911 to become the New Middlesex Theatre of Varieties, it increased its capacity from 500 to 3,000.

The Canterbury was rebuilt in 1876 as a three-tier theatre, with a bar which became celebrated as a rendezvous for music-hall artistes.

The Alhambra on Leicester Square had been opened in 1854 as an exhibition centre, the Royal Panopticon of Science and Art *(ill. 112)* but reopened in 1858 as a circus and again in 1860 as a music hall, seating 3,500 in four tiers. Leotard and Blondin *(see p132)* both made sensational London debuts there in 1861. In 1870 it lost its licence for presenting 'an indecent dance' – the can-can. In 1871 the Alhambra *(ill. 113)*, a name it retained through various incarnations as Palace of Varieties, Music Hall, Theatre etc., was granted a dramatic licence for the first time. Burned down in 1882, it reopened a year later to specialize in lavish ballets.

Expansion was often matched by a managerial drive for greater respectability, matched by the petty bourgeois correlates of safety, decent sanitation and stylish comfort. At the same time improved, cheap public transport in the form of trams and double-decker buses, coupled with better street-lighting made it safer to venture out at night. The Royal Cambridge Hall of Varieties on Commercial Street aimed at a better sort of clientele. Serving premium Bass's bitter in the balcony, it also offered champagne, cigars and its own brand of cigarettes to patrons of the stalls. This was in clear breach of the 1843 Act which was, however, cheerfully ignored with impunity by most East End houses. Anxious to maintain its tone the management of the Royal Cambridge invited patrons to report any vulgarities on the part of performers or dishonesty on the part of the waiters. In the East End some managers paid for policemen to sit among the audience as Sir Richard Mayne, Chief Commissioner of the Metropolitan Police informed the Select Committee on Theatrical Licences and Regulations in 1866, when quizzed about behaviour in music halls:

112. *The Panopticon in Leicester Square began in 1854 as a place to exhibit science and art. It failed in 1856 and was then used for circus shows. The Moorish building burned down in 1882.*

" There are a great number in some parts of the town, especially in the eastern parts, where the audiences are a very low class of people, and many of them are very young, but they are well-behaved. There are police, I believe, employed in every house; the usual course is for the manager to apply for the police to attend to prevent any disorder or decorum and I think the system works satisfactorily so far."

Another crucial factor in prompting rebuilding was a growing concern with public safety. In 1878 the Metropolitan Board of Works imposed a requirement for places of public performance to obtain a Certificate of Suitability. This led to the closure of some two hundred venues but also to the flotation of joint-stock companies to raise the capital needed for the luxurious and large-scale venues which would

be viable under the new regime.

Ambition was not always matched by certainty of direction. The four-tier Royal English Opera House, opened at Cambridge Circus in 1891, soon flopped as an opera venue but was rescued by Charles Morton to be relaunched as the Palace Theatre of Varieties. The Tivoli in the Strand, opened in 1890 as a theatre, was likewise turned around as a music hall by the indefatigable Morton, with bills lasting four hours and featuring up to twenty-five turns.

Sadler's Wells itself went through an extended phase of uncertainty. In 1878, after being used as a skating-rink and a boxing-ring, it was closed down as a dangerous structure. In 1879 it came under the co-management of Mrs. Sidney Bateman (1823-81), who restored it expensively with the hope of reviving its past glories under Phelps. Virtually reconstructed inside its old

113. The Alhambra in Leicester Square, c. 1904.

114. What became the Palace Theatre in Cambridge Circus, c. 1896

115. The Camberwell Palace of Varieties, 1896.

walls, it was redecorated in cream, crimson, gold and sky blue. Scarcely had the work been completed than Mrs. Bateman died, heavily in debt. After further changes of management in 1886, 1890, 1893, the Wells was relaunched as 'Sunny Old Sad's', alternating programmes of music hall with reliable melodramas like *East Lynne* or *Sweeney Todd*. After that "having undergone complete reconstruction, reseating and redecoration", the house reopened as North London's Popular Picture Theatre. When its licence was given up, the building once more slipped into dereliction.

Several suburban projects rivalled West End ventures in their scale and ambition. At Camberwell the Metropole (1894), later the Empire, was intended to be not a music hall but a straight theatre, complete with private boxes. More or less opposite was the Oriental Palace of Varieties (1896), relaunched in 1899 as the Camberwell Palace of Varieties, with seating for two thousand.

The New Cross Empire, designed by Frank Matcham and opened in 1899, could also seat two thousand and was valued at £1,250,000. Its opening playbill promised 'Two Complete and Distinct Performances Nightly' (6.50-8.50 and 9.10-11.10) and 'An Entire Change Of Programme Every Week'. Admission prices ranged from threepence in the gallery to 10/6d for a box for four.

Stars

The stars of the halls came from a variety of backgrounds. Albert Chevalier (1861-1923) was born into bourgeois comfort at 17 (then 21) St. Ann's Villas, Royal Crescent on the up-market Norland estate beyond Notting Hill. His own given names imply bourgeois pretension as well – Albert Onesime Britannicus Gwathveoyd Louis. Having taken part in 'penny readings' from the age of eight, he played for fourteen years on the 'legitimate' stage, including spells under the Bancrofts and Sir George Alexander *(see p144),*

116. The New Cross Empire. It was demolished in 1958.

117. Albert Chevalier.

118. *Gus Elen.*

119. *Dan Leno.*

before shocking his professional colleagues to become a superstar of the 1890s with coster songs such as *Knocked 'em in the Old Kent Road* and *My Old Dutch*, many written by his brother and manager. In all Chevalier wrote some eighty songs and nearly twenty plays. He brought to the music hall the wit and polish of a trained professional actor, enabling him to be, in the title of one of his own songs, *Funny Without Being Vulgar*, a quality which endeared him to the toffs and led to many invitations to perform in drawing-rooms. Chevalier was married to Florrie, the daughter of George Leybourne.

Many performers were, however, born of the same working-class that constituted the mass of their audience. Jenny Hill and Marie Lloyd *(see p131)* both started out in one of the most exploitative of 'sweated industries', making artificial flowers. Gus Elen (1862-1940) was born in Pimlico and was variously a draper's assistant, egg-packer and programme-seller at the Royal Aquarium while he worked his way onto the professional stage via singing in pubs and even on the streets. In the 1890s he was able to secure his position by exploiting the craze for comic ditties in the Cockney mode created by Albert Chevalier. Elen's most celebrated number, a typically sardonic mock-celebration of the frustrations of working-class life was *If it wasn't for the 'ouses in-between*, which reiterates what a splendid view his home might have enjoyed if it hadn't been where it actually was.

Dan Leno (George Galvin) (1860-1904), generally regarded as the greatest performer of the golden age of music hall, was the offspring of minor music-hall artists, born in a slum whose site was covered by St. Pancras station shortly afterwards. Both his father and stepfather were alcoholics. He made his debut at four at the Cosmotheca music hall in Paddington. In his youth Leno, who took his stage-name from his stepfather, learned the skills of the comedian, contortionist, clog-dancer and 'character vocalist'. Experienced and energetic, he was also imaginative and characteristically capable of peopling the stage with invisible personalities with whom he conducted convincing one-sided conversations. He made his solo adult London debut at the Foresters in Mile End in 1885, appearing in drag as a Dickensian nurse-maid. By 1886 he was in *Jack and the Beanstalk* at the Surrey. From 1888 he appeared in fifteen consecutive Christmas shows at Drury Lane. In 1901 he played a command performance at Sandringham for the Royal Family in consequence of which the press hailed him as 'The King's Jester'. Leno's last years were clouded by deafness, drink and large financial losses, followed by complete mental and physical collapse.

Little Tich (Harry Relph) (1868-1928) made his debut at twelve in blackface at one of London's last pleasure-grounds, the Rosherville, near Gravesend. His early experience included years in America, pantomime and burlesque. Instantly recognisable by the preposterously elongated boots which were his trademark, he developed a panorama of caricatures – the Ballerina, the Territorial Soldier and the Gas Inspector. At just over four foot tall he was indeed little. He also had an extra finger on each hand. Linguistically gifted, he worked so successfully in Paris that in 1910 he was made an officer of the Academie-Francaise. He was an important influence on Charlie Chaplin.

Harry Lauder (Henry MacLennan) (1870-1950) became, in 1919, the first music hall star to be knighted, in recognition of his initiative in organising the first front-line entertainment for British troops during the Great War *(see p162)*. Earlier, Lauder had worked in a flax mill and in coal mines for ten years. Although he became known as the personification of Scotsmen, he began as a singer of Irish songs. His London debut in 1900 was at Gatti's-Over-The-Water as an extra turn. Ironically he turned to Scottish material in response to encores which ran through his regular offerings. Lauder was a star overnight and became the highest paid British performer of his day.

Lauder's fellow Scot, Harry Tate (Ronald Macdonald Hutchison) (1872-1940) began as a mimic, impersonating music hall stars such as

120. *Harry Lauder.*

Dan Leno, Gus Elen and George Robey but switched to sketches and perfected the art of creating utter chaos on stage, whether ostensibly fishing, driving a car or playing golf. W.C.Fields learned much from him.

Kate Carney (1868-1950) dressed as a 'Pearly Queen' with a monstrous feather hat. Australian-born Florrie Forde (Florence Flanagan) (1876-1940) doubled as a 'Principal Boy' in pantomime and belted out such perennials as *Down at the Old Bull and Bush, Has Anybody Here Seen Kelly?* and *Hold Your Hand Out, Naughty Boy*. Albert Whelan (Waxman) (1875-1961) was another Australian; the first artist to use a signature tune, he whistled it as he sauntered on stage immaculate in evening dress, then with studied elegance deposited onto a piano his coat, cane, top-hat, gloves and scarf, reversing the procedure as his turn came to its end.

Some artists managed to spin an entire career out of the same material Charles Coborn (Colin

121. (top left) Harry Tate.

122. (bottom left) Albert Whelan.

123. (top right Florrie Forde.

Whitton McCallum) (1852-1945) was known for *Two Lovely Black Eyes* and *The Man Who Broke the Bank at Monte Carlo*. The first time he sang *Two Lovely Black Eyes* he was booed off the stage at the Trocadero. He recorded both songs in 1924, at the age of seventy-two and went on singing them for almost another twenty years. Harry Champion (1866-1942) was likewise indissolubly linked with *I'm 'Enery the Eighth I am* and *Boiled Beef and Carrots*.

124. Marie Lloyd.

The Queen of the Halls

When asked to name the three greatest women of the age the writer and wit Max Beerbohm, half-brother of Herbert Beerbohm Tree, nominated Queen Victoria, Florence Nightingale – and Marie Lloyd. T.S. Eliot hailed her as the authentic voice of the people.

Born in Hoxton, Marie Lloyd (Matilda Wood) (1870-1922) made her debut as Bella Delmare. She initially made her name with Nelly Power's wistful ballad *The Boy I Love Is Up in the Gallery* but soon became renowned for saucy songs with suggestive titles like *She'd Never Had Her Ticket Punched Before*. From 1891 until 1893 she starred in pantomime at Drury Lane until an improvised piece of stage business involving a search for a supposedly missing chamber-pot so outraged the manager Sir Augustus Harris *(see p143)* that she was never asked back. Although Marie Lloyd was certainly no stranger to innuendo or *double*

entendre her suggestiveness lay far more in her delivery than in her material. Apart from a cheery vitality and infectious laugh, she had an alluring figure and dressed superbly in gowns of her own making.

The traumas of Marie Lloyd's private life belied her chirpy *persona*. Her first husband, Percy Courtenay, was a man-about-town who beat her. After their divorce she lived and toured with, then married, a mild-mannered, soft-voiced music hall singer, Alec Hurley. Her celebrity so overshadowed him that they, too, drifted apart. These marital mishaps, coupled with her high-profile support for striking artists during their struggle against the music hall managers, ensured that she was not invited to take part in the first Royal Command Variety Performance in 1912. Unabashedly proclaiming that she appeared every night by command of the people, as her figure filled out and her looks faded she skilfully refashioned her stage self to become a plump, middle-aged Cockney housewife. Her most popular numbers referred to the quotidien disasters of working-class life. *My Old Man Said Follow the Van* refers to a 'moonlight flit' from rooms with weeks of rent outstanding. *I'm One of the Ruins That Cromwell Knocked Abaht a Bit* relates to wife-battering, a subject on which Marie had become even more of an expert. At the wedding of her only daughter Marie had been flattered by the attentions of Bernard Dillon, a successful jockey half her age. Three months after Alec's death in 1913 they were married. Dillon proved to be even more violent than her first husband. Apart from the maltreatment she received at her husband's hands, Marie further undermined her health with a tireless round of engagements entertaining troops during the Great War. After a nervous breakdown and a period of semi-retirement, Marie returned to the stage in 1920 but collapsed as the final curtain fell at the Edmonton Empire one night in October 1922. She died three days later. Fifty thousand people lined the streets of London to pay their respects to her funeral cortège.

Speciality Acts

The patter-song, reflecting the very specific local circumstances and experiences of working-class life remained at the core of the music hall's bill of fare. Its very authenticity made it unsuitable for export. In 1897 Dan Leno himself, billed as 'the funniest man in the world', rather injudiciously as it turned out, took on New York audiences and had a real struggle on his hands. Acts which depended on visual rather than verbal material proved far more capable of crossing cultural barriers. Although singers and comics might make up more than half the two dozen or more 'turns' of a typical evening's offering, they might be interspersed with illusionists, animal acts, gymnasts and virtuoso instrumentalists, many of Continental or American origin.

The agile and graceful Jules Leotard (1838-70) was the son of a French gymnastics instructor and, after an engagement at the Alhambra, became immortalized in song as *The Daring Young Man on the Flying Trapeze*. Unlike the gaudy spangles traditionally worn by acrobats and strongmen he wore the severe, unadorned costume named after him. Leotard's only feasible rival was another Frenchman, Charles Blondin (Jean Francois Gravelet) (1824-97) whose wire-walking feats defy belief. Having crossed Niagara Falls blindfolded and then pushing a man in a wheelbarrow, he made his London debut at the Crystal Palace for a fee of £100 per performance. Cinquevalli (Paul Kestner) (1856-1918) was of German stock, although born in Poland, began as an acrobat but, after a 75-foot fall and eight months in hospital, was obliged to reinvent himself to become possibly the greatest juggler of all time. First seen in London in 1885, he typically concluded his act by catching a cannon ball on the nape of his neck.

Ventriloquist Fred Russell (Thomas Frederick Parnell) (1862-1957) made his first appearance with his Cockney doll 'Coster Joe' in 1896. Russell played a leading part in the establishment of the Variety Artists' Federation, of which he became president at the age of ninety. Fourteen members of his family went into show-business, notably

125. Vesta Tilley.

his sons, the ventriloquist Russ Carr (1899-1973) and the impresario Val Parnell (1894-1972).

Vesta Tilley (Matilda Powles) (1864-1952) brought the art of the male impersonator to perfection, although she was also a celebrated principal boy. The vague erotic unease which might have been inspired by her skilfully assumed masculinity and immaculately correct tailoring was disarmed by her unmistakably soprano rendering of *Following in Father's Footsteps*. Particularly expert at rendering soldiers, she played an enthusiastic role in recruiting Tommies during the Great War.

Few recruits to music hall came farther or less intentionally to the music hall stage than Yukio Tani (1881-1950), scion of a dynasty of teachers of ju-jitsu. Tani came to London in 1900 at the behest of engineer Edward Barton-Wright, who had spent three years in Japan and, on returning to London, had opened a martial arts academy, where Tani and his elder brother were

126. *Max Miller.*

127. *Max Wall.*

recruited to teach. But he also wanted them to appear on the halls. Tani's elder brother went home in disgust at this proposed debasement of his ancestral heritage but Yukio had no such reservations. Tani pursued the music-hall route with immense success. The moment was historically perfect. The signature of the Anglo-Japanese alliance of 1902, followed by Japan's stunning victories over Russia in the war of 1904-5, created a craze for all things Japanese. Tiny Tani's routine and seemingly effortless trouncings of hefty boxers and wrestlers seemed to be quite magical as well as a complete incarnation of plucky little Japan's startling overthrow of the Russian bear. Tani's prodigious earnings as a top-of-the-bill artist should have made him not just secure, but rich. But he was an alien in an alien world, entirely bereft of the familiar social anchors of family and neighbourhood. He gambled and spent lavishly, thinking nothing of hiring a Thames steamer and inviting an entire company out for supper and a cruise. By 1914 Tani's show-biz career had run its course and he was content to stay on as the instructor he had originally come to be.

The End

Although the advent of the cinema and the wireless sounded the death-knell of the halls they were decades a-dying and could still nurture major talents for whom they were a natural environment even as they adjusted to performance on radio and film.

'The Cheeky Chappie' Max Miller (Thomas Sargent) (1895-1963) worked his way up through amateur concert parties, the circus, army entertainment units and provincial touring to make his London debut in 1922. By 1926 he was top of the bill at the Holborn Empire. In the authentic tradition of music hall he evolved a bizarrely individualised trademark constume consisting of two-tone shoes, kipper tie, white trilby and an outrageously coloured and patterned suit with plus-four trousers. The overall effect was, like his act, loud and cheerfully vulgar. Sex was his constant stage preoccupation. Appearing to act on the unquestioning assumption that this was just as true for every member of his audience made them complicit in his open conspiracy of illicit indulgence. An absolute master of comic timing, Miller blended the uncompleted punch-line, the implied rhyme and the all-too-meaningful pause, into a confiding flow of insinuation and braggadocio that he kept on flowing until his final appearances at the Metropole Edgware Road in the late 1950s.

Max Wall (Maxwell George Lorimer) (1908-90) was a lugubrious incarnation of the comic droll, apparently disarticulating his limbs to anarchic effect and delivering mordant observations in a tone of limitless flatness. Moving from music hall through radio to the 'legitimate' stage, he starred, appropriately, at Greenwich in 1974 as Archie Rice, the personification of cynically naff comedy, in *The Entertainer*. In the same year he launched his own one-man show *Aspects of Max Wall* and went on to display a special affinity for playing the works of Samuel Beckett.

The Prime Minister of Mirth

Born in Kennington, south London, as George Edward Wade, son of a civil engineer, the future George Robey (1869-1954) had a peripatetic childhood in consequence of his father's work as an installer of tramway systems. Having lived for years in Dresden and Leipzig he came to speak German and to admire the country and its culture. When re-settled in Birmingham he found relief from a routine clerical job by performing comic songs at charity shows and smoking concerts and thus acquired a hunger for applause. Returning alone to London at twenty-two, he sought further evening engagements, while cautiously keeping to a clerical day job. Aware of his family's potential disapproval, he adapted the name of a Birmingham firm to become George Robey.

A short spell as stooge to a stage hypnotist was followed by Robey's debut at the Oxford Music Hall, Oxford Street in July 1891. This secured him an immediate twelve month contract. By the end of 1892 he was topping the bill and had already perfected an instantly recognisable stage *persona* – red nose, heavily-blacked eyebrows, arched variously in mock-shock, pretended dismay or assumed distaste, a bald-fronted wig, topped by a black, pseudo-clerical hat with a flattened crown, and a collar-less coat, reminiscent of a priest's *soutane*, the ensemble completed by a short, spring 'swish' cane. The effect was calculatedly ambiguous, a sort of stylish shabbiness, as of authority past its peak.

As if in contradiction of his carefully-crafted air of self-importance, Robey bustled and crackled on stage, commanding his audience as he put it "to the last man in the gallery". Dashing between as many as five music halls in a single evening, he would hurl himself on stage and attack an audience which was already laughing before he had spoken a word. When the words came they did so as a sparkling flow enunciated with an uncompromised middle-class clarity which an awed Laurence Olivier characterised as "whiplash diction". Hecklers were brushed aside with crushing repartee. Much of Robey's patter, which he wrote himself, was phrased in deliberately over-wrought and archaic vocabulary, as in his constant injunction to "Kindly temper your hilarity with a modicum of reserve" or, even more frequently, to "Desist!"

Commanding the extensive vocabulary of a self-educated man who had made a good job of it, Robey was a master of innuendo, a magician of the unspoken word. He would, however, in his autobiography, vehemently protest a firm distinction between "honest vulgarity" (what he did) and "smut" (what other comedians did). Complementing his not-quite-clerical persona Robey also developed a range of 'characters', ranging from the Prehistoric Man to the Mayor of Mudcumdyke and The District Nurse. His songs were supplied by others. *If you were the only girl in the world,* sung with Violet Loraine in 1916 in the long-running revue *The Bing Boys are Here,* was the only one which became a 'standard'.

An inevitable choice for the first royal command variety performance in 1912, Robey worked tirelessly fund-raising for charity during the First World War but modestly declined a knighthood as excessive and agreed only to accept the CBE. Accepted by general assent as the consistently best pantomime dame over a period of forty years, Robey also managed the Shaftesbury Theatre (1927-9), and, in his sixties, daringly made a successful stab at operetta (1932)

and at film (1934), playing Sancho Pancho opposite Chalyapin under the direction of Pabst. In 1935 he was acclaimed as Falstaff, a role he reprised in Olivier's 1944 *Henry V*.

Seedy and subversive on stage, in private life Robey was seemingly conformist and, compared with most populist performers, highly cultured – a knowledgeable collector of Oriental art, a philatelist, he also made violins and painted watercolours exhibited at the Royal Academy. His intellectual interests ranged from Egyptology to comparative religion. Robey was also an energetic and versatile sportsman, once playing cricket against W.G. Grace, making guest appearances with Chelsea and Aston Villa and also participating in athletics, rugby, tennis and, in old age, golf. Robey's children were aimed for conventional success. His son became a barrister and magistrate, his daughter inherited his talent as a painter. For all his talents and interests, however, Robey did have a weakness - women - which atrophied his marriage over the years. At the age of sixty he fell deeply in love with Blanche Littler, a member of the famed theatrical dynasty. Thirty years younger than he, she became his fierce protectress, business manager, and in retirement, nurse. When Robey finally divorced in 1938, they were swiftly married. Robey retired, reluctantly, just short of eighty. He finally acepted a knighthood just months before his death in 1954.

128. George Robey.

CHAPTER NINE

Golden Age

etween Irving's take-over of the Lyceum in
1878 and the outbreak of war in 1914
theatre in London enjoyed what was in
several respects a golden age. More Londoners,
both in absolute numbers and as a proportion of
the capital's ever-rising population, went
regularly to some form of theatrical entertainment
than they ever had done before or have since. The
number of actors and actresses more than
quadrupled between the 1860s and the end of
the century. Over twenty new theatres were built,
with increasing splendour in their appointments
and increasing sophistication in their
equipment. The scene was dominated by
swashbuckling actor-managers, several of
whom, led by Irving, achieved the supreme
accolade of a knighthood. Many productions
achieved runs of hundreds of performances.
Novel efforts were also made to experiment with
drama as a form. Writers like Percy Fitzgerald
and Robert Lowe brought more scholarly
standards to the investigation of theatrical
history. The theatrical industry became better
institutionalised. And after more than a century
of largely indifferent fare, the plays got a lot
better. Even the critics were better.

Writing in 1879 the Anglophile American
Henry James (1843-1916) observed with the acute
eye of the detached novelist:

"this interest in histrionic matters almost reaches
the proportions of a mania ... the London world
is apparently filled with stage-struck young
persons ... Plays and actors are perpetually talked
about, private theatricals are incessant and
members of the dramatic profession are 'received'
without restriction. They appear in society and

129. W. S. Gilbert

the people of society appear on the stage; it is as
if the great gate which formerly divided the
theatre from the world had been lifted off its
hinges."

Theatres

The Savoy Theatre, opened in 1881, was the first
public building in London to be lit by electricity.
Designed by C.J. Phipps *(see p113)*, it was financed
by impresario Richard D'Oyly Carte to stage the
operas of Gilbert and Sullivan. So closely did the

130. Sir Arthur Sullivan.

131. Charles Hawtrey.

two become identified with one another that the G & S *oeuvre* became known as 'the Savoy operas' and their performers as 'Savoyards'. Opening with *Patience*, the Savoy enjoyed an unbroken series of hits, most notably *The Mikado* (1885), which set a West End record for a run which stood for thirty years. In 1890 Gilbert famously quarrelled with Carte over the expense of the production of *The Gondoliers*, most notably about the sum spent on re-carpeting the theatre foyer. Sullivan sided with Carte and the fruitful partnership of composer and librettist broke up. Adjoining the theatre, the Savoy Hotel, inspired by the sort of luxury establishments Carte had experienced on tour in the USA, was completed in 1889 to the designs of T.E. Collcutt. Managed by Cesar Ritz, with the legendary Auguste Escoffier as chef, it proved so successful that in 1903-4 another block was added on. The Savoy became a confirmed favourite with show-business luminaries such as Sarah Bernhardt and Dame Nellie Melba. Irving actually moved in.

The Comedy Theatre in Panton Street also opened in 1881 and at first also concentrated on comic operas. Under Charles Hawtrey (1888-92, 1896-9) the focus was on farces and comedies. Marie Tempest appeared regularly in comedies from 1907 to 1909. *Peg O'My Heart*, opening in 1914, ran for 710 performances.

What became the Empire Theatre in 1884 began in 1881 as The Royal London Panorama. Financed by a French company, it opened with panoramic scenes from the Crimean war but failed within a year and was handed over to Thomas Verity for conversion. Re-opened in 1884, after redecoration it reopened yet again in 1887 as a music hall but finally found a winning formula with spectacular ballets, led by such legendary *danseuses* as Adeline Genee. In 1894 the theatre became the focus of a famous fracas thanks to the efforts of purity campaigner Mrs. Ormiston Chant. The promenade of the Empire having become a notorious cruising-ground for prostitutes, the newly-established London County Council required the theatre, as a

132. The Empire Theatre, Leicester Square, c.1904.

precondition of renewing its licence for public performance, to erect a screen between the auditorium and the promenade. On the opening night after their installation a crowd of boisterous young men, urged on by a Sandhurst cadet named Winston Churchill, tore down the flimsy canvas screens and paraded sections outside in triumph.

Theatre speculator Sefton Parry opened the Playhouse Theatre on recently-built Northumberland Avenue in the expectation that the site would be required by the South Eastern Railway Company, whose trains ran into adjacent Charing Cross station. Opened in 1882, it passed into the hands of actor-manager George Alexander *(see p144)* in 1891 and in 1894 staged the first production of Shaw's *Arms and the Man*. In 1905 part of the station collapsed on the theatre, killing six people and necessitating major rebuilding.

The Kingsway Theatre in Great Queen Street, also opened in 1882, was designed by Thomas Verity with comedies in mind. It was therefore ironic as the chosen venue for the British premiere of Ibsen's *A Doll's House*. In a production of *Sins of the Night* actor Temple E. Crozier was accidentally stabbed to death.

The Theatre Royal, Stratford East opened inauspiciously in 1884 when proprietor and producer William Charles Dillon had to reprove the East End audience's rowdy reaction to Bulwer-Lytton's heavyweight drama, *Richelieu*.

The Prince of Wales Theatre, Coventry Street, also opened in 1884, as Prince's. It was designed by the prolific C.J. Phipps for actor-manager Edgar Bruce, who had made so much out of *The Colonel* at the Scala (1880-2) that he could afford to treat himself to his own theatre.

Terry's (1887) in the Strand was built for

133. *The Playhouse Theatre in 1882, then called the Royal Avenue.*

134. *The Theatre Royal, Stratford c. 1904.*

135. Edward Terry.

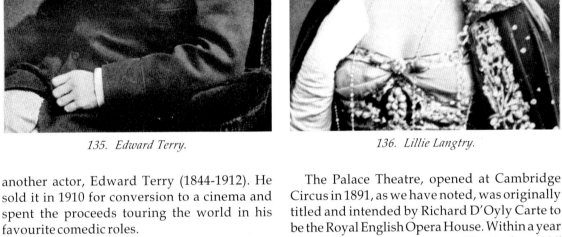

136. Lillie Langtry.

another actor, Edward Terry (1844-1912). He sold it in 1910 for conversion to a cinema and spent the proceeds touring the world in his favourite comedic roles.

The Lyric (1888) on Shaftesbury Avenue, another Phipps design, was financed by Henry J. Leslie with profits he had made from the comic opera *Dorothy* at the Prince of Wales's, transferring the play to the Lyric with Marie Tempest in the lead. For the next decade The Lyric, appropriate to its title, specialised in comic operas, although it was also the venue chosen for the London debut of Eleanora Duse *(see p151)* in *La Dame aux Camelias*.

A Lyric Opera House opened in Hammersmith in 1890 under the proprietorship of Charles Cordingley, owner and editor of the local *West London Advertiser*. Almost completely rebuilt by Frank Matcham in 1895, it reopened with a prologue spoken by Lillie Langtry but within a decade it had become known as 'The Blood and Flea Pit' and was more often closed than open.

The Palace Theatre, opened at Cambridge Circus in 1891, as we have noted, was originally titled and intended by Richard D'Oyly Carte to be the Royal English Opera House. Within a year it was passed on to Augustus Harris *(see p144)* who re-launched it as the Palace Theatre of Varieties. Russian ballet dancer Anna Pavlova chose it for her London debut in 1910.

The Duke of York's Theatre, opened in 1892 as the Trafalgar Square Theatre, was the first to be built on St. Martin's Lane and in 1904 staged the first ever performance of *Peter Pan*, which became an annual Christmas fixture for the next decade.

At its opening in 1898 The Coronet at Notting Hill Gate was proclaimed to be "a theatre of which the whole County of London may be proud." Built for impresario Edward George Saunders, to the designs of W.G.R. Sprague, it featured a Japanese touring company in 1900 and witnessed performances by Bernhardt, Irving, Langtry and Mrs. Patrick Campbell but by 1916 had been converted to a cinema.

137. The Hippodrome in Charing Cross Road, c. 1904.

for impresario Oswald Stoll on a lavish scale. It was the first theatre in England to have a revolving stage and the first in Europe to be equipped with lifts. With a seating capacity of over 2,500 it remains London's largest theatre. 1905 witnessed the addition of no less than three theatres in a single year. The Aldwych was designed by Sprague for Charles Frohman *(see p98)* and Seymour Hicks *(see p146)*, who ran it until 1910. The Strand was originally known as the Waldorf and designed by Sprague as a symmetrical offset to match his Aldwych. Marie Wilton's Scala, which had been used as a Salvation Army hostel from 1866 to 1903, was rebuilt on an enlarged site by Verity but by 1911 was being used as a cinema and afterwards became a venue for amateur players. The Globe on Shaftesbury Avenue, designed by Sprague, was another Frohman-Hicks venture and until 1909 was known as the Hicks. Its twin, the Queen's (1907) was also by Sprague.

The Little Theatre (1910) in John Adam Street was what its name claimed, with seating for just 250. Converted from the banking hall of a branch of Coutts & Co., it was the brainchild of actress Gertrude Kingston (1866-1937) and opened with Laurence Housman's version of Aristophanes' *Lysistrata*, herself playing the title role. In 1911 Noel Coward, then twelve, made his stage debut there. In the same year Shaw had his first commercial success with *Fanny's First Play*, followed in 1912 by *Captain Brassbound's Conversion*. Shaw acknowledged his debt by writing *Great Catherine* specially for her, which she played at the Vaudeville in 1913. Her memoirs were engagingly entitled *Curtsey While You're Thinking*.

What became the Shaftesbury Theatre on Shaftesbury Avenue was first (1911) known as the New Prince's Theatre, soon abbreviated to Prince's. The last pre-war house to be built, again by Sprague, was the Ambassador's on St. Martin's Lane.

Wyndham's on Charing Cross Road, also designed by Sprague, was built for Sir Charles Wyndham *(see p143)*. In 1903 it staged the first English performance of Rostand's *Cyrano de Bergerac. An Englishman's Home* (1909) filled the house for six months and is alleged to have substantially boosted recruitment to the newly-reorganized Territorial Army. The Hippodrome, diagonally opposite Wyndham's, was built (1900) as a circus and incorporated a huge water-tank for aquatic spectacles. Reconstructed as a music-hall in 1909, in 1910 it staged the first English performance of Tchaikovsky's *Swan Lake*.

More than a dozen more theatres were to be added to the London total between the turning of the century and the outbreak of the Great War.

The Apollo, designed for musicals, opened in 1901. The Albery (1903) was built on St. Martin's Lane by Sprague for Wyndham. The London Coliseum (1904) was designed by Frank Matcham

138. The Waldorf (later the Strand) Theatre, c. 1904.

Actors, Managers and Actor-Managers

Charles Wyndham (né Charles Culverwell) (1837-1919) was already a qualified doctor when he made his debut on the professional stage at twenty-five. Medicine, however, soon reclaimed him as he emigrated to the USA and served as a surgeon in the Union army during the American civil war. From 1870 to 1872 Wyndham toured the theatres of the mid-West with his own company. Returning to London, he used the intimate Criterion to present society farces. Wyndham's own favourite role was the name part in Robertson's *David Garrick*, which played for the opening of the theatre Wyndham named after himself. Knighted in 1902, Wyndham remained handsome into old age. In 1916, just shy of eighty, he married his long-time mistress and leading lady, Mary Moore (1869-31), widow of the playwright James Albery.

Augustus Harris (1852-96) came of a great theatrical lineage. His grandfather, Joseph Glossop, had built the Coburg Theatre ('Old Vic') and managed La Scala, Milan. His father,

139. Charles Wyndham.

140. Augustus Harris surrounded by characters from plays by John Davidson. Design by Aubrey Beardsley, 1894.

Harris's pantomimes featured top-line music-hall stars, including Little Tich, Dan Leno, Marie Lloyd and Vesta Tilley. They were also noteworthy for monster processions; one depicted twenty-one sports and pastimes, another twenty-eight nursery rhymes. The 'high brow' productions ranged from Shakespeare to Wagner and the Comedie Française. In the interests of verisimilitude Harris hired the then Major Kitchener to drill marching extras and reproduced a real cigarette factory in Seville for the staging of *Carmen*. In 1888 he decided to take over Covent Garden and bought the *Sunday Times* to use as a weapon against hostile critics.

At Covent Garden Harris initiated the production of operas in their original language, not just Italian, and arranged personal visits by Mascagni and Puccini. Royal approval was signalized by the organization of command performances at Windsor Castle in 1893 and 1894. Harris also somehow found time to serve as a member of the newly-constituted London County Council and as Sheriff of the City of London, for which, rather than for his undoubted services to the theatre, he was knighted in 1891. A combination of overwork, diabetes and cancer carried off the colourful impresario at just forty-three.

Johnston Forbes-Robertson (1853-1937) actually wanted to be an artist but thought acting a better bet when Samuel Phelps *(see p103)* took him on at six guineas a week and became his mentor and voice coach. Forbes-Robertson worked for Buckstone and the Bancrofts before accepting Irving's invitation to join the Lyceum company. Graceful and gifted with voice of outstanding quality, Forbes-Robertson at forty-four became the definitive Hamlet of his generation and by general assent the inheritor of Irving's mantle as the senior actor of the British stage. Occupying a suitably dignified Georgian residence in Bedford Square, he was knighted and retired in 1913. His autobiography *A Player Under Three Reigns* asserted that he had never really enjoyed acting.

Born George Samson, George Alexander (1858-1918) worked under Irving (1881-9) before

also Augustus Harris (1826-73) had made his stage debut at eight, married a theatrical costumier and managed the Princess's and Covent Garden. Harris himself had been born in Paris and was brought up to speak both French and German. Beginning as a touring actor in the provinces, he was quickly promoted to stage manager. At twenty-seven, on borrowed cash, he took over the lease of Drury Lane. Unashamedly catering to popular taste, he devised a seasonal programme which began with melodrama and ended with 'high-brow' plays but centred on a gorgeous pantomime, the profits from which subsidised the other elements. Harris co-wrote and acted in his first melodrama *The World* (1880), whose baffling plot was mitigated by enthralling staging and effects.

141. Johnston Forbes-Robertson.

142. George Alexander.

buying the lease on the St. James's Theatre and retaining it until his death. Unlike many of his contemporaries Alexander's declared policy as a manager was to support the writing of new plays by British authors. He was the first English producer of Oscar Wilde with *Lady Windermere's Fan* (1892) and himself played the first Jack Worthing in *The Importance of Being Earnest* (1895). His boldest – and hugely worthwhile – gamble was Pinero's *The Second Mrs. Tanqueray* (1893), which made a star of Mrs. Patrick Campbell *(see p151)*. Henry James's *Guy Domville* (1895), by contrast, had a famously disastrous first night and was soon withdrawn. When Wilde was disgraced Alexander removed the author's name from the playbills of *Earnest* but took pains to secure the play's performing rights for the benefit of Wilde's children. Shrewd, efficient and punctiliously fair, Alexander was knighted in 1911.

Herbert Beerbohm Tree (1853-1917) defied parental opposition to make his professional debut in 1878. Entering management to run the Haymarket (1887-96), he liked to provoke and thus presented Wilde's *A Woman of No Importance* (1893) and Ibsen's *An Enemy of the People* (1893). Tree appeared himself as the hypnotist Svengali in *Trilby*, the sensation of 1895 and also played an acclaimed Falstaff (1896). Tree's private opinion of *Trilby* was that it was 'hogwash' but it made him so much money that he was able to finance the building of his own theatre, opposite the Haymarket.

From 1897 until 1915 Tree managed His Majesty's Theatre, which he had planned himself and where he occupied a penthouse apartment. Under his direction it became renowned for lavish productions of Shakespeare which took stage 'naturalism' to such extremes as putting real rabbits on stage in *A Midsummer Night's*

143. Herbert Beerbohm Tree.

144. Seymour Hicks.

Dream and decking the set of *Twelfth Night* with terraces of real grass. Tree's concern for his craft was not always appreciated, as a disgruntled former colleague made clear:

"With the amount of personal attention, Mr. Tree, which you give to all your presentations, and the care you bestow on every detail I really don't think you need an actual producer. Nor, with the constant supervision you so thoroughly exercise, have you any use for a stage manager. What you really require are a couple of tame, trained echoes."

A master of make-up, Tree also created a great costume role for himself as *Fagin* (1905). As Henry Higgins in the first (1914) English production of Shaw's *Pygmalion*, he was, however, more than matched by Mrs. Patrick Campbell's Eliza Doolittle. Despite maintaining two separate families simultaneously, Beerbohm Tree was knighted in 1907.

Edward Seymour Hicks (1871-1941) toured America before producing *Under the Clock* (1893), the first revue staged in London. A versatile performer, he was also a prolific writer of light comedy and Christmas fare. Both the theatres he built, the Aldwych and the Globe, opened with performances of his own plays. In 1931 Hicks was awarded the Legion d'Honneur for his efforts to present French drama on the English stage. He was knighted in 1935.

Making the London Coliseum synonymous with spectacle, Australian-born Oswald Stoll (1866-1942) also acquired control of the Hackney, New Cross and Shepherd's Bush Empires and Croydon Hippodrome as well as several provincial halls. Joining Walter Gibbons' Variety Theatres Consolidated in 1911, he became responsible for some twenty-nine halls. Cold and shrewd, with a Darwinian ruthlessness in his approach to business, Stoll was knighted in 1919.

145. *Sir Oswald Stoll.*

Avenues of Talent

Whereas Brompton was one of the most preferred residential areas for theatricals in the first half of the nineteenth century, in the second half, despite still being the chosen residence of Beerbohm Tree, Ellen Terry and Brandon Thomas, Brompton was increasingly overshadowed in this respect by St. John's Wood and Maida Vale, a district also renowned for its population of painters, sculptors and singers. While the respectability of most residents was indisputable its characteristic detached villas and discreet high garden walls made it also notorious as the favoured residence of the most well-kept mistresses or of such Bohemians, like the novelist George Eliot, who lived in irregular unions. Sometime residents of this quintessentially up-market suburb included J.L. Toole, Charles Fechter, Charles Wyndham, Sir Squire Bancroft, Sir George Alexander, Sir Augustus Harris and Sir Arthur Pinero.

John Hollingshead (1827-1904), who lived at 14 North Bank, by Regent's Park, came late to theatrical management, having been on the staff of Dickens' *Household Words* and worked as drama critic of the *Daily News* and a freelance for

Punch. As stage manager of the Alhambra he was instrumental in introducing the can-can to London. Taking over the Gaiety in 1868, he relied mainly on burlesques, many penned by ex-civil servant Robert Reece (1838-91), another resident of St. John's Wood. Hollingshead also pioneered the novel notion of matinee performances and staged London's first playing of Ibsen *(see p156).* Having made a considerable fortune, Hollingshead lost it speculating in provincial theatres and devoted his retirement to writing affectionate memoirs about the Gaiety.

Hollingshead's near neighbour on North Bank was the famed novelist George Eliot, who lived with the polymath journalist George Henry Lewes (1817-78), a gifted linguist and dabbler in business, law and medicine, who could turn his hand to novels, biography, philosophy and popular science. Variously described as resembling an "unkempt Polish refugee" and "an old-fashioned French barber or dancing-master" and characterised as "a man of conscience wearing a mask of flippancy", this "very ugly, very vivacious and very entertaining" character, habitually dressed in a combination of morning and evening clothes "combining the less pleasing points of both." An amateur actor of some talent, Lewes played with Dickens' company *(see p102)* and in the provinces but never appeared professionally on stage in London. Lewes also collaborated with Charles Mathews the Younger on plays and wrote over a dozen more himself under the pseudonyms Slingsby Lawrence and Frank Churchill. As an influential drama critic Lewes shared Dickens' dislike of Charles Kean and was one of the first to hail Irving as an outstanding talent. A selection of Lewes's criticism was published as *On Actors and the Art of Acting* (1875).

The Eliot-Lewes mansion was later the home of melodrama specialist Wilson Barrett (1846-1904). Taking over the Princess's Theatre, he had a huge hit with *The Lights o' London* (1881), written by George R. Sims (1847-1922), who lived in Hamilton Terrace. It not only had a long run but then toured the world. Barrett's own fortune was made and his acting career pretty much

146. Wilson Barrett.

147. George R. Sims

148. William Terriss.

blighted by his own play *The Sign of the Cross* (1896) – "a melodrama of frantic spirituality" – in which he played Marcus Superbus to such acclaim and financial reward that he was unable to escape the part thereafter.

William 'Breezy Bill' Terriss (1847-97) was actually born in a house in Circus Road, St. John's Wood. Following a disastrous provincial debut in 1867 and a brief spell with the Bancrofts, he tried his hand as merchant seaman and a tea-planter before settling in the Falkland Islands as a sheep-farmer. During this exile he fathered a daughter, Ellaline (1871-1971), who would have her own stage career and marry Sir Seymour Hicks. Returning to the stage in 1873, Terriss was drawn into Irving's company before transferring to the Adelphi where his muscular talent for swashbuckling hero parts in melodramas like George R. Sims' *The Harbour Lights* (1885) won him the punning sobriquet 'No. 1 Adelphi Terriss'. Terriss was sensationally murdered at his own stage-door when an actor

149. Ellaline Terriss.

150. Lilian Baylis.

whom he had sacked literally stabbed him in the back.

Edward Smith Willard (1853-1915) made his London debut in Sims' *The Lights o' London* and went on to specialise in villains. In 1889 Willard took over the Shaftesbury and formed a company which toured North America annually.

John Martin-Harvey (1863-1944) served an extended apprenticeship under Irving before forming his own company to tour a dramatised version of Dickens' *A Tale of Two Cities*, *The Only Way*, in which he played Sydney Carton, for forty years. Modelling himself on Irving he alternated histrionic hokum with standard Shakespeare favourites. In 1912, when he was living at 30 Avenue Road, Martin-Harvey gave the performance of his life in *Oedipus Rex* at Covent Garden. Knighted in 1921, he carried on touring until 1939, the last of the Victorians.

Whereas there was a certain expansive style common to the actor-manager as a type Lilian Baylis (1874-1937) was one of a kind. In the words of Ronald Bergan – "an irritating, God-intoxicated, 'undereducated', unmarried,

bespectacled woman who hardly ever saw a play through." A musical child prodigy, she lived (1890-8) in South Africa before returning to her native London to assist her aunt, Emma Cons *(ill. 151)*, in the management of the Old Vic, which she had been running as a "cheap and decent place of amusement on strict temperance lines" for the local working-class community of Lambeth since 1880. A social worker and the first woman member of the London County Council, Emma Cons was deeply committed to the uplifting of an area then synonymous with some of the worst deprivation in London. In 1900 they put on their first opera, *The Bohemian Girl*. Opera, and later ballet, would remain Lilian Baylis's first love but it was through theatre that she would initially establish her unique standing in the world of the arts. In 1912 Emma Cons died and the intensely devout and equally single-minded Baylis took sole control of management, boldly determined to raise the standard of the Old Vic's offerings *(see p163).*

151. Emma Cons (see p149).

152. Marie Tempest.

Grandes Dames

The rising status of the actor was matched by a growth in both the numbers and standing of actresses. Whereas in 1851 actors had outnumbered actresses by roughly two to one by 1881 women were outnumbering men in the profession.

New York-born Genevieve Teresa ('Lucy') Ward (1838-1922) acquired the title Countess of Guerbel by an early marriage and made her professional debut as an opera diva under the name of Ginevra Guerrabella but lost her voice through illness and turned to acting, appearing as Lady Macbeth in 1873. Twenty years later, at Tennyson's direct request, she played opposite Irving in *Becket*. Her stage appearances after 1900 were rare although her farewell appearance was not until 1920. In 1921 she was created D.B.E., the first actress to be so honoured.

Madge Kendal (Margaret Sholto Robertson)(1848-1935) was the youngest of twenty-two children, of whom the playwright T.W. Robertson was the eldest. Noted for playing comedy at the Haymarket under Buckstone's management, at twenty-one she married the actor W.H. Kendal (1843-1917). As 'the Kendals' they starred together on stage and became efficient joint managers of the St. James's (1879-88). *The Cambridge Guide to Theatre* characterises Mrs. Kendal as "less notable as an actress than as a theatrical grande dame, the sort who inaugurates charity benefits, unveils plaques and opens fetes." She was appointed DBE in 1926

Marie Tempest (1864-1942) also trained as a singer and initially appeared in musical comedies before switching to comedy, enjoying repeated success with plays written by her second husband Cosmo Gordon-Lennox (1869-1921), notably the coquettish name role in *Becky Sharp* (1901), based on Thackeray's *Vanity Fair* and *The Marriage of Kitty* (1902). Noel Coward wrote the part of feckless actress Judith Bliss in

153. Mrs Patrick Campbell.

154. Sarah Bernhardt.

Hay Fever (1925) especially for her. She was subsequently directed by her third husband W. Graham Brown (1870-1937). Appointed DBE in 1937, she made her last appearance in *Dear Octopus* in 1938.

Witty, eccentric, temperamental, imperious Mrs. Patrick Campbell (Beatrice Tanner) (1865-1940) became a slightly belated overnight star when she created the name role in *The Second Mrs. Tanqueray* (1893), reprising success with Pinero's follow-up *The Notorious Mrs. Ebbsmith* (1895). Encouraged by a smitten Johnston Forbes-Robertson, 'Mrs. Pat' progressed to Shakespeare in which she proved erratic and to Ibsen, in which she disappointed. Shaw, with whom she shared a long, passionate but platonic correspondence, wrote *Caesar and Cleopatra* specifically for her and Forbes-Robertson but she never performed it. She did, however, create Eliza Doolitle in *Pygmalion* (1914), another role which Shaw had written for her. He advised her to "write a true book entitled WHY, THOUGH I

WAS A WONDERFUL ACTRESS, NO MANAGER OR AUTHOR WOULD EVER ENGAGE ME TWICE IF HE COULD POSSIBLY HELP IT."

With a voice likened to "a golden bell", a consummate talent to match it and a tempestuous private life Sarah Bernhardt (1844-1923) was more than a star, she was a phenomenon. An accomplished painter and sculptor, she also wrote poetry and plays and toured not only in Britain and the USA but as far as Russia, Africa and Australia. Her London debut came with the Comedie Française in 1879. She later went into management on her own account, naming her Paris theatre after herself. Transcending the normal run of 'breeches roles', she successfully played Hamlet. Unchecked by bankruptcy, 'the divine Sarah', as Oscar Wilde dubbed her, also defied the amputation of a leg in 1915 to go on playing until the year before her death.

Born into an Italian family of players Eleanora Duse (1858-1924) endured years of gruelling tours and was tempted to abandon the family tradition until seeing Bernhardt convinced her to persevere. She later formed her own company, touring worldwide. Chekhov found Duse captivating as Cleopatra and Shaw hailed her as "the first actress whom we have seen applying the method of the great school to characteristically modern parts". Duse first visited England in 1894 and played a command performance before Queen Victoria at Windsor. A year later she played in London opposite Bernhardt. An electrifying presence and painstaking preparation enabled her to overcome a frail but graceful physique. Apparently able to blush or turn pale at will, she scorned the use of stage make-up.

After learning her craft with touring companies Lilla McCarthy (1875-1960), joined Tree through whom she met Shaw, who became a great admirer and cast her for leading roles in the first performances of *John Bull's Other Island* and *Man and Superman* (1905) and *The Doctor's Dilemma* (1906), then marrying the director of these plays, Harley Granville-Barker *(see p157)*. Taking over The Little Theatre in 1911, she presented Ibsen's *The Master Builder*. McCarthy also played in the celebrated 1912 production of *Oedipus Rex*. She later took over the Kingsway Theatre but quit the profession on her second marriage.

Playwrights

Arthur Wing Pinero (1855-1934) left school at ten to work in his father's law office and then left there to become an actor, excelling in what Ellen Terry called 'silly ass' roles. Pinero wrote fifteen plays before giving up the stage in 1884 to concentrate on writing. As a dramatist Pinero was then to enjoy success in two quite distinctly different fields, with a succession of farces like *The Magistrate* (1885) and *Dandy Dick* (1887) and the sentimental *Sweet Lavender* (1888), which ran for 684 performances, and a series of 'problem' plays focusing on the double standards which beset women in a man's world, most notably the sensationally successful *The Second Mrs. Tanqueray* (1893), in which the beleaguered

155. Arthur Wing Pinero.

heroine obligingly tidies up the plot by committing suicide. Pinero had, unusually, managed to write a 'serious' English play which actually made money, scrutinising conventional morality without actually crossing the line of good taste by challenging it outright. He also impressed the more analytical critics by his skill in completely dispensing with such conventional devices as the soliloquy and the aside. Pinero's best comedy *Trelawny of the 'Wells'* (1898) was an unashamedly nostalgic celebration of the mid-century theatrical world. Pinero was knighted in 1909 but thereafter his career was a disappointing coda of declining reputation and inventiveness as his mode of writing was overshadowed by the work of Shaw.

A Scot by birth and education J.M. Barrie (1860-1937) came to London via journalism in Nottingham and successfully established himself as a novelist in his twenties but his first two plays were indifferently received. Recognition came with J.L. Toole starring in *Walker, London* (1892) and was confirmed with a dramatisation of his novel *The Little Minister*

156. J. M. Barrie.

157. Oscar Wilde.

(1897), followed by society comedies like *The Admirable Crichton* (1902) and *What Every Woman Knows* (1908). The work that would forever be associated with Barrie's name, *Peter Pan* (1904), was another dramatisation of a Barrie novel, originally published as *The Little White Bird* (1902). Barrie's characteristic blend of fantasy and sentimentality featured again in *Dear Brutus* (1917). *Shall We Join the Ladies?* (1922), originally intended as the opening of a full-length murder mystery, was staged as a one-act play which became a favourite of amateur companies. Barrie was knighted in 1913 and subsequently awarded the Order of Merit.

A brilliant classicist, Oscar Wilde (1854-1900) first established his public reputation as a poet and mannered lecturer on aesthetic and literary topics and was well enough known by 1881 to be satirized by Gilbert and Sullivan in *Patience*. His early melodrama about anarchists and costume tragedy in verse were both first staged in the USA, to little notice. Success came in 1892 with *Lady Windermere's Fan*, billed as a "New and original play of modern life". Wilde's theatrical arrival was confirmed by *A Woman of No Importance* (1893). 1895 proved the year of the playwright's greatest triumph and personal undoing with the success of *An Ideal Husband* (1895) and his masterpiece *The Importance of Being Earnest* (1895) followed by the unmasking of the author's homosexual life, with its merciless retribution in the form of disgrace, imprisonment, the loss of his family and early death in a penurious Parisian exile. The one-act *Salome* which Wilde penned in gaol was staged in Paris in 1896 but banned in Britain until 1931.

The early plays of John Galsworthy (1867-1933) *The Silver Box* (1906), *Strife* (1909) and *Justice* (1910) dealt respectively with legal injustice, industrial unrest and solitary confinement and were all produced by Harley Granville-Barker. *Justice* made a profound impression on Winston Churchill, then Home Secretary and had a salutary effect on the improvement of prison conditions. *The Fugitive* (1913) dealt with the victimization of women,

158. *John Galsworthy*

159. *Harley Granville-Barker, a sketch by Sava in 1936.*

while *The Mob* (1914) denounced war hysteria. Galsworthy's plays made him sufficiently wealthy to be able to complete his magnum opus, the multi-volume *Forsyte Saga*. In 1932 he was awarded the Nobel Prize for Literature, mainly for his novels. Galsworthy refused a knighthood but accepted the Order of Merit.

Nowadays (William) Somerset Maugham (1874-1965) is also better remembered for his novels than his plays. Trained as a doctor, he had his first play staged in 1903 and by 1908 had four running in London simultaneously. Further cynical, witty comedies of manners flowed from his facile pen for another quarter of a century. Arnold Bennett (1867-1931) was a third novelist whose career as a dramatist paralleled Maugham's to include both romantic comedies and stage versions of his novels.

Of all the dramatists of the period it was to be George Bernard Shaw (1856-1950) who would

have the most enduring impact on the British stage. Quitting his native Dublin for London at twenty, he established a public profile as a provocative speaker on behalf of of the newly-formed Fabian Society of socialist intellectuals. The son of a professional singer, he made a literary impact as an iconoclastic book reviewer and music critic and with an essay on *The Quintessence of Ibsenism* (1891). Abandoning novels for the drama, with the encouragement of the drama critic William Archer *(see p156)*, he crafted *Widowers' Houses* (1892) as an attack on slum landlords. He also switched from being a music critic to becoming an equally acerbic critic of the drama (1895-8) for the *Saturday Review*. Shaw's concern to deal confrontationally with uncomfortable issues made his plays unlikely to appeal to theatrical knights who depended on the bourgeoisie to keep them in spats and monocles and forced him to promote his output through readings, publication and private productions until he was seriously taken up by Granville-Barker at the Royal Court (1904-7).

Shaw progressed, over the course of his very long life, from gadfly to sage, seldom losing the opportunity to punt his pet passions, from vegetarianism to the radical reform of English spelling. As a director he earned the admiration of actors and was also one of the first dramatists to realise that the performance of plays on radio would demand a complete different style of acting. In the printing of his plays he paid meticulous attention to both their layout and typography and provided extensive stage directions as well as lengthy prefaces elaborating their (usually didactic) themes. In 1925 Shaw was awarded the Nobel Prize for Literature. By 1932 his stature was such that his drama criticism of over three decades previously was published in three volumes as *Our Theatres in the Nineties.*

The Cutting Edge

In 1881 the theatrical company led by Georg II, Duke of Saxe-Meiningen (1826-1914) and his morganatic wife, the acress Ellen Franz (1839-1923) presented *Julius Caesar, Twelfth Night* and *The Winter's Tale* at Drury Lane – in German. Representing one of the most conservative of European dramatic traditions, the court theatre, the Meiningen Company paradoxically also represented a radically innovatory approach to direction and staging. The Duke not only directed but also designed both costumes and scenery with a close attention to historical accuracy which even extended to the actors' voice production and gestures, thus incarnating the concept of the director as creative and interpretative supremo. Particular attention was paid to ensemble acting, especially in relation to crowd scenes which were composed in detail like the massive panoramic paintings with archaeologically 'correct' details so favoured by contemporary academic artists. Steps and rostrums were deployed to keep action moving quite literally at different levels. The emphasis was on team-work, with even spear-carriers being treated as actors in their own right, and

major players being periodically rotated to minor roles. The Meiningen philosophy thus incarnated the very opposite of the individualistic actor-manager egotism personified by Irving. But, even if Irving was unmoved by the philosophy, he was immensely impressed by the stagecraft and, like many of his contemporaries adopted the Meiningen compositional technique in arranging stage groupings thereafter.

The standard of English experimentalism was borne by William Poel (né Pole) (1852-1934) who, in complete contrast to the Meiningen insistence on visual verisimilitude, advocated a return to the bareness of the Elizabethan stage, unadorned by scenery and bereft of machinery or effects. In 1881 Poel himself played Hamlet on a raised platform in St. George's Hall. In 1893 he presented *Measure for Measure* on an attempted reconstruction of the stage of the Elizabethan Fortune theatre set within the proscenium arch of the Royalty Theatre. By founding the Elizabethan Stage Society in 1894 Poel was able to undertake productions on a more regular basis and to broaden his range from Shakespeare to

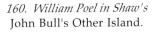

160. William Poel in Shaw's John Bull's Other Island.

Marlowe, Beaumont and Fletcher, Middleton etc. Beginning with *Twelfth Night* in 1895 he continued his crusade in the unsympathetic surroundings of halls, courtyards and lecture-rooms for a decade, ending with *Romeo and Juliet* in 1905. Apart from the works of Shakespeare and his contemporaries Poel also staged Milton's *Samson Agonistes* and possibly had his greatest triumph with the medieval *Everyman*. Although not financially viable, Poel's campaign was artistically vindicated and exerted an immediate influence on other directors, most notably Harley Granville-Barker. A fully paid-up member of the awkward squad to the very end, Poel continued to rescue long-neglected scripts into the 1920s. In 1929 he even rejected a knighthood on the grounds that "it was inconceivable that my name could be added to the long list of theatrical knights not one of whom was in sympathy with an Elizabethan method of presentation."

The most influential critic of the period, and certainly one of the most cerebral, was the Scot, William Archer (1856-1924). Having spent years of his boyhood in Norway, Archer made an early acquaintance with the works of Ibsen, whose translator and champion he became. Archer became a London drama critic in 1879, writing for several papers. His translation of Ibsen's *Pillars of Society* became in 1880 the first Ibsen play to be staged in London but it made little impression. In 1882 Archer published a study of *English Dramatists of Today*, followed by a critical, not to say hostile, account of *Irving* (1883), whom he regarded as a nugatory influence on the drama. In 1888 he published an analysis of the place of emotion in acting, *Masks or Faces?*

When Archer's translation of Ibsen's *A Doll's House* was staged in 1889 its theme aroused much hostile reaction, compounded still further by *Ghosts* and *Hedda Gabler* in 1891. In 1890 Archer published a study of Macready, in 1891 a five volume edition of Ibsen's prose dramas in translation and in 1892 a translation of *Peer Gynt*. His own collected criticism was sufficiently well regarded to appear in volume form in 1897 as *A Theatre World*, followed a decade later by Ibsen's collected works in a hefty eleven volumes.

161. The critic, Clement Scott.

As well as Ibsen Archer also promoted the work of Shaw, who acknowledged this support by featuring Archer as Mr. Gunn in *Fanny's First Play* (1911).

In 1907 Archer collaborated with Harley Granville-Barker to draw up detailed proposals for the establishment of a National Theatre (see p177) and in 1919 helped to establish the New Shakespeare Company at Stratford-upon-Avon. Archer's *The Old Drama and the New* (1923) reasserted the cause of 'new' dramatists such as T.W. Robertson, Ibsen, Shaw and Galsworthy and protested against what he saw as the indiscriminate English tendency to overvalue old plays and undervalue new ones. In 1921 Archer's own play *The Green Goddess*, a rather improbable melodrama, was staged to acclaim in the USA. When it was put on at the St. James's in 1923 it ran for 416 performances.

Clement Scott (1841-1904) of the *Daily Telegraph* headed the traditionalist school of critics and also founded and edited (1877-90) the widely-read journal *The Theatre*. A virulent opponent of 'Ibscenity', he finally went too far with the observation that "it is nearly impossible for a woman to remain pure who adopts the stage as a profession" and was sacked from the *Telegraph*.

The London visit of Andre Antoine's Theatre Libre from Paris in 1891 inspired another critic J.T. Grein (1862-1935) to found the Independent Theatre, its name chosen to signify that it intended to be independent both of the Lord Chamberlain's censorship and of the commercial pressures of the conventional theatre. The Independent made *Ghosts* its opening production, provoking Scott to denounce the work as "an open drain; a loathsome sore unbandaged; a dirty act done publicly". In 1892 the Independent Theatre launched Shaw's dramatic career by presenting his *Widowers' Houses* and in the same year staged a Poel revival of Webster's *The Duchess of Malfi*. Following the demise of the Independent in 1898, the progressivist banner was taken up by The Stage Society, established in 1899. To make use of professional actors, the Society gave performances on Sunday night when theatres were normally closed. As the Society successfully claimed that it was using a theatre as a private place it was able to stage plays like Shaw's *Mrs. Warren's Profession* (1902), which dealt with prostitution and had been refused a licence by the Lord Chamberlain.

Another Stage Society production was *Waste* (1907), which referred to abortion, by Harley Granville-Barker who gained his early training as an actor and director with Poel and with the Society. As artistic director of the Royal Court Theatre (1904-7) with J.E. Vedrenne as business manager Granville-Barker staged eleven of Shaw's plays, as well as Ibsen, Yeats, Galsworthy three new translations of Euripides and his own play *The Voysey Inheritance*. In 1910 he directed an experimental repertory season at the Duke of York's, which served as further confirmation of his belief in the need for public subsidy if the theatre was to free itself from its dependence on unchallenging conventional material. At the Savoy Theatre in 1912-14 he reached a directorial pinnacle with productions of *The Winter's Tale, Twelfth Night* and *A Midsummer Night's Dream*. which, in complete contrast to Tree's lavish

162. *Edward Gordon Craig.*

spectaculars, impressed with their fast pace, pared down simplicity, impressionistic costumes and the strength of their ensemble playing. Granville-Barker gave up the stage after divorcing Lilla McCarthy to marry a wealthy American who collaborated with him on translating Spanish plays. His posthumous fame largely rests on his influential six volumes of *Prefaces to Shakespeare* (1927-47). Even the famously egotistical Shaw judged Granville-Barker to have been "altogether the most distinguished and incomparably the most cultured person whom circumstances had driven into the theatre."

After eight years as an actor under Irving Ellen Terry's son Edward Gordon Craig (1872-1966) edited *The Page* (1898-1901) which he illustrated with his own wood-cuts. He also attended lectures by the fashionable academic painter Hubert von Herkomer. After directing small-scale, experimental projects in London Craig found the prevailing theatrical context so unsympathetic that he moved into a self-imposed Continental exile to develop his own *avant-garde* approach to lighting and stage-design. Like Shaw he found himself having to campaign through print rather than productions, publishing *The Art of the Theatre* in 1905 and *Towards a New Theatre* in 1913. In 1908 in Florence he founded a quarterly theatrical journal *The Mask* as a vehicle for his own views, writing most of its contents himself under a dozen or more pseudonyms. He later published a definitive study of *Irving* (1930). Craig took an exalted view of the role of the director, virtually reducing the actor to the level of a marionette, a posture which not unnaturally did not recommend his philosophy to actors. Rejecting the naturalism of his day, Craig looked for an abstract or ritualistic theatricality parallel to that of the Japanese *noh* theatre. Craig did design settings for a production of Ibsen's *Rosmersholm* for Eleonora Duse and worked fruitfully with Yeats in Dublin and Stanislavsky in Moscow but had little immediate influence on the London he had abandoned.

Getting Organised

Perhaps because so many of them were recruited from the ranks of the working classes and played largely to working-class audiences, music hall performers began to organise in defence of their collective interests some twenty years ahead of performers of the 'legitimate theatre', establishing a Music Hall Artists' Association as early as 1885 and, after a bruising dispute with management in 1906, creating the stronger Variety Artists' Federation which secured some slight improvements in working conditions and contractual rights.

Henry Irving served as president of the first Actors Association, formed in 1891, but both it and the Actors' Union founded in 1905 by his own son and Seymour Hicks had a short life.

There were more enduring developments on the social front. In 1889 the Grand Order of Water Rats was founded as a showbiz charity. Over the succeeding century it was to make a special contribution to schemes for the benefit of children.

The Eccentric Club was founded in 1890 by theatrical costumier Jack Harrison. Early members included both giants of music hall, like Dan Leno and George Robey, and theatrical grandees like Sir George Alexander and Sir Charles Wyndham. Initially based at No. 21 Shaftesbury Avenue, in 1914 they moved to 9

163. *Equity, the trade union for actors, was formed in 1930 by some West End performers. It now has its office in Upper St Martin's Lane.*

Ryder Street, whose previous incarnation as the Dieudonne Hotel could have provided inspiration for a hundred bedroom farces. The Water Rats also had a suite of rooms there.

The Royal Academy of Dramatic Art, founded in 1904, was largely the initiative of Beerbohm Tree and was initially housed in Her Majesty's Theatre before finding a permanent home on Gower Street in Bloomsbury. The Central School of Speech and Drama, founded in 1906 by the actress Elsie Fogerty (1866-1945), had its first home in the Royal Albert Hall. In 1911 actress Italia Conti (1874-1946) was asked to train children for the fairy play *Where the Rainbow Ends* and went on to found the stage school named after her and to devote the rest of her life to it.

The London Academy of Music and Dramatic Arts (LAMDA) had been founded as long before as 1861. Based usually in west London, it moved to Earl's Court in 1946 and then in 2005 it found larger premises in Talgarth Road. In addition, the Macowan Theatre in Logan Place, Earl's Court was specially built for productions.

First Knight

*" a romantic actor, highly intellectual, of magnetic personality and originality
of conception, but of mannered elocution and gait."*
Oxford Companion to English Literature

Henry Irving (John Henry Brodribb) 1838-1905), the first British actor to be knighted, was born remote from the London theatre in every sense and was obliged to escape both his native Cornwall and the disapproval of his strict Methodist family. After initial refuge in a London counting-house, he made his professional stage debut at eighteen and worked the provinces for the following decade, allegedly portraying some 428 characters on stage in just his first three years. In 1867 Irving acted for the first time opposite Ellen Terry (1847-1928), in Garrick's *Katharine and Petruchio*, an abbreviated version of *The Taming of the Shrew*. It was another comic role in 1870, however, as Digby Grant, that first signalled Irving as an exceptional talent.

Confirmation of Irving's greatness came in 1871 with the agreement of H.L. Bateman *(see p98)* to present *The Bells*, a version of *Le Juif Polonais* by the lawyer Leopold Lewis, which Irving himself had further honed and polished after securing the rights for himself. The plot involves murder, deception, guilt, fear of discovery, hypnotism, delusions and retribution. Irving made the guilt-ridden burgomaster Mathias a trademark role for the rest of his professional life but the audience at the half-empty Lyceum that November night was as much mystified by the play as mesmerized by Irving. When the final curtain fell a stunned silence was followed by rounds of applause which brought up the curtain to reveal Lewis wringing Irving's hand in congratulation. The editor of the *Daily Telegraph*, who had been in the audience, sent

164. Sir Henry Irving.

instructions to his drama critic Clement Scott – "Tonight I have seen a great actor at the Lyceum – a great actor. There was a poor house. Write about him so that everyone shall know he is great." On the way home by brougham at Hyde Park Corner Irving's wife, Florence asked "Are you going to make a fool of yourself like this all your life?" Irving stopped the cab, got out and never spoke to Florence again, although the fiction of a marital union was maintained. In 1872 Irving moved into a flat at 15A Grafton Street, just off New Bond Street. This was to be his home until 1899. The relationship that developed between Irving and Ellen Terry was managed with the utmost discretion.

Irving repeated the secret guilt motif in an 1873 adaptation of Bulwer-Lytton's novel *Eugene Aram (see p93)* and mesmerized in the name part in a revival (1873) of the same author's *Richelieu*. Irving's playing of Hamlet (1874) as a figure of acute sensitivity was too far from the accepted norm to be immediately accepted as the classic portrayal that it was. What the public came to expect of Irving was the sinister, as in Philip II in Tennyson's *Queen Mary* (1876) or the villainous, as in *Richard III* (1877).

In 1878 Irving bought out the management interest that Bateman's widow *(see p98)* had retained in the Lyceum. Henceforth that theatre became a sacred shrine to the arts of Thespis, with Irving self-cast in the role of magus. The intellectual critic J.T. Grein *(see p157)* hailed Irving's Lyceum as "the embodiment of all that is refined, sumptuous and noble in English histrionic art".

Irving opened with a revival of *Hamlet,* casting Ellen Terry as Ophelia. There followed a series of shared triumphs – Shylock and Portia (1879), Iago and Desdemona (1881), Benedick and Beatrice (1882), although they failed as Romeo and Juliet (1882), perhaps already too larger-than-life to be convincing as nerve-jangled young lovers. In 1893 they had another great success with Tennyson's seldom-attempted *Becket* (1884). George Bernard Shaw, then working as a drama critic, was forcefully struck by the contrast and complementarity of their characters – "she, all brains and sympathy, scattering them everywhere and on everybody; he, all self, concentrating that self on his stage as on a pedestal ... Everything went from her and everything came to him."

Passionate as an actor, Irving was painstaking as a producer. He commissioned special music from Sir Arthur Sullivan (*Macbeth*) and Edward

165. *The Lyceum in 2006, home to the long-running musical* The Lion King.

German (*Henry VIII*). He commissioned set designs from leading artists renowned for their scholarly credentials, such as Sir Lawrence Alma-Tadema and Sir Edward Burne-Jones. He rehearsed both lighting-effects and crowd scenes without the distracting presence of principal actors.

Irving was better placed than any other person to raise the standards of English drama but, as Shaw consistently complained, made little attempt to do so, indifferent to the larger scene – "Of the theatre at large he knew almost nothing; for he never left his own stage." Irving was obsessed with acting and devoted to the theatre but indifferent to drama, at least as literature. What mattered was not what a play contributed to the explication of the human condition but whether it had parts in it to shock or move an audience. He stuck to Shakespeare and melodrama and produced not a single new play of any significance. Irving did, however, transform the standing of actors in the regard of both the general public and the British 'establishment'. The conferment of his knighthood in July 1895 was the incontrovertible confirmation of this. During the ceremony itself the Queen, not by then known for any sweetness of temper, pronounced herself "very, very pleased" to be honouring him.

Henry Irving presented his last (1905) London season at Drury Lane but died in a Bradford hotel after performing *Becket*. His body rested for days in the Stratton Street home of his friend Baroness Angela Burdett-Coutts, reputedly once the wealthiest woman in Britain and certainly the most philanthropic, so that members of the public could pay their respects. A memorial service was held at Westminster Abbey and the body was cremated at the recently-established (1902) crematorium at Golders Green, the first there of a major celebrity. Irving's ashes were interred at the Abbey. With remarkable rapidity a fund was established which raised money on both sides of the Atlantic for the erection of a public statue. Unveiled in 1910, it was designed by the most favoured sculptor of the day, Thomas Brock, who would be knighted for sculpting the Victoria Memorial. Irving's statue stands in Charing Cross Road, opposite the Garrick Theatre and in the shadow of Britain's Valhalla, the National Portrait Gallery. Immediately adjacent is Irving Street, which appropriately leads up to the half-price ticket booth on Leicester Square.

Irving's elder son, known professionally as H. B. Irving (1870-1919), married Dorothea Baird (1875-1933) the first actress to play the name role in George Du Maurier's *Trilby* (1895). He formed his own company the year after his father's death and toured in many of his roles. Laurence Irving (1871-1914) wrote as well as acted. In 1899 Irving had indulged him by mounting his adaptation of *Robespierre* from the French at enormous expense, employing no less than 355 performers and musicians, supported by 236 technical staff and 48 administrators and assistants. Laurence drowned in a shipwreck en

166. Ellen Terry.

route to Canada. H.B. Irving's son, also Laurence (1897-1983) became a set designer and biographer of his illustrious grandfather.

Ellen Terry, born into a theatrical family, had been thrust onto the stage at nine and at seventeen made a disastrous marriage to the reclusive painter G.F. Watts, from which he declined for decades to give her legal release. Irving initially considered her charming but frivolous. Her beauty, magically captured in 1864 by the pioneering photographic portraitist Julia Margaret Cameron, was undeniable. From 1868 until 1875 Terry lived with the married architect E.W. Godwin, giving birth to two future theatrical phenomena Edith Craig and Edward Gordon Craig *(see p157)*. After Irving's death Ellen Terry completed *The Story of My Life* (1908), lectured on Shakespeare's heroines, appeared to indifferent effect in five silent films and was finally (1925) appointed DBE. Sir John Gielgud was among her many descendants.

CHAPTER TEN

War and Inter-war

Despite a conspicuous absence of governmental support or direction, much less subsidy, the theatrical world rallied to the nation's cause when war broke out in August 1914.

The conflict inevitably brought major disruptions, through shortages, through governmental interference and simply as a by-product of the general atmosphere of uncertainty. The government ordered West End theatres to close by 9.30, although it later relented to allow 10.30 closing. Train, bus and taxi services were restricted by the diversion of transport workers, trains, vehicles and horses to military purposes. This not only had an impact on potential audience attendance but significantly limited possibilities for London-based touring companies.

Acting talent was in no way officially recognised as an asset essential to the maintenance of national morale, whose possessors might better soldier on where they were. Beerbohm Tree reckoned that by 1915 some 1,500 actors had joined up. Members of the theatrical profession served in a range of capacities. The novelist and dramatist Arnold Bennett (1867-1931) was Director of Propaganda for the Ministry of Information. Drama critic Ashley Dukes (1885-1959) rose from private to major in the Machine Gun Corps. Robert Winthrop (Chaim Reeven Weintrop) (1896-1968) served in the Royal Field Artillery, survived gassing and retrospectively revenged himself on a malicious sergeant-major by adopting his name to become Bud Flanagan. Playwright Guy Du Maurier (1865-1916), elder brother of the actor Gerald Du Maurier and author of *An Englishman's Home (see p142)* was killed on active service, although over fifty. Actress Susan

Richmond, who had been taken on by Tree and under-studied on Broadway, gave up a promising career to became a VAD nurse in France for over a year before being recruited into Lena Ashwell's troupe *(see p162)* touring around Abbeville to entertain British troops.

Vesta Tilley donned a succesion of well-cut uniforms to persuade the music hall masses to join up. Prussian-born strongman Eugen Sandow, physical training adviser to the Territorial Army and King George V, lay down

167. Eugen Sandow, strong man used to persuade army volunteers.

162

on a music hall stage and allowed volunteers off to the front to march across his chest. Ivor Novello *(see p166)* supplied troops with a sentimental anthem in *Keep the Home Fires Burning*. Marie Lloyd, George Robey and dozens of other music hall artists threw themselves into the task of entertaining troops in camps at home and abroad and, at even greater emotional cost, doing what they could to liven the spirits of the disabled, disfigured, blinded and gassed. Lena Ashwell (Lena Margaret Pocock) (1872-1957) organised no less than twenty-five companies to entertain troops in France and later Germany and eventually became one of the first female recipients of the newly-instituted Order of the British Empire.

In 1916 belated recognition of such efforts led the Navy and Army Canteen Board to establish an Entertainments Department to help make appropriate venues and facilities available to touring companies visiting garrisons, camps and depots. In the same year, however, the government slapped an Entertainments Tax on theatre takings. On New Year's Day 1917 Harry Lauder received a telegram to inform him that his son, Captain John Lauder, had been killed in action three days previously. His response was to take a touring company and thousands of packets of cigarettes to the Western Front and to launch the Harry Lauder Million Pound Fund for Maimed Men, Scottish Soldiers and Sailors.

Despite the fact that theatre advertising was officially deemed non-essential and paper for posters was unavailable, London theatres had no trouble finding audiences. On any evening there were tens of thousands of servicemen on leave in the capital, seeking diversion and having every inclination to spend their pay and very little incentive to save it. Many of these were foreign soldiers, some with little or no English, others from English-speaking countries which did not share British assumptions about class and culture. Music, glamour and spectacle were self-evidently best fitted to surmount such barriers. The eventual recruitment of five million men into the services ensured full employment on the home front and, over the course of the war,

real wages rose by about a fifth, giving London's own large population of workers spare cash to spend.

Given the nature of what they offered – songs, skits and patter – music halls were able to adjust their programmes much faster than theatres, although a play to boost recruiting, entitled *The Man Who Stayed Behind* was on the boards before the end of 1914. This was followed by a flow of hastily-drafted patriotic and propandist pieces whose simplistic messages were summarised in such titles as *The Invisible Foe, The Enemy in Our Midst, Loyalty, The War Baby, Brave Women Who Wait, Home on Leave*. Tree, more thoughtfully, as might be expected, revived an historical pageant about Sir Francis Drake. But it soon became apparent to theatre managements that while Hun-hating might accord with the popular mood the real demand was for undemanding escapism, perhaps spiced with a little naughtiness. *A Little Bit Of Fluff*, which opened at the Criterion in 1915, ran for 1,241 performances. The musical *Chu Chin Chow*, which opened in 1916, set a record of 2,238 performances, which was not to be surpassed for forty years. Given the prevalence of packed houses, managers might have been forgiven for failing to notice an ultimately ominous trend, a continuing increase in the number and size of cinemas, playing to equally packed audiences.

At the Old Vic Lilian Baylis trod her own distinctly individualistic path, beginning in 1914 a project, unprecedented in the history of theatre anywhere, to present the entire works of Shakespeare, and at popular prices. The enterprise took until 1923 to complete but already, by the end of the war, the Old Vic had become established in general regard as one of London's leading theatres. Recognition of its peculiar virtues was affirmed by the receipt of substantial charitable donations and grants from the City Parochial Foundation and the Carnegie United Kingdom Trust. In the closing weeks of the war the hundredth anniversary of the opening of the Old Vic was marked by a visit from Queen Mary and the Princess Royal.

Time itself took its own casualties. Tree died

in 1916, Sir George Alexander in 1917. Their passing signalled the ending of the dominance of the old-style actor-manager. With West End theatre rents and production costs quadrupling over the course of the war years those that survived, like Martin-Harvey, would be forced to seek salvation touring the provinces or the Empire. The post-war theatre - few guessed that inter-war would be more accurate - faced new challenges, notably the cinema, and would pretty much try to meet them in the old way.

New Theatres ....

While British industry was entering a prolonged period of disruption and contraction in what were variously referred to as 'the regions' or less blandly as 'distressed areas', London throughout the inter-war period prospered from its expanding service sector, a massive boom in house-building and the extension and upgrading of its transport system with the Underground pushing out into the suburbs. On its periphery the metropolis benefited from the new growth industries of the period, symbolized in the east by the great Ford plant at Dagenham and in the west by the Art Deco factories of Firestone, Gillette and Hoover. Given London's relative economic buoyancy there were still investors for the building of new West End theatres, although some foundered swiftly, especially with the advent of the 'talkies' in 1928. The Carlton, opened in 1927, was converted into a cinema in 1929. The Dominion, opened in 1929, made the conversion in 1931.

The old Middlesex Music Hall, at the northern end of Drury Lane, reopened in 1919 as the Winter Gardens Theatre. Dominated by vehicles for the musical comedy star Leslie Henson (1891-1957), it also introduced Londoners to the music of George Gershwin and the rumbustious talents of Sophie Tucker and Gracie Fields.

The historically - and optimistically- named Fortune, opened in Russell Street, at the rear of Drury Lane in 1924. Despite its favourably central location, with seating for only 424, it was almost bound to struggle commercially and by the 1930s was being used by amateur companies.

168. Gracie Fields.

The Piccadilly in Denman Street, opened in 1928 with a musical, then became a cinema before reverting to theatre in 1929 with a revival of *The Student Prince*, found a precarious viability taking over long runs at reduced prices and closed on the outbreak of war in 1939.

The Duchess, in Catherine Street by Drury Lane, opened in 1929, also seated less than five hundred but survived thanks to being taken over for their own plays by J.B. Priestley *(see p168)* and Emlyn Williams *(see p168)*.

1930 was remarkable for the opening of no less than four new venues. The Cambridge Theatre in Seven Dials enjoyed some success with French plays and French touring companies. The Phoenix, off Charing Cross Road, opened with Noel Coward's *Private Lives* and remained associated with him. The Prince Edward in Old Compton Street, Soho was used

ARTHUR RISCOE. VIOLA TREE. BOBBY HOWES. OLGA LIN O. ALFRED DRAYTO

169. *The stylish entrance to the new Saville Theatre in Shaftesbury Avenue*

for musicals, revue and pantomime before becoming the London Casino which, despite its name, was a combined restaurant and cabaret. The Whitehall, just off Trafalgar Square, with 628 seats managed to survive on straight plays. In the same year the Savoy was rebuilt.

Three theatres opened in 1931. The Saville on Shaftesbury Avenue followed the musical comedy and revue formula. The Windmill, in Great Windmill Street, Soho, reversed the apparently ordained order of things, being converted to a theatre from a cinema of 1910. Seating just 326, it found a winning formula by presenting non-stop (2.30-11.00) variety, featuring nude tableaux punctuated by stand-up comedians. The Westminster, in Palace Street, Victoria was another conversion, from chapel via cinema and, despite seating only six hundred, managed to survive with an intellectually challenging series of pieces by Pirandello, Granville-Barker, Eugene O'Neill, Dorothy L. Sayers and T.S. Eliot.

In 1931-32 Sadler's Wells was completely rebuilt to become exclusively a home for opera

170. *An early 20th-century view of a Tudorised Sadler's Wells. It was rebuilt in the 1930s.*

171. Ivor Novello.

172. Charles Laughton.

and ballet *(see p176)*. In 1933 the Open Air Theatre opened in Regent's Park to become a permanent feature of the London summer scene, often featuring Shakespeare's comedies.

... Old Theatre

The new breed of commercially-driven managers sought long runs to maximise returns on their investment in sets and costume. Lavish musicals in exotic settings could pay off handsomely, as in the case of *Rose Marie* (1925), *The Desert Song* (1926), *The Student Prince* (1926) and *White Horse Inn* (1931). Actor and composer Ivor Novello (David Ivor Novello Davies) (1893-1951), turned out four successive musical hits for Drury Lane - *Glamorous Night* (1935), *Careless Rapture* (1936), *Crest of the Wave* (1937) and *The Dancing Years* (1939). The critic Ivor Brown congratulated him

for being able to "wade through tosh with the straightest face ... Both as actor and as author he can pursue adventures too preposterous even for the films...".

C.B. Cochran (1872-1951) was something of a breed apart, eclectic enough to undertake projects ranging from Ibsen, ballet and boxing to circus, rodeo and roller-skating, he possessed the bravura style of a true showman, which enabled him to transcend the pursuit of mere profit. He also knew quality and commissioned designs from set-designers of quality, including Oliver Messel, and Rex Whistler. Famed for revues, 'Cocky' also put on the first London showing of a play by Eugene O'Neill, which doubtless helped him go bust for a second time. In 1925 he published the first of four volumes of memoirs, aptly entitled *The Secrets of a Showman*. A fruitful collaboration with the rising talent of Noel Coward recouped his position. In 1929 he presented another of his essays into highbrow territory Sean O'Casey's *The Silver Tassie*, featuring a young Charles Laughton, a set by the Bohemian portraitist Augustus John and direction by the Canadian actor Raymond Massey (1896-1983).

Plays with a small cast and a single set obviously represented a much safer bet than big musicals. Social comedies about the 'Bright Young Things' with whom the Twenties were synonymous, fitted the bill, although setting one in a smart London apartment in front of an audience, many of whom would be going home to just such an apartment, demanded high standards of accuracy in set-dressing. The same economic parameters favoured the murder mystery set in a country house or similarly closed environment (convent, luxury liner, Oxbridge college etc.). The ultra-prolific, free-spending novelist Edgar Wallace (1875-1932) assiduously re-cycled his thrillers for the stage and in 1928 had three in performance simultaneously.

'Problem plays' likewise tended to make modest demands in terms of setting and costume. *A Bill of Divorcement* (1921) by the ambiguously-named Clemence Dane (Winifred Ashton) (1888-1965) dealt sympathetically with the predicament of divorce on grounds of insanity and made so much money for the author that she could give up acting as Diana Cortis and write plays about Shakespeare and the Brontés, novels about the theatre and a history of the Covent Garden area. An excellent sculptor, she also made the bust of Ivor Novello which stands in the foyer of Drury Lane. Galsworthy's last important play *Escape* (1927) applauded characters who defied the law by helping a convict on the run. *A Sleeping Clergyman* (1933) by James Bridie (Osborne Henry Mavor) (1888-1951) drew on his training as a doctor to confront issues of medical ethics. Drama critic and ex-manager of Dublin's Abbey Theatre St. John Ervine (1883-1971) addressed the issues of working women and birth-control in '*Robin's Wife* (1937).

173. *Terence Rattigan.*

A resolute determination to avoid any serious or problematic issue was the consistent hallmark of the hugely popular series of 'Aldwych farces' crafted by Ben Travers (1886-1980) between 1925 and 1933, starting with *A Cuckoo in the Nest* and including *Rookery Nook* (1926) and *Thark* (1927), which also became great favourites with amateur companies. Frederick Lonsdale (1881-1954) exploited a less absurdist vein in equally popular comedies of contemporary manners such as *Aren't We All?* (1923) and T*he Last of Mrs. Cheyney* (1925), reflecting the lives of the wealthy, worldly and well-bred who were assumed to reflect the aspirations of the average West End theatre-goer.

Terence Rattigan (1911-71) had a huge hit with his second effort, a light comedy *French Without Tears* (1936), which ran for over a thousand performances. This was matched by *Dear Octopus* (1938) by Dodie Smith (1896-1990) starring Marie Tempest as the matriarch presiding over the reunion of her 'octopus'

174. *J. B. Priestley (right) with novelist Horace Walpole.*

family, it opened in 1938 and was still running when war broke out in September 1939.

J.B. Priestley (1894-1984) began his translation to dramatist with a stage version (1931) of his best-selling novel (1929) about a travelling amateur troupe *The Good Companions. Dangerous Corner* (1932) explored the role of chance in determining a personal tragedy. *I Have Been Here Before* and *Time and the Conways* (both 1937) exploited his fascination with the supposed circularity of time and were followed by a rollicking Yorkshire farce *When We Are Married* (1938). By then his earnings from the stage were over £30,000 a year, enough to buy an entire avenue of the 'semis' in the burgeoning suburbs which doubled the built-up area of London in the years between the wars.

Welsh actor-writer Emlyn Williams (1905-87) ratcheted up the routine whodunnit to an altogether more scary level of psychological intimidation with *A Murder Has Been Arranged* (1930) and *Night Must Fall* (1935), which featured a psychopathic killer who carries around with him the head of his last victim. The versatile

175. *Emlyn Williams.*

Williams also demonstrated his range with a farce *The Late Christopher Bean* (1933), a drama about Shakespeare's drama, *Spring 1600* (1934) and a semi-autobiographical study of a Welsh miner liberated by a dedicated teacher, *The Corn is Green* (1935) which ran for two years with himself in the lead role.

The most prolific and versatile creative new talent of the inter-war period was generally conceded to be Noel Coward (1899-1973), a youthful master of deft comedies distinguished by brittle wit and implicit sexually knowingness, starting with *The Young Idea* (1923) and including *Fallen Angels, Hay Fever* (both 1925) and *Private Lives* (1930), in which Coward himself starred memorably opposite Gertrude Lawrence. In retrospect his much more intense exploitation of an anguished mother-son relationship in *The*

Vortex (1924) may be read as autobiographical in inspiration and its dark 'secret' revealed not as drug-taking but homosexuality. In 1925, when he had five productions running simultaneously in London, Coward wrote his first revue for C. B. Cochran *On With the Dance*. *Cavalcade* (1931) was an unashamedly patriotic parade of recent British history, subsequently reprised on film as a war-time morale-booster.

There was little encouragement for dramatists to analyse the war, on which there was a general cultural moratorium for a decade. *The Conquering Hero* (1924), written by the Manchester Guardian drama critic Allan Monkhouse (1858-1936) tells the story of a reluctant recruit, humiliated in battle, who returns to the irony of a triumphal welcome. Somerset Maugham's *For Services Rendered* (1932) was really about post-war disillusionment. *Journey's End* (1928), focused realistically on the reactions of a small group of men just before an attack, provided an early leading role for a youthful Laurence Olivier (1907-89) and immediately made the reputation of its author, R.C. Sheriff (1896-1975). Initially presented on a Sunday evening by the Stage Society, it was taken to the Savoy Theatre by

176. Noel Coward – 'The Master'.

177. R. C. Sheriff's first and abiding love was rowing – in fact he began writing plays in the hope of raising funds for the Kingston Rowing Club, of which he was captain. He is seen here coaching the Kingston School rowing club, to which he bequeathed a substantial sum when he died.

178. Dame Sybil Thorndike.

179. Peggy Ashcroft as Rosalind in As You Like It *in 1932.*

another of its leading players, Maurice Browne (1881-1955). The play ran for two years and was widely translated. Noel Coward's *Post-Mortem* (1930) was not performed until 1968.

Shakespeare

The Bard also generally proved to be safe, yet still gave scope for experiment and for displaying the extraordinary talents of an extraordinary generation of players including Sybil Thorndike (1882-1976), Edith Evans (1888-1976), Ralph Richardson (1902-84), Flora Robson (1902-84), Peggy Ashcroft (1907-91) and Laurence Olivier. In 1930 there were no less than four West End productions of *Hamlet* on offer, as well as Richard III and a sensational *Othello* starring Peggy Ashcroft and the multi-talented Afro-American Paul Robeson (1898-1976). An outstanding American football player and a graduate of Columbia Law School, Robeson had burst onto the English stage as Joe in the London staging of *Showboat* (1928) when he made *Ol' Man River* his lifelong personal anthem.

John Gielgud (1904-2000) revealed not only an elegant and expressive stage presence but also a precocious talent for direction. Having played under Granville-Barker in 1921, he had his first London success at twenty-one in *The Cherry Orchard*. Instantly acclaimed for the clarity of his speech in his first Shakespearean role at the Old Vic in 1929, he showed his gift for comedy as Jack Worthing in a 1930 production of *The Importance of Being Earnest*. In 1932 he directed *Romeo and Juliet* for the Oxford University Dramatic Society, a version which he revised and reprised at the New Theatre in 1935 with Olivier and Edith Evans to achieve a record 186 performances. In 1932 he directed a gorgeously-costumed production of Daviot's *Richard of Bordeaux*. In 1934 he directed and starred in a much-praised *Hamlet*. After further triumphs in *The Seagull* (1936) and *The Three Sisters* (1937), he directed the remarkable 1938-9 Queen's Theatre season, co-ordinating the contributions of Angela Baddeley (1904-76), Michael Redgrave (1908-85), Anthony Quayle (1913-) and Alec Guinness (1914-2000).

Of the established figures suave Gerald Du Maurier (1873-1934) was the model, one might say modal, actor of the day. He began his career under Forbes-Robertson and Tree, with whom

180. Ralph Richardson and Edith Evans as Iago and Emilia in Othello, *1931.*

181. John Gielgud.

182. Gerald du Maurier and Marie Lohr.

he played a small part in *Trilby*, which had been written by his own father, the artist and writer George Du Maurier (1834-96). He established his name in the premieres of *The Admirable Crichton* and *Peter Pan* and came to specialise in officer class heroes like Raffles and Bulldog Drummond. He took over the management of Wyndham's in 1910 and was knighted in 1923.

Looking back from the perspective of 1967 Laurence Olivier would observe with ambiguous humility that Du Maurier had had "the most disastrous influence on my generation, because we really thought, looking at him, that it was easy; and for the first ten years of our lives in the theatre nobody could hear a word we said. We thought he was being really natural; of course he was a genius of a technician giving that appearance, that's all."

Outside the Mainstream

In 1918 the happily-named Nigel Playfair (1874-1934) took over that notoriously flawed enterprise, the Lyric, Hammersmith and followed a strategy that looked anything but safe to transform it into both an artistic beacon and a commercially viable business. Playfair, an experienced actor, opened with a specially-commissioned Christmas entertainment, *Make Believe*, which was the first stage piece attempted by A.A. Milne (1882-1956), who was to inherit Barrie's mantle for whimsy. Playfair's breakthrough came with his 1920 imaginative revival of Gay's *The Beggar's Opera,* staged on a single stylised set by the brilliant but short-lived Claude Lovat Fraser (1890-1921), which managed to reconcile modernist motifs with an authentic Georgian feel. The production ran for an unprecedented 1,463 performances and did

183. Norman MacDermott, founder of the Everyman Theatre at Hampstead.

1925 presented twenty-six plays by Shakespeare's contemporaries and Restoration successors. Enjoying the enthusiastic support of many actors and actresses, the Society also showcased the potential of its two permanent but adaptable sets.

The Everyman Theatre at Hampstead, originally a drill hall for Volunteer riflemen, was converted to a theatre in 1920 under Norman MacDermott (1890-1977) and enjoyed six years of glory with eight Shaw revivals, plays by Ibsen, Pirandello and O'Neill and Coward's *The Vortex*, which transferred to the West End. After 1929 the Everyman was used intermittently by students until its conversion to an art house cinema in 1947.

Initially opened in 1925, with seating for 96 on the top floor of a warehouse in Floral Street, Covent Garden, the Gate Theatre enjoyed its first success a year later with *From More to Midnight*, translated from the German by Ashley Dukes. After mounting thirty-two productions in two years the Gate relocated to Villiers Street, Charing Cross to occupy part of Gattis'-Under-the-Arches. The company continued to present challenging material as well as witty revues, starring Hermione Gingold and pieces which transferred to commercial theatres, such as *Oscar Wilde*, starring Robert Morley.

The Barnes Theatre, also opened in 1925, attracted attention with a stage version of *Tess of the D'Urbervilles* prepared by Thomas Hardy himself, succeeded by Chekhov's *Uncle Vanya*, directed by the wayward Russian genius Theodore Komisjarevsky (1882-1954), who went on to direct Gielgud in *Three Sisters* and Charles Laughton in Gogol's *The Government Inspector*.

The Arts Theatre opened in Great Newport Street, off St. Martin's Lane in 1927. Seating 327, it was intended for the production of unlicensed and experimental plays for audiences consisting of subscribing members. Several of its productions transferred to commercial theatres, most notably Gordon Daviot's *Richard of Bordeaux* (1932).

The Mercury Theatre at Notting Hill Gate was opened in 1933 by Ashley Dukes in a former

much to reawaken interest in Restoration and eighteenth-century texts, enabling Playfair to present revivals of Congreve, Farquhar, Goldsmith and Sheridan and, for the first time since 1768, Isaac Bickerstaffe's *Lionel and Clarissa* (1925), as well as staging Chekhov. He was able to draw on such rising talents as Edith Evans, Charles Laughton and John Gielgud as well as presenting Ellen Terry's last stage appearance. Fraser was succeeded as Playfair's designer by such talents as Charles Ricketts and Doris Zinkeisen. Playfair's achievement was recognized within a decade by the conferment of a knighthood (1928). Following his withdrawal from theatre in 1933 the Lyric was used only occasionally for more than a decade.

The Phoenix Society, constituted in 1919 as an offshoot of the Stage Society *(see p157)*, had by

184. The Byfield Hall at Barnes, which became in 1925, the Barnes Theatre under the direction of Philip Ridgeway. The business manager was the 17-year-old Hugh 'Binkie' Beaumont. Here was produced the first performance of Hardy's own adaptation of Tess of the Durbevilles, *starring the young Gwen Ffrangcon-Davies.*

185. The former Mercury Theatre at Notting Hill Gate.

186. *Tyrone Guthrie, directed at the Old Vic in the 1930s. (see p. 176)*

187. *Alec Guinness appeared as Hamlet at the Old Vic in 1938.*

Congregational church Sunday School building. The purchase was funded by Dukes' earnings from *A Man with a Load of Mischief*. Intended as a showcase for new and uncommercial plays, it also served as a base for the ballet company run by his wife, Marie Rambert, thus becoming the first ever permanent home of ballet in England. The co-presence of the two was significant. In 1938 critic Arthur Haskell praised the Mercury for showing 'that a dancing school must be something more than a physical-training ground; it must be a cultural centre.' On the dramatic side Haskell also recognised that whereas large theatres with large overheads could not afford to take too many risks a miniature one had to do so in order to survive because it could not compete with commercial giants on their terms. In 1935 the first London production of T.S. Eliot's *Murder in the Cathedral* ran for 2225 nights before transferring to the West End. In 1937 came the first London showing of Auden and Isherwood's *The Ascent of F.6*.

The energetic Lena Ashwell, who had managed the Kingsway Theatre in Holborn, attempted to replicate her war-time efforts in organising entertainment for the sort of people who wouldn't normally think of going to a West End theatre. In 1925 she based herself in Westbourne Grove at the Bijou Theatre, where she had made her own stage debut with Tree in 1891, and which she re-named the Century. From here Ashwell attempted to bring drama into the suburbs. Having absorbed Irving's conviction that the theatre must be a spiritual rather than merely just a commercial, force in life, she skilfully enlisted the support of London's mayors to get permission to use town halls and public baths for performances on payment of a merely nominal fee. She also used the Century to present her own adaptations of Dostoevsky's *Crime and Punishment* and R.L. Stevenson's *Dr. Jekyll and Mr. Hyde*. The outreach scheme enjoyed initial success but was crushed by the introduction of a government entertainment' tax in 1929, so she gave up the stage to write her autobiography, *Myself a Player* (1936).

At the Old Vic Lilian Baylis continued to work herself and her staff and actors hard, paying but poorly, stretching shoe-string budgets and gathering plaudits for her extraordinary achievement. In 1923 the theatre received another royal visit to mark the tercentenary of the publication of the First Folio. In 1924 Oxford made her only the second woman outside the university itself to receive an honorary M.A. In 1929 she was appointed Companion of Honour. In 1931-2 Lilian Baylis undertook the complete reconstruction of Sadler's Wells to make it a home for an opera company which eventually became the English National Opera and a ballet company, led by Ninette de Valois, which would eventually become the Royal Ballet. At the Old Vic Tyrone Guthrie (1900-71) presented Charles Laughton (1933) and Emlyn Williams (1937) in *Measure for Measure*. Guthrie's 1937 *Hamlet* with Olivier later played at Elsinore and in 1938 he directed Alec Guinness in a modern dress version. At Christmas 1937 and 1938 he presented *A Midsummer Night's Dream* with the ballet dancer Robert Helpmann as Oberon and music by Mendelssohn.

By the time of her death in 1937 Lilian Baylis had made the Old Vic the 'National Theatre' in fact if not in name.

Amateurs

The British Drama League was founded in 1919 by Geoffrey Whitworth (1883-1951), supported by Lena Ashwell, to promote the development of Theatre. Its aims included the foundation of a National Theatre *(see p177)*, the introduction of drama into the school curriculum and the promotion of public support for the arts. It also accumulated a large collection of play-scripts, including a bequest from William Archer *(see p156)* and promoted research into theatre history.

Amateur companies proliferated across the nation in the post-war period, perhaps encouraged by the fact that many ex-servicemen had discovered an unsuspected talent (or at least passion) by taking part in a concert party to entertain their comrades or a play at one of the ten 'garrison theatres' imaginatively devised by

188. *The first Questors Theatre in an old Catholic church in Ealing, shortly before demolition in 1958. It was replaced by the present building.*

repertory pioneer Basil Dean (1888-1978). Although amateur dramatic groups were more prominent in the provinces London did have a few notable companies. The Tavistock Repertory Company, founded in 1932, was led by Duncan Marks and housed at the Mary Ward Settlement, Tavistock Square. Questors Theatre was founded in 1929 by Alfred Emmet and in 1933 adapted a disused chapel in Mattock Lane, Ealing for its productions.

Lena Ashwell's theatre, renamed the Twentieth Century in 1936, was used by the local Notting Hill Players and amateur groups from the D.H. Evans and Harrod's department stores.

In the 1930s a left-wing amateur group, the St. Pancras People's Theatre, acquired a converted church hall in Britannia Street, King's Cross and opened it in 1936 as the Unity Theatre. Their brief sojourn there was notable for Paul Robeson playing the lead in Ben Bengal's *Plant in the Sun*. Eighteen months later the company moved to a small theatre for two hundred in Goldington Street, St. Pancras. Their experimental work included a documentary about striking London bus-drivers and a political pantomime *Babes in the Wood*. In 1938 they presented the first play by Bertolt Brecht to be seen in London, *Senora Carrer's Rifles*.

A National Theatre

The story of the creation of London's Royal National Theatre could provide enough material not just for a play but for a saga - interpolated by farce. The aspiration to establish a national theatre goes back at least as far as David Garrick. A concrete proposition first emerged in 1848 when the publisher Effingham Wilson suggested that a theatre and drama school should be built, not in London, but, in deference to Shakespeare's standing as "the world's greatest moral teacher", in Stratford-upon-Avon. Supporters recruited to the cause included the playwright and MP Edward Bulwer Lytton, Henry Irving and Alfred Lyttelton. In 1879 the poet and influential literary critic Matthew Arnold was converted after seeing the Comedie Française for the first time. Arnold's essay *The French Play in London*, which appeared in the influential periodical *The Nineteenth Century*, proclaimed with all the zeal of a convert that "The theatre is irresistible, organise the theatre!"

It was not until 1907, however, that a detailed scheme, including financial estimates, was finally advanced by the critic William Archer and the director Harley Granville-Barker. A Shakespeare Memorial National Theatre Committee was formed and raised £100,000 within five years. In 1913 a Private Member's Bill was introduced in the House of Commons proposing that this sum should be topped up from the public exchequer to enable the venture to go ahead. The Bill was passed and a site was bought on Gower Street in Bloomsbury. The outbreak of the First World War put a halt to all idea of immediate further action.

The cause was then taken up by the British Drama League. The Bloomsbury site was sold in favour of a Kensington location opposite the Victoria and Albert Museum. Sir Edwin Lutyens drew up plans for a suitably imposing building and George Bernard Shaw laid the foundation stone. In an era of economic depression, however, neither public funds nor private generosity became available to enable building to begin. (In more recent years the empty site was used to build the Ismaili Centre opposite the V & A Museum.) Instead supporters of the Old Vic theatre, which had assumed the *de facto* role of presenting Shakespeare in London on a regular basis, actively opposed the campaign for a Shakespeare Memorial National Theatre. Reconciliation between the two sides during World War Two enabled a revitalised effort to enlist the support of both Parliament and, just as crucially, the London County Council, then the ruling body of the metropolis with responsibility for planning decisions. A Bill passed in 1948 allocated £1,000,000 of public money for the establishment of a national theatre on the south bank of the Thames. Architect Brian O'Rorke was commissioned to produce a fresh design. In 1951 the then Princess Elizabeth, standing in for the ailing George VI, laid a third foundation stone – in what afterwards turned out to be the wrong place.

Further delay was finally ended by the appointment of Laurence Olivier as the National Theatre's first Director. It was decided that a National Theatre company should be formed forthwith and operate from the Old Vic until its own purpose-built home should be completed on the proposed South Bank site, now confirmed as a significant cultural location by the building of the Royal Festival Hall as a permanent legacy of the 1951 Festival of Britain.

190. The National Theatre in 2006.

189. Sir Laurence Olivier as Justice Shallow in
Henry IV, pt. 2

The first National Theatre season, at the Old Vic in 1963, began with *Hamlet* and was followed by such highlights as Olivier's *Othello*, Peter Shaffer's *The Royal Hunt of the Sun* and a revival of Farquhar's *The Recruiting Officer*.

Meanwhile, back at the drawing-board, responsibility for the design of a suitable permanent home had been reassigned to Denys Lasdun, a proponent of the then fashionable 'brutalist' school of architecture. His brief included the requirement to accommodate no less than three theatres – one with an open stage (the Olivier), another with a proscenium arch (the Lyttelton) and a 'black box' (the Cottesloe) for experimental works, plus generous allocations of space for foyers, dressing rooms,

workshops, restaurants and state of the art stage technology. Rising construction costs in an era of rapid inflation inflicted further delays on completion. In 1973 Olivier gave way as Director to Peter Hall, creator of the Stratford-based Royal Shakespeare Company. Controversies arose as publicly-funded regional theatres and West End commercial managements criticised the subsidies provided to National Theatre productions. Critics could with justice point out that the National had gone beyond its original brief of presenting a repertoire of classics to make deals with commercial theatre companies which could siphon off the bulk of any profits. Tainted by reality and obliged to open in phases in 1976-7, the National Theatre under Peter Hall's guidance nevertheless managed to establish itself as the Blue Riband of the British theatre, rivalled only by the Royal Shakespeare Company. The Olivier was inaugurated with a production of Marlowe's *Tamburlane*, directed by Peter Hall, who was knighted in 1977.

CHAPTER ELEVEN

People's Theatre?

"In London, audiences have notoriously resisted the will of the critics."
Encyclopaedia Britannica

On the day war broke out the BBC broadcast an official announcement that "All places of entertainment will be closed until further notice." George Bernard Shaw wrote to the newspapers to denounce the stupidity of this bureaucratic knee-jerk reaction, pointing out that, apart from the obvious implications for theatrical employment and civilian morale, on any evening for the foreseeable future London would be crowded with thousands of young servicemen on leave and without any other legitimate diversion open to them they would simply throng into public houses, drink to excess and generally make a nuisance of themselves. Whether or not Shaw's argument carried any force the absolute ban was lifted within a week.

Calculations in Whitehall weighed the chances of a direct hit on a theatre or cinema, possibly causing up to two thousand casualties, against the certainty that the congregation of two thousand theatre-goers meant a saving of the energy which would otherwise have been used heating a thousand or more homes for the evening. In the event the Shaftesbury, Queen's and Little Theatre were all completely destroyed in the blitz and the Duke of York's, Royal Court and Old Vic severely damaged. But none of these blows occurred during a performance. As the writer and Auxiliary Fireman William Sansom observed,

"night opening in the West End was a matter of permission. However, this was usually granted, although concern was felt in some quarters at the danger of large congregations assembled under bombardment. Westminster, with the greatest concentration of theatres and cinemas in England, was extraordinarily fortunate in this respect. There were no major disasters at places of entertainment ....".

Evening performances were re-scheduled to begin at six and end by nine. Donald Wolfit (1902-68), the very last incarnation of the Victorian actor-managers, offered extracts from Shakespeare at a hundred lunch-time performances throughout the Battle of Britain. Given the hazards of travelling through the black-out, however, most suburban Londoners hurried home after work and contented themselves with a visit to their local 'flea-pit'. At Drury Lane where Ivor Novello's *The Dancing Years* had been playing to packed houses the stalls were so empty one Saturday evening that Novello invited the occupants of the gallery to come down and fill them. Early evening schedules allowed no time for theatregoers to go home to change out of their day clothes. Evening dress, formerly *de rigeur* for the dress circle and stalls, was abandoned, never to reappear.

Once the blitz got under way in September 1940 theatre attendances fell even more markedly. There were widespread closures. The Prince Edward became the Queensberry All Services Club. The Hippodrome became a rendezvous for American service personnel as The Rainbow Club. *The Dancing Years* transferred to the provinces, as did *The Corn is Green*. Playgoers in Nottingham could relish the distinctly unusual opportunity of seeing Rex

Harrison or John Gielgud in the flesh. The Old Vic played remote Kendal. Only two theatres could truthfully boast complete continuity of opening. One, famously was The Windmill ('We never clothed'). The other was the Unity, which had a topical revue on stage within forty-eight hours of the outbreak of hostilities.

As in the previous conflict many members of the theatrical profession rallied to the colours. Ex-regular officer David Niven returned from Hollywood to join the Rifle Brigade before being released to film the inspirational *The Way Ahead*. Glen Byam Shaw (1904-86) was wounded with the Royal Scots in Burma. George Devine *(see p183)* serving as a captain of artillery, also in Burma, was twice mentioned in dispatches. Lieutenant Peter Daubeny (1921-75) of the Coldstream Guards, an alumnus of the London Theatre Studio, lost an arm at Salerno. Rex Harrison served in RAF flight control. Ben Travers became a censor for the RAF attached to the Ministry of Information. Laurence Olivier joined the Fleet Air Arm and, having severely damaged or destroyed five aircraft in seven weeks was reassigned to less lethal duties before being released to make his morale-boosting film of *Henry V*. Ralph Richardson likewise earned the sobriquet of 'pranger Richardson' but still rose to the rank of Lieutenant Commander. Terence Rattigan drew on his experience of service in the RAF to write *Flarepath* (1942) about the wives of bomber crews, which ran for eighteen months. Noel Coward wrote a supernatural comedy, *Blithe Spirit* (1941), scripted, directed and starred in a stirring naval film epic *In Which We Serve* (1942) and wrote a typically understated but fervent ballad anthem for the blitzed city, *London Pride*. J.B. Priestley broadcast a series of radio essays which ranked second only to Churchill's speeches as an affirmation and clarification of national purpose. He also wrote a play about war aims for the Army Bureau of Current Affairs, *Desert Highway*, which reprised *Journey's End* in the claustrophobic setting of a stranded tank, rather than a trench. Intended for performance in camps, it transferred to The Playhouse on Northumberland Avenue in 1944. Priestley also

wrote a rather lighter piece for ENSA *(see below) How Are They at Home?*, illustrating the impact on a staid country house of a cohort of Land Army Girls

Theatre-going recovered with the ending of the blitz in May 1941. *Blithe Spirit* went into a long run, as did Agatha Christie's stereotypical country-house murder mystery *Ten Little Niggers* and the macabre comedy *Arsenic and Old Lace*. There were successful revivals of escapist musicals like *The Merry Widow* and *Lilac Time*. Rattigan's *While the Sun Shines* (1943) was unusual in actually being set in wartime London. Despite a highly implausible plot involving an earl serving in the Royal Navy as an ordinary seaman, his ex-mistress, the daughter of an impoverished duke and officers from the American and French forces, its self-authenticating references to spam, the Beveridge Report and razor-blade shortages carried it through more than a thousand performances. Esther McCracken's paean to the Home Front housewife *No Medals*, opened in October 1944, likewise ran on well into the peace. As during the Great War revue proved extremely popular, requiring no expensive sets and allowing for numerous topical references to the irritations and frustrations of wartime life. *The Dancing Years* returned from the provinces to run and run. *Sweet and Low* was predictably followed by *Sweeter and Lower*.

The V-bomb campaign of June 1944- April 1945 saw theatre attendances drop again. On one occasion, when comedian Arthur Askey was playing at the Prince's Theatre a V-1 fell on Holborn swimming baths opposite – "the theatre shook and dust from the ornate carvings on the walls and ceilings of the theatre floated down onto the audience ... The show went on."

Over the course of the war the state took control of virtually every aspect of national life, theatre included. Basil Dean, who had invented 'garrison theatres' in the Great War took over Drury Lane as the headquarters of the organisation he headed, the Entertainments National Services Association (ENSA). Despite the accusation that the acronym stood for Every

191. Sir Laurence Olivier, leader of the Old Vic season at the New Theatre in 1944-45. He gave memorable performances in Richard III *and* Lear.

impresario Prince Littler (1901-73) was by no means idle. City centre properties, self-evidently most vulnerable to aerial destruction, could often be got for giveaway prices. Littler took advantage of the situation to add to his already extensive holdings by taking over both Moss Empires and the Stoll theatre chain. He thus came to control almost half the active London theatres and also had a majority holding in the H.M. Tennent theatrical management company, headed by Hugh 'Binkie' Beaumont (1908-73). This concentration of control secured many properties against the possibility of demolition or conversion to non-theatrical uses, but also invested Littler and Beaumont with enormous influence over what was performed. Primarily astute businessmen, they naturally tended to caution and conventionality, interpreting their purpose as pleasing audiences rather than challenging them. Perhaps the most eloquent comment on their influence was the fact that by 1955 a third of London houses were hosting American plays or musicals.

Austerity
The post-war Britain of continuing shortages and bureaucratic controls was itself quite challenging enough. This social sub-text is neatly illustrated by the success of *The Chiltern Hundreds*, written by William Douglas Home (1912-) in which a by-election enables a butler to defeat a self-proclaimed socialist aristocrat. Terence Rattigan proved expert at exploiting middle-class emotional reticence in *The Winslow Boy* (1946), in which a family risks ruin over an allegation of a child's petty theft and *Separate Tables* (1954) in which an ex-officer is charged with sexual molestation. Other writers of the post-war decade included the still youthful Peter Ustinov, who specialised in whimsy, and the novelists Graham Greene and Enid Bagnold. The ensemble company led by Brian Rix found a secure niche with a run of contemporary farces which made the name of the Whitehall Theatre as synonymous with the genre as the Aldwych had been two decades previously. As austerity gradually gave way to a modest prosperity West

Night Something Awful, ENSA could draw on such established talents as Jessie Matthews and Leslie Henson and liberated such unsuspected ones as Joyce Grenfell and Tony Hancock. The highbrow end of the market was the concern of the Council for the Encouragement of Music and the Arts (CEMA) which eventually sponsored sixteen touring companies. In London it supported the Old Vic company which returned from exile in Lancashire to take up residence in the New Theatre under the supervision of Sir Bronson Albery and Tyrone Guthrie and the leadership of Olivier who, supported by Ralph Richardson, made the season of 1944-45 memorable with his own Richard III, Hotspur, Justice Shallow and Lear and presentations of *Oedipus*, Sheridan's *The Critic* and *Uncle Vanya*. In 1946 CEMA was placed on a permanent basis as the Arts Council, thus signifying the state's acceptance of the legitimacy of public subsidy for the arts, and thus reviving the notion of a National Theatre *(see p177)*.

If the state extended its influence over society throughout the war capitalism in the shape of

192. *Peter Ustinov as Sergeant Dohda in* Love in Albania, *which he also directed in 1949.*

193. *The sad remains of the Bedford Music Hall in Camden Town in the 1960s.*

End theatres benefited from block-booked coach parties from the suburbs and commuter towns whose numbers qualified them for substantial discounts on seat prices. A rollicking farce was just the ticket for such groups. Another beneficiary proved to be Agatha Christie's *The Mousetrap*, which was indifferently received on its opening in 1952 but would set a world record by still being in performance over half a century later.

The 'classics' were another safe bet, involving only modest expenditures on sets and costumes and, even more important, until 1950 qualifying for exemption from the still extant wartime Entertainments Tax. In 1949 Wolfit played a majestic Macbeth at the old Bedford music hall in Camden Town. In the same year Olivier took over management of the St. James's and memorably played opposite his then wife, Vivien Leigh in *Antony and Cleopatra*, reprising their success with Shaw's *Caesar and Cleopatra* and Tennessee Williams' *A Streetcar Named Desire*.

Beginning with *Oklahoma!* a succession of American musicals achieved hit status.

Successful British-made ripostes included Sandy Wilson's *The Boy Friend* (1953) and Julian Slade's *Salad Days* (1954), both of which became firm favourites with amateur companies, and Lionel Bart's *Oliver!* (1960).

At the Mercury Theatre Martin Browne (1900-80), Whitworth's successor as Director of the British Drama League, sought to re-establish the house's reputation as a home for verse and religious drama. *A Phoenix Too Frequent* (1946) by Christopher Fry (1907-) and *Happy as Larry* (1947) by Donagh MacDonagh (1912-68) both transferred successfully to the West End.

Another base for non-conventional work was the Old Vic Centre, created by Michel Saint-Denis in bomb-damaged premises off the Waterloo Road. Glen Byam Shaw headed its school of acting and George Devine (1910-65) its 'Young Vic' company. Despite much valuable work the Centre failed to attract support and foundered in 1951.

In 1953 the itinerant Theatre Workshop at last secured a permanent base at the Theatre Royal, Stratford East, a decayed and detached venue

194. Brendan Behan.

which, under the aggressive direction of Joan Littlewood (1914-2002) became a powerhouse of innovation. From necessity the company themselves redecorated and repaired the theatre but this also symbolised both their artisan affinities and 'can do' philosophy. Opening with *Twelfth Night*, by 1955 Theatre Workshop was already sufficiently distinguished to be invited to represent Britain at the international theatrical festival organised in Paris by UNESCO, where they reprised their Edinburgh Festival successes, Lillo's version of the anonymous Elizabethan *Arden of Feversham* and Jonson's *Volpone*. In 1956 they filled the Moscow Art Theatre to capacity. A succession of commissioned plays with working-class themes and settings then transferred to the West End on which Littlewood had so resolutely turned her back – *The Quare Fellow* (1956) and *The Hostage* (1958) by the iconoclastic Irish ex-con Brendan Behan (1923-64), Shelagh Delaney's *A Taste of Honey* (1958) and the Cockney musicals *Fings Ain't Wot They Used T'Be* (1959) by ex-con Frank Norman and Lionel Bart and *Sparrers Can't Sing* (1960) by Stephen Lewis. A climactic triumph was reached with Charles Chilton's *Oh, What a Lovely War!*

(1963) a devastating satire on the Great War in the guise of a stylised seaside concert party. The very process of West End transfer, while essential to provide funding for the Workshop's characteristic and time-consuming process of creative improvisation through rehearsal simultaneously bled it of its best talents and constantly undermined the formation of a stable ensemble company. Not the least of their losses were the talented designers John Bury and Sean Kenny.

At the Arts Theatre Alec Clunes (1912-70) had taken over in 1942 and, producing over a hundred plays in the course of a decade, had raised it to the status of a 'pocket national theatre'. Clunes' successor Peter Hall (1930-) was responsible for staging the English premiere (1955) of Samuel Beckett's *Waiting for Godot*, which left audiences bemused but ran for three hundred performances. In 1960 the Arts also staged *The Caretaker* by Harold Pinter (1930-), which transferred to the West End for a long run.

Anger
The formation of the English Stage Company was intended to provide a platform for contemporary plays by establishing a 'writers' theatre'. The moving spirits behind the venture were actor George Devine, playwright Ronald Duncan, director Tony Richardson and businessman Neville Blond. Its first season, 1956, at the Royal Court Theatre was dominated by the phenomenal success of John Osborne's *Look Back in Anger*, which is conventionally credited with inaugurating an era of 'kitchen sink' dramas turned out by 'angry young men', railing against the bourgeois world-view and its archetypal cultural manifestation the 'well-made play' on the West End stage. Osborne (1929-2006) continued to supply the Royal Court with such successes as *The Entertainer* (1957), a post-Suez allegory of imperial decline personified by a seedy music hall comedian, *Luther* (1961) in which the name role was compellingly played by a youthful Albert Finney and *Inadmissible Evidence* (1964) which provided the same sort of opportunity for Nicol Williamson.

195. George Devine, who led a new wave of playwrights at the Royal Court, Chelsea.
Photo: John Haynes.

196. John Osborne. Photo: John Haynes.

Whereas Osborne was previously an unknown Arnold Wesker (1932-) had already established a reputation at Coventry's post-war civic theatre with an autobiographical history of an East End Jewish socialist family *Chicken Soup with Barley* (1958), *Roots* (1959) and *I'm Talking about Jerusalem* (1960) which transferred readily to the Royal Court. *The Kitchen* (1959) and *Chips with Everything* (1962) were similarly autobiographical, drawing on the author's experiences as a chef in the RAF. Under Devine's successors the Royal Court maintained its commitment to 'new drama', fostering the work of David Storey (1933-) and Edward Bond (1934-). Bond's play *Saved* (1965) caused a populist rather than a critical furore in depicting a baby being stoned to death. The same author's *Early Morning* (1968) was set in a cannibalistic heaven. The addition of a Small Theatre Upstairs (1969)

provided a facility for staging low-budget new plays by unknown young writers.

In 1960 Peter Hall became director of the Shakespeare Memorial Company, based in Stratford Upon Avon. Within a year he had changed its name to the Royal Shakespeare Company, introduced long-term contracts for a core company and acquired a second, London base at the Aldwych, where he could mount modern plays and classics not written by Shakespeare. In 1962 he also ran an additional experimental season at the Arts Theatre. Successful Stratford productions were transferred to London and RSC troupes were sent to tour the world. In 1965 the company established Theatregoround, a stripped-down outfit suited to performing in halls, schools and factories. Hall also persuaded Peter Brook and Michel St. Denis to join him as associate directors.

St. Denis remained largely an *eminence grise* but Brook won a place in theatrical history with two productions in particular. *The Persecution and Assassination of Marat as Performed by the Inmates of the Asylum of Charenton under the Direction of the Marquis de Sade* (1964) – understandably abbreviated in common parlance to *Marat-Sade* – translated from the German of Peter Weiss, starred Patrick Magee, Ian Richardson and Glenda Jackson in a play-within-a-play of spectacular effects, rendered with an intensity that challenged the equanimity of the audience and, according to Jackson, the sanity of the players. Brook's swan-song before moving to Paris was an acrobatic take on *A Midsummer Night's Dream* set in an adult adventure playground complete with stilts, trapezes and conjurors.

Hall's expansionist policy soon turned the company's hard-won financial surplus into a deficit and increasing reliance on Arts Council grants. It also trebled audiences and massively boosted its reputation to make it a worthy rival to the National Theatre. New talents which emerged through the ranks included Ian Holm, Ian Richardson, David Warner, Janet Suzman and Glenda Jackson.

Trevor Nunn (1940-), who succeeded Hall in 1969, continued to blend revivals (*London Assurance* 1970) with premieres and opened studio theatres for experimental work at The Place (1971-4) off Euston Road and the Warehouse in Covent Garden (1977-82) as well as fostering such talents as Ben Kingsley, Patrick Stewart, Ian McKellen and Judi Dench. In Willy Russell's *Educating Rita* (1979), first presented at The Warehouse, the RSC continued its tradition of accidental success as it transferred to a long West End run and then a screen version, also starring the original Rita, Julie Walters. A nine-hour marathon adaptation of *Nicholas Nickleby* (1980) proved a legendary *tour-de-force*. Even the habitually barbed pen of critic Bernard Levin praised the adaption as "so richly joyous, so immoderately rife with pleasure, drama and entertainment, so life-enhancing ... so ... Dickensian." In 1982 the RSC relocated to a new

home in the Barbican and found itself with another unexpected hit on its hands, *Peter Pan*, which ran for three successive Christmases. Almost Nunn's final coup was the 1985 production of *Les Miserables*, a co-production with commercial management, which transferred to the Palace Theatre where it ran through the decade and beyond. In 1990, however, the RSC left the Barbican.

In 1968 the literary, left-wing MP Michael Foot, steered a Private Member's Bill through Parliament which abolished the powers of the Lord Chamberlain to ban or censor any play. One of the first fruits of the new atmosphere of 'liberation' was a proliferation of stage nudity, variously manifested in the imported American 'love-rock musical' *Hair!* (1968) and the domestically produced *Pyjama Tops* (1969) and *Oh! Calcutta!* (1970). In the longer run abolition eased the emergence of works addressing gay and lesbian concerns.

The rampant inflation of the 1970s and unbridled commercialism of the Thatcherite 1980s necessarily obliged the West End theatres to reassess their offerings. The advent of the wide-bodied long haul jet had further boosted London's unsolicited emergence as a global tourist venue and thus put a premium on shows which could appeal to audiences of which a substantial constituent had only a slender grasp of the English language. (A development unmistakably acknowledged by Sir Alec Guinness who adamantly shunned the West End stage). Musicals were an obvious answer and Andrew Lloyd Webber (1948-) proceeded to build a mega-fortune by supplying a seemingly endless stream of long-running spectaculars. His reputation had been established with *Joseph and the Amazing Technicolour Dreamcoat* (1968), which became a mainstay of school production efforts, and was confirmed by *Jesus Christ Superstar* (1970) and *Evita* (1976, revived 2006). These were followed by *Cats* (1981), *Starlight Express* (1984-2000), *The Phantom of the Opera* (1986) and *Aspects of Love* (1989).

Audiences with a fully competent command of English, by contrast, could avail themselves of

197. A revival of Andrew Lloyd-Webber's Evita *in 2006.*

While the 'Angry Young Men' of the 1950s challenged post-war Britain's comfort-seeking conformism by direct confrontation, the creators of the ground-breaking satirical review *Beyond the Fringe* opted for insouciant irreverence, nonchalantly lampooning venerated national institutions ranging from the royal family and the prime minister to Shakespeare and the veterans of World War Two. Written for the 1960 Edinburgh Festival, *Beyond the Fringe* was the product of a novel combination of Oxford and Cambridge talents. Peter Cook (1937-95) Of Pembroke College, Cambridge wrote most of the sketches, while Dudley Moore (1935-2002) of Magdalen College, Oxford contributed the musical parodies, accompaniments and interludes. Alan Bennett (1934-) and Jonathan Miller (1934-) set aside incipient careers in academia and medicine to perform. *Beyond the Fringe* transferred to London in May 1961 and, with a take-over cast, ran until 1964. The original cast took it to New York in October 1962 where another take-over cast carried it through until 1966. Prime Minister Harold Macmillan and President John F. Kennedy both went to see it.

Initially startled by their success, the four progenitors of what became labelled as 'the Sixties satire boom', each developed remarkable individual careers. As 'Pete and Dud' the lofty, public-school-educated Cook and diminutive scholarship boy from Dagenham 'Cuddly Dudley' Moore achieved cult status as TV sketch performers. Cook also founded London's first comedy club, became proprietor of *Private Eye* magazine and a writer and performer of unrivalled, if sometimes uneven, brilliance, posthumously honoured by a television poll as Britain's greatest ever comedic talent, a verdict endorsed by such disciples as the multi-talented Stephen Fry and Terry Jones of 'Monty Python' fame. A victim of ennui and alcohol, Cook is memorialised today by a foundation (www.petercook.org) devoted to helping young adults with learning difficulties. Moore, a classical organist and superb jazz pianist, became an Oscar-nominated film actor before succumbing to an horrific degenerative disease.

plays in which casts of modest size in sets of modest expense relied on verbal fireworks supplied by the likes of Tom Stoppard, Michael Frayn or, most bankable of all, Scarborough-based Alan Ayckbourn, who proved that, given the opportunity, he could out-sell Shakespeare at the National.

Economic considerations – in plain language cheapness – favoured the one-man shows of Australian humourist Barry Humphries or Roy Dotrice's personification of seventeenth-century pocket biographer John Aubrey's *Brief Lives*. Veteran farceur Ray Cooney proved that comedy could still be made to pay. Another tactic was the importation of sitcom stars from television, like Penelope Keith, or Hollywood stars, like Dustin Hoffman, who played *The Merchant of Venice* at the Phoenix in 1989. Following in his footsteps came Charlton Heston, Sharon Gless, Macaulay Culkin, Kathleen Turner and in 2006, Al Pacino, to play Shylock.

198. Four musicals which brought back audiences to London's theatres.

The self-deprecating Bennett, superficially the archetypical northern droll, became the outstanding television dramatist of his generation, an Oscar-nominated scriptwriter, unofficial Laureate of the desperate and depressed and a 'National Treasure'. The polymathic Miller dazzled as a television presenter, writer, lecturer, sculptor and challengingly cerebral opera director, honoured with a CBE and a knighthood. An unanticipated by-product of the collective success of these Oxbridge superstars was the perhaps belated recognition of the elite universities as an entry route to showbiz stardom, a path that was to become open to critics and writers like Clive James and Germaine Greer, as well as to performers.

New Theatres. New 'Spaces'

Attempts to establish new theatrical venues met with mixed fortunes. Perhaps their most interesting aspect has been their variety, ranging from the appropriation of a synagogue and a railway engine-shed, to purpose-built constructions in association with a library or a multi-storey car park, to a proliferation of 'pub theatres', to the revival or reconstruction of historic theatrical locations.

The Prince Edward in Old Compton Street reopened as a theatre in 1946 with a Christmas pantomime, *Mother Goose*, followed by a revival of Novello's *The Dancing Years* and seasons of revue. Adapted for wide-screen *Cinerama* (1954-74), the Prince Edward reverted to theatrical use for the Andrew Lloyd Webber-Tim Rice musical *Evita*, which ran for eight years, followed by another Lloyd Webber blockbuster, *Chess* and a Broadway transfer *Crazy for You*. A £3,500,000 refurbishment was subsequently justified by the success of the Abba tribute *Mamma Mia!*, followed by *Mary Poppins*.

The creation of the Mermaid Theatre was very much an act of faith on the part of its founder, actor-director Sir Bernard Miles (1907-91). It began in 1951 in an abandoned school hall at the back of his house in Acacia Road, St. John's Wood, converted to an Elizabethan style acting-space. The opening production was Purcell's opera *Dido and Aeneas*, featuring Kirsten Flagstadt, whose salary was a bottle of beer a day. This was followed by *The Tempest* and Middleton's *A Trick to Catch the Old One*. In 1953 to mark the coronation of H.M. Queen Elizabeth II, the Mermaid was given a temporary home in the Royal Exchange at the heart of the City of London. This proved so successful that a campaign was begun to establish a permanent Mermaid presence in the City. This involved taking over a bombed Victorian warehouse at Puddle Dock, Blackfriars and adapting it into a modern theatre, which was achieved by 1959. The Mermaid became noted for an adventurous eclecticism, ranging from Brecht, Shaw and O'Casey to Bill Naughton (*Alfie, Spring and Port Wine*) and a musical biography of Noel Coward (*Cowardy Custard*) which ran for a year. An optimistic, if architecturally unsympathetic, reconstruction (1978-81) and the adoption (1987) of the theatre as a second London home for R.S.C. productions proved, however, insufficient to maintain its viability. Despite such intriguing ventures as *A Midsummer Night's Dream* in kabuki style, spoken in Japanese, the Mermaid was eventually converted into a conference centre.

Hampstead Theatre, founded in 1959 by James Roose-Evans (1927-), committed itself to promoting the work of new writers and bringing international work to London, a policy vindicated in its very first season with its productions of Pinter's *The Room* and *The Dumb Waiter*, which transferred to the Royal Court. Subsequent notable productions have included works by Ionesco, Havel, Frayn and Friel. An ordained Anglican priest, Roose-Evans, who remained Artistic Director until 1971, made prize-winning adaptations of Helen Hanff's *84 Charing Cross Road* and Laurie Lee's *Cider with Rosie*, as well as founding a spiritual retreat in Wales and writing what became a standard text on *Experimental Theatre*, a series of children's books and other works on theatre and spirituality.

Originally based in Moreland Hall, the home of a local Scout troop, the Hampstead Theatre

199. The new Hampstead Theatre at Swiss Cottage.

moved into a Portakabin at Swiss Cottage in 1962 and in 1970 to new premises seating 157. The Hampstead's current – RIBA award-winning – home seats 325 with state-of-the-art disabled access and with its 'Michael Frayn Space' has acquired a subsidiary performance area and a venue for educational workshops and community activities.

Built on the site of the former London Opera House/ Stoll Picture Theatre/ Stoll Theatre, The Royalty in Portugal Street, Kingsway opened in 1960, became a cinema in 1961 but reverted to theatrical use for the nude revue *Oh! Calcutta* (1970-4) and the musical *Bubbling Brown Sugar* (1977). In 1981 it became a television studio.

In 1961 Arnold Wesker took over a disused early Victorian (1847) locomotive shed, known as the Round House (it had a turntable for turning round locomotives) at Chalk Farm, Camden Town to serve as the home of his projected 'Centre 42', a focal point for the diffusion of the arts with the backing of the trade unions (42 referring to an enabling TUC resolution in concurrent union discourse). Although that specific essay in utopian socialism foundered in what its supporters would doubtless have seen as the

wilderness of Wilsonian pragmatism, the Round House became a noted location for risky ventures, ranging from an experimental *Themes on the Tempest* (1968) by Peter Brook to works by Kafka, Genet and *Richard III* in Georgian

The Greenwich Theatre can trace its history as a place of entertainment back to the 1850s in the Large Room of the still adjacent Rose and Crown pub. Attached premises opened in 1871 as Crowder's Music Hall and were rebuilt in 1895 as the Greenwich Hippodrome. After use as a cinema (1924-49) the building became a warehouse and was threatened with demolition in 1962. Years of campaigning led to reconstruction and a reopening in 1969. The stability of the venture was guaranteed by an immediate succession of transfers to the West End - a musical biography of Marie Lloyd, *Sing a Rude Song*, John Mortimer's *A Voyage Round My Father*, Peter Nichols' *Forget-Me-Not-Lane* and Alan Ayckbourn's trilogy *The Norman Conquests*.

The Lyric Hammersmith proved another phoenix. Closed from 1939, reopened in 1944 by CEMA, the Lyric staged the first plays of both Harold Pinter (*The Birthday Party,* 1958) and John Mortimer (*Dock Brief* 1958) but closed in

200. The bar of the sadly-decayed Collin's Music Hall, Islington in the 1950s. Surrounded by mementoes of the past, the last customers paid for trashy shows and nude entertainment. Most of the theatre was destroyed by fire in 1958. In a building on part of the site with a facade remarkably like the old theatre is now a Waterstone's bookshop.

201. A welcome incentive to go to the theatre was the establishment of a cut-price ticket kiosk in Leicester Square.

1966. The exuberant Frank Matcham plasterwork of the interior was subsequently transferred to a new Lyric in King Street, opened in 1979. Down by the Thames in Hammersmith the Riverside Studios flourished for a decade as a London venue for avant-garde touring companies like Joint Stock and their counterparts from Poland (Tadeusz Cantor) and Italy (Dario Fo). Originally (1933) a film studio, latterly used for BBC recordings (*Dixon of Dock Green, Hancock's Half Hour*) the name of the Riverside later became synonymous with its restaurant, which specialised in Italian regional cooking.

The Shaw Theatre (1971), built by Camden Council as an integral part of a new library building on Euston Road, memorialises George Bernard Shaw's services as a local councillor for the borough of St. Pancras, which was absorbed in the newly-created London Borough of Camden in 1965. Its primary purpose, once it was built, was to provide a home for the National Youth Theatre, founded in 1956 by former actor and teacher Michael Croft (1986). Croft, appropriately, had been a teacher at Alleyn's School, a subsidiary of Edward Alleyn's foundation and the first intakes were drawn from his school and Dulwich College. The National Youth Theatre's resident dramatist Peter Terson wrote the most popular school play to date, *Zigger-Zagger* (1967), an exploration of emotion on the football terrace. NYT alumni include Sir Derek Jacobi and Dame Helen Mirren.

In 1971 at The King's Head, Islington American producer Dan Crawford opened a pub theatre in a back room seating 120. In 1975 Robert Patrick's *Kennedy's Children* transferred to the Arts Theatre as the first 'fringe theatre' production originating in a pub to go to the West End - and subsequently to Broadway and on tour across the USA. King's Head policy has, however, traditionally been less confrontational than many of the other pub theatres inspired by it and has concentrated on six-week runs with a penchant for mini-musicals.

202. David Drummond's theatrical memorabilia shop has been in Cecil Court, off Charing Cross Road, since 1967.

The Half Moon Theatre opened in an Aldgate synagogue in 1972, moved to a converted Methodist chapel at Stepney Green in 1979. It relocated, very slightly, to a new 400-seat theatre adjacent in 1983 and is now in Limehouse as a 'Young People's Theatre'.

The New London at the northern end of Drury Lane stands on the site of the 'Old Mo' music hall, subsequently the Winter Gardens Theatre, which was demolished in 1965. In 1973 it opened as part of a complex which included, typically for that period, a restaurant and a multi-storey car-park. Reduced to the role of a TV studio (1977-80), it found salvation in 1981 with an Andrew Lloyd Webber vehicle *Cats*, based on the poems of T.S. Eliot. To avoid confusion with the newcomer the New Theatre in St. Martin's Lane changed its name to the Albery - and has since become the Noel Coward.

Built (1837) as reading rooms and a lecture hall for Islington's Literary and Scientific Institution, what is now the Almeida Theatre was subsequently a music hall (1874), a Salvation Army facility (1904) and a factory for making carnival novelties (1956). Saved by its architecture (listed Grade II) as a by-product of

203. The new auditorium of the Almeida Theatre, Islington. Photo: Bridget Jones.

204. *The renovated and rejuvenated Old Vic. Completely refurbished by the generosity and enthusiasm of Ed Mirvish, it is now directed by the actor Kevin Spacey.*

Islington's renaissance as a desirable residential area, it opened as a theatre in 1980 as a venue for an annual international festival of contemporary music. In 1990 actors Jonathan Kent and Ian McDiarmid took over and within a decade made it an award-winning institution (forty-five awards by 2004), attracting a staggering roll-call of talent and outstanding performances – Diana Rigg as Medea (1994), Ralph Fiennes as Hamlet (1995), Kevin Spacey and Tim Piggott-Smith in *The Ice Man Cometh* (1998) ....

The reconstruction of Shakespeare's Globe on Bankside is almost entirely to the credit of Chicago-born Sam Wanamaker (1919-93, who established the Globe Playhouse Trust in 1970. At this time Bankside was a befouled and redundant confusion of wharves and warehouses entirely devoid of interest to tourists and, indeed, to most Londoners. In 1972 Wanamaker opened a temporary theatre in a tent there for a summer season which included a modern dress *Hamlet* by Keith Michell. In 1973 Vanessa Redgrave played Cleopatra in *Antony and Cleopatra* before the tent was wrecked by a storm. Undeterred, Wanamaker persisted with a

205. *The Donmar Warehouse in Covent Garden. A former banana warehouse, the Donmar was bought in 1961 as a ballet rehearsal studio by Donald Albery and Margot Fonteyn. Since 1992 it has been a self-styled 'producing theatre'.*

207. A local hero – a plaque commemorating Sam Wanamaker who, sadly, died before the completion of his project.

206. The gates to the rebuilt Globe on Bankside.

structure of tubular steel. By 1986 it was possible for Theo Crosby to begin drawing up designs for a reconstruction. A location, two hundred yards from the original site, was finally acquired in 1989. Construction began in 1993 and was completed in 1995. As far as possible materials and methods followed the standards of Shakespeare's day e.g. pegs not nails. Neither Theo Crosby nor Sam Wanamaker, however, lived to see their dream fulfilled. Wanamaker was, before his death, appointed Commander of the British Empire and honoured with an honorary doctorate by the University of London. There is also a memorial in his honour beneath the Shakespeare window in Southwark Cathedral. The official opening of the Globe by the Queen in 1997 was marked by a production of *Henry V*. Apart from Shakespeare the Globe Theatre Company has presented plays by Middleton, Fletcher and Dekker as well as visiting companies' versions of a Zulu *Macbeth*, a Cuban *Tempest*, a kathakali *King Lear* and a Japanese kyogen *Comedy of Errors*. Productions are complemented by extensive programmes of education and outreach and the world's most comprehensive exhibition about Shakespeare and his world – which, if not quite back to the beginning of this story, seems a fitting point of conclusion.

Chronology

1665   Red Bull demolished
        Nell Gwyn leads in John Dryden's *The Indian Queen*
1665-6 Great Plague closes theatres for sixteen months
1668   John Dryden *Essay of Dramatic Poesy*
1669   Nell Gwyn retires from the stage
1672   Theatre Royal, Drury Lane burned down (reopened 1674)
1674   William Wycherley *The Country Wife*
1675   John Dryden *Aurengzebe*
        Thomas Otway *Alcibiades*
1676   Sir George Etherege *The Man of Mode*
1678   John Dryden *All For Love*
1681   King's Company and Duke's Company merge as the United Company
1682   Thomas Otway *Venice Preserv'd*
1694   William Congreve *The Double Dealer*
1695   William Congreve *Love for Love*
        Thomas Southerne *Oroonoko*
1697   Sir John Vanbrugh *The Provok'd Wife*
        Sir John Vanbrugh *The Relapse*
1698   Jeremy Collier *A Short View of the Immorality and Profaneness of the English Stage*
1700   William Congreve *The Way of the World*
1705   Her Majesty's Theatre opened as the Queen's
1706   George Farquhar *The Recruiting Officer*
1707   George Farquhar *The Beaux' Strategem*
1708   Thomas Downes *Roscius Anglicanus*
1709   Nicholas Rowe's edition of Shakespeare
1717   John Rich inaugurates annual pantomimes
1719-20 Sir Richard Steele edits *The Theatre*
1720   Little Theatre in the Haymarket opened
1722   Sir Richard Steele *The Conscious Lovers*
1728   John Gay *The Beggar's Opera*
1729   Goodman's Fields theatre opened
1730   Colley Cibber appointed Poet Laureate
1731   George Lillo *The London Merchant*
1732   John Rich builds Theatre Royal, Covent Garden Theatre
        Goodman's Fields reopened after rebuilding
1733-4 Lewis Theobald's edition of Shakespeare
1737   Lord Chamberlain assumes responsibility for theatrical censorship
1740   Colly Cibber *An Apology for the Life of Mr. Colly Cibber, Comedian*
1741   Monument to Shakespeare unveiled in Westminster Abbey
        Charles Macklin plays Shylock
1742   David Garrick first appears at Theatre Royal, Drury Lane
1746   David Garrick becomes joint manager of Theatre Royal, Drury Lane
1765   Sadler's Wells rebuilt in stone
1766   David Garrick and George Colman the Elder *The Clandestine Marriage*
        Samuel Foote gains a limited patent for The Little Theatre in the Haymarket

1768   Edward Capel's edition of Shakespeare
1769   David Garrick's *The Jubilee*
1770   Grimaldi's first stage appearance, aged two, at Sadler's Wells
1775   R.B. Sheridan *The Rivals*
1777   R.B. Sheridan *The School for Scandal*
1779   R.B. Sheridan *The Critic*
1789   Boydell's Shakespeare Gallery opened in Pall Mall
1794   R.B. Sheridan rebuilds Theatre Royal, Drury Lane
1806   Adelphi Theatre opens as the Sans Pareil
1808   Covent Garden Theatre burns down
1809   Theatre Royal, Drury Lane burned down
1810   Debut of William Macready as Romeo
1812   Theatre Royal, Drury Lane reopened
        Sarah Siddons' farewell performance
1814   Edmund Kean's debut performance as Shylock at Theatre Royal, Drury Lane
1815   Sarah Siddons retired from the stage
1817   William Hazlitt *The Characters of Shakespeare's Plays*
        Lyceum and Drury Lane stages lit by gas
1818   William Hazlitt *A View of the English Stage*
        Coburg Theatre opened
1821   Theatre Royal, Haymarket rebuilt
        William Moncrieff's *Tom and Jerry* exceeds 100 consecutive performances
1823   J.R. Planche designs historically accurate costumes for Kemble's *King John*
1828   Grimaldi makes his last appearance on stage at Theatre Royal, Drury Lane
1834   Britain's first mechanical sinking stage installed at the Adelphi theatre
1837   William Macready takes over Covent Garden
1841   Dion Boucicault *London Assurance*
1843   Abolition of patent theatre monopoly
1844   Samuel Phelps becomes manager of Salder's Wells (to 1862)
1847   J. Maddison Morton *Box and Cox*
1848   London publisher Effingham Wilson proposes a National Theatre
1853   John Buckstone becomes manager of the Theatre Royal, Haymarket
1856   Covent Garden Theatre burns down
1860   Dion Boucicault *The Colleen Bawn*
1861   Dion Boucicault *The Octoroon*
        T.W. Robertson *Caste*
1863   Tom Taylor *The Ticket-of-Leave Man*
1864   T.W. Robertson *David Garrick*
1866   John Oxenford *East Lynne*
1870   Royal Court Theatre opened as the New Chelsea Theatre in a converted chapel
        Vaudeville Theatre opened
1871   Leopold Lewis *The Bells*
        Hengler's Grand Cirque opened
1874   Criterion Theatre opened
1875   G.H. Lewes *On Actors and the Art of Acting*

H.J. Byron *Our Boys* (to 1878 1,362 performances)
1878 Professional debut of Herbert Beerbohm Tree
Henry Irving takes over the Lyceum
1879 Comedie-Francaise visits London
1880 Emma Cons takes over the Coburg Theatre as the Royal Victoria Hall and Coffee Tavern
Squire Bancroft becomes manager at the Haymarket
1881 Savoy Theatre completely lit by electricity
Comedy Theatre opens as the Royal Comedy Theatre
Duke of Saxe-Meiningen visits London
1882 William *Archer English Dramatists of Today*
Playhouse Theatre opened as the Royal Avenue Theatre
1884 Prince of Wales Theatre opened as the Prince's Theatre (renamed 1886)
1885 Marie Lloyd makes music hall debut
Arthur Wing Pinero *The Magistrate*
Music Hall Artists' association formed
1887 Royal Court Theatre rebuilt
Beerbohm Tree becomes manager of the Haymarket Theatre
1888 William Archer *Masks or Faces?*
Lyric Theatre opened
1889 Garrick Theatre opened
Dan Leno makes his debut at Theatre Royal, Drury Lane
1890 George Alexander becomes manager of the St. James's Theatre
1891 Palace Theatre opened as the Royal English Opera House
J.T. Grein's Independent Theatre Society founded
1892 Brandon Thomas *Charley's Aunt*
Oscar Wilde *Lady Windermere's Fan*
Duke of York's Theatre opened as the Trafalgar Square Theatre
1893 Arthur Wing Pinero *The Second Mrs. Tanqueray*
Oscar Wilde *A Woman of No Importance*
Daly's Theatre opened
London debut of Eleanora Duse
1894 G.B.Shaw *Arms and the Man*
William Poel founds the Elizabethan Stage Society
1895 William Poel presents *Twelfth Night* in a reconstructed Elizabethan stage setting
Oscar Wilde *An Ideal Husband*
George du Maurier *Trilby*
Henry Irving knighted
1897 J.M. Barrie *The Little Minister*
Beerbohm Tree opens Her Majesty's Theatre
William Terriss murdered at the stage door of the Adelphi
Squire Bancroft knighted
Charles Frohman takes over the Duke of York's
1898 Coronet Theatre opened at Notting Hill Gate
1899 The Incorporated Stage Society founded
Wyndham's Theatre built

1900 G.B.Shaw *Captain Brassbound's Conversion*
First performance of John Milton's *Samson Agonistes*
Arthur Bourchier becomes manager of the Garrick Theatre (to 1915)
Japanese company at Coronet Theatre
1901 Apollo Theatre opened
1902 J.M.Barrie *The Admirable Crichton*
Licensing laws ban the sale of drink from a theatre auditorium
Charles Wyndham knighted
1903 Albery Theatre opens as the New Theatre
1904 J.M. Barrie *Peter Pan*
G.B.Shaw *John Bull's Other Island*
(Royal) Academy of Dramatic Art founded
London Coliseum opened with Britain's first revolving stage
1904-7 J.E. Vedrienne and H. Granville-Barker manage Royal Court Theatre
1905 G.B. Shaw *Man and Superman*
Dissolution of the Elizabethan Stage Society
Royal Academy of Dramatic Art moves to Gower Street
Aldwych Theatre opened
Scala Theatre opened
Actors' Union formed
Strand Theatre opened as the Waldorf (renamed 1909)
London debut of John Barrymore at the Comedy Theatre
1906 G.B.Shaw *The Doctor's Dilemma*
Globe (now Gielgud) Theatre opened as The Hicks (renamed 1909)
Variety Artists' Federation established
1907 Queen's Theatre opened
1908 Jerome K. Jerome *The Passing of the Third Floor Back*
1909 London debut of Sybil Thorndike
Beerbohm Tree knighted
First London performance of Chekhov's *The Cherry Orchard*
1910 John Galsworthy *Justice*
London Palladium opened as the Palladium (renamed 1934)
Harley Granville-Barker and William Archer – *The National Theatre: A Scheme and Estimates*
1911 Edward Gordon Craig *On the Art of the Theatre*
New Middlesex Theatre of Varieties opened
Shaftesbury Theatre opened as the Prince's Theatre
First Royal Command Variety Show held at the Palace Theatre
George Alexander knighted
1912 Lilian Baylis becomes manager of the Old Vic
1913 Desmond McCarthy becomes drama critic of the *New Statesman*
Beerbohm Tree *Thoughts and Afterthoughts*

Edward Gordon Craig *Towards a New Theatre*
Ambassadors Theatre opened
Sir Johnston Forbes-Robertson makes his farewell appearance

1914   Thomas Hardy *The Dynasts*
Lilian Baylis stages Shakespeare at the Old Vic
G.B. Shaw *Pygmalion*
C.B.Cochran presents revue *Odds and Ends*

1915-23 Old Vic becomes the first theatre in the world to stage all the plays in Shakespeare's First *Folio*

1915   *A Little Bit of Fluff* at the Criterion (1,241 performances)

1916   Entertainments Department of Armed Forces started
Harold Brighouse *Hobson's Choice*
St. Martin's Theatre opened
Coronet Theatre becomes a cinema
Frank Benson knighted by George V at Drury Lane with a props sword

1916-21 Frederick Norton *Chu-Chin-Chow* at Her Majesty's Theatre (2,238 performances)

1917   J.M.Barrie *Dear Brutus*
Frederick Lonsdale *The Maid of the Mountains*

1918   Nigel Playfair takes over the Lyric, Hammersmith (to 1934)
C.B. Cochran becomes manager of the London Pavilion (to 1931)

1919   Geoffrey Whitworth establishes the British Drama League
Arthur Bourchier becomes manager of the Strand Theatre
Actors' Association re-formed as a trade union

1920   Nigel Playfair revives *The Beggar's Opera* (1,462 performances)

1921   Clemence Dane *A Bill of Divorcement*

1923   William Archer *The Old Drama and the New*
William Archer *The Green Goddess*
James Agate becomes drama critic of *The Sunday Times* (to 1947)

1924   Noel Coward *The Vortex*
Sybil Thorndike leads in the first London production of Shaw's *Saint Joan* at the New (Albery) Theatre
Fortune Theatre opened
Westminster Theatre opened as St. James's Picture Theatre in a converted Chapel (theatre 1931)

1925   Ben Travers *A Cuckoo in the Nest*, the first of the 'Aldwych farces'
Noel Coward *Hay Fever*
Rose Marie at Theatre Royal, Drury Lane
Nigel Playfair *The Story of the Lyric Theatre, Hammersmith*
Ellen Terry appointed DBE
Paul Robeson's London debut in *The Emperor Jones* at the Ambassador's
Non, No, Nanette at the Palace Theatre (655 performances)

1926   Margaret Kennedy and Basil Dean *The Constant Nymph*
Ben Travers' *Rookery Nook*
Theatre Managers' Association formed

1927   Ben Travers' *Thark*
The Desert Song at Drury Lane

1928   R.C. Sherriff *Journey's End*
Nigel Playfair knighted
Show Boat at Theatre Royal, Drury Lane
Piccadilly Theatre opened

1929   Foundation of British Actors' Equity
Duchess Theatre opened
Savoy Theatre reconstructed
Lilian Baylis appointed Companion of Honour
A.A.Milne *Toad of Toad Hall*
Sean O'Casey *The Silver Tassie*

1930   Paul Robeson plays opposite Peggy Ashcroft in *Othello*
Rudolph Besier *The Barretts of Wimpole Street*
Apollo Victoria opened as the New Victoria Cinema
Cambridge Theatre opened
Phoenix Theatre opened
Prince Edward Theatre opened
Whitehall Theatre opened
Noel Coward *Private Lives*
Adelphi rebuilt

1931   Noel Coward *Cavalcade*
Ronald Mackenzie *Musical Chairs*
White Horse Inn at the Coliseum (651 performances)
The Land of Smiles at Drury Lane
J.B. Priestley *The Good Companions*
Sadler's Wells rebuilt
Sybil Thorndike appointed DBE

1932   First Crazy Gang Show at the London Palladium
Royal Court Theatre becomes a cinema
Gordon Daviot (Josephine Tay) *Richard of Bordeaux*

1933   Ashley Dukes opens the Mercury Theatre in Notting Hill Gate
Open Air Theatre opened in Regent's Park
J.B. Priestley *Laburnum Grove* (355 performances)

1934   Norman Marshall becomes director of the Gate Theatre
Gielgud's Hamlet plays a record 155 performances

1935   Ivor Novello *Glamorous Night*
Ronald Gow and Walter Greenwood *Love on the Dole*
Emlyn Williams *Night Must Fall*
George Robey plays Falstaff
Seymour Hicks knighted

1936   Ivor Novello *Careless Rapture*
Terence Rattigan *French Without Tears* at the Criterion Theatre (1,039 performances)
Unity Theatre Club established

Alhambra demolished

1937 Noel Gay *Me and My Girl* (1,046 performances)
J.B. Priestley *Time and the Conways*
Gerald Savory *George and Margaret*
Marie Tempest appointed DBE
Mile End Empire demolished

1938 Dodie Smith *Dear Octopus* includes last London appearance of Marie Tempest
Emlyn Williams *The Corn is Green* at the Duchess Theatre (to 1939)

1939 Ivor Novello *The Dancing Years*
Noel Coward *Design for Living*
T.S. Eliot *The Family Reunion*
Council for the Encouragement and Music and the Arts founded
ENSA formed
Criterion Theatre becomes a BBC sound studio (to 1945)
Old Vic closes (to 1950)

1940 Daphne du Maurier *Rebecca* at the Queen's Theatre (bombed out, closed to 1959)
Old Vic bombed

1941 Noel Coward *Blithe Spirit*

1942 Terence Rattigan *Flare Path* at the Apollo Theatre (to 1944) (670 performances)
Kesselring's *Arsenic and Old Lace* at the Strand Theatre (1,337 performances)
Prince Edward Theatre becomes the Queensbury All Services Club
Whitehall Follies features stripper Phyllis Dixie (to 1947)
Alec Clunes becomes Artistic Director of the Arts Theatre

1943 Noel Coward *Present Laughter*
Noel Coward *This Happy Breed*
Duke of York's Theatre reopened after bomb damage

1945 Walter Greenwood *The Cure For Love*
Ivor Novello *Perchance to Dream*

1946 Warren Chetham-Strode *The Guinea Pig*
Terence Rattigan *The Winslow Boy*
J.B. Priestley *An Inspector Calls*
Edith Evans appointed DBE
Arts Council incorporated

1947 Vivian Ellis and A.P.Herbert *Bless the Bride*
William Douglas Home *The Chiltern Hundreds* (to 1950)
John Dighton *The Happiest Days of Your Life*
Norman Marshall *The Other Theatre*
Annie Get Your Gun (to 1950)
Laurence Olivier and Ralph Richardson knighted
Harold Hobson becomes drama critic of the *Sunday Times* (to 1976)
Crazy Gang in residence at the Victoria Palace (to 1962)

1948 Terence Rattigan *The Browning Version*
Christopher Fry *The Lady's Not for Burning* at the

Arts Theatre

1949 Vivien Leigh leads in *A Streetcar Named Desire* at the Aldwych
National Theatre Bill allocates £1,000,000
Ivor Novello *King's Rhapsody* at the Palace Theatre (to 1951)

1950 Old Vic reopened
Brian Rix inaugurates 'Whitehall Farces' at the Whitehall Theatre (to 1967)
Terence Rattigan *Seagulls over Sorrento* at the Apollo Theatre (to 1950)
Roussin's *The Little Hut* at the Lyric Theatre (1,261 performances)

1951 Desmond McCarthy knighted
Bernard Miles founds the Mermaid Theatre in St. John's Wood
Foundation stone of National Theatre laid
J.C. Trewin *The Theatre since 1900*
Playhouse Theatre becomes a BBC studio (to 1975)

1952 Agatha Christie's *The Mousetrap* opens at the Ambassador's Theatre
Terence Rattigan *The Deep Blue Sea*
Frederick Knott *Dial 'M' for Murder*
Royal Court reopened as a theatre

1953 Wolf Mankowitz *The Bespoke Overcoat*
Sandy Wilson *The Boy Friend* (2,078 performances)
John Gielgud knighted
Theatre Workshop settles at Theatre Royal, Stratford

1954 Dorothy Reynolds and Julian Slade *Salad Days*, Vaudeville Theatre (2,329 performances)
Desmond McCarthy *Theatre*
George Robey knighted
Comedy Theatre reconstructed
Prince Edward Theatre converted to a cinema for wide-screen *Cinerama*

1955 Michael Croft founds National Youth Theatre
Michael Redgrave *The Actor's Ways and Means*
Sailor Beware at the Strand Theatre (1,231 performances)
Samuel Beckett *Waiting for Godot*

1956 English Stage Company established at the Royal Court Theatre
New Watergate Theatre Club established at the Comedy Theatre
John Osborne *Look Back in Anger*
New Cross Empire demolished
Peggy Ashcroft appointed DBE

1957 John Osborne *The Entertainer*
Norman Marshall *The Producer and the Play*
N.F. Simpson *A Resounding Tinkle*
Michael Flanders and Donald Swann *At the Drop of a Hat* at the Fortune Theatre (733 performances)
Donald Wolfit knighted

Willesden Hippodrome and Ilford Hippodrome demolished

1958 Harold Pinter *The Birthday Party*
Wolf Mankowitz *Expresso Bongo*
Brendan Behan *The Hostage*
Michael Redgrave *Mask or Face*

1959 Mermaid Theatre opened at Puddle Dock
John Arden *Serjeant Musgrave's Dance*
Frank Norman *Fings Ain't Wot They Used T'Be*
Bernard Miles and Lionel Bart *Lock Up Your Daughters*
Alec Guinness and Michael Redgrave knighted
John Gielgud reopens the Queen's Theatre with solo recital *The Ages of Man*

1960 Willis Hall and Keith Waterhouse *Billy Liar* (to 1962)
Harold Pinter *The Caretaker*
Robert Bolt *A Man For All Seasons*
Lionel Bart *Oliver!* (Runs at the New (Albery) Theatre until 1966)
Terence Rattigan *Ross*
Stephen Lewis *Sparrers Can't Sing*
Flora Robson appointed DBE
Peter Hall appointed director of RSC
The Aldwych Theatre becomes the London home of the RSC (to 1982)
Piccadilly Theatre reconstructed as the first London theatre with air-conditioning
Demolition of the Chiswick Empire, Woolwich Empire, Holborn Empire and Lewisham Hippodrome

1961 John Whiting *The Devils*
John Osborne *Luther*
Beyond the Fringe at the Fortune Theatre (1,184 performances)
The Sound of Music opened at the Palace Theatre (to 1967)
Tyrone Guthrie knighted

1962 David Ruskin *Afore Night Come*
Arnold Wesker *Chips With Everything*
Terence Rattigan's *Boeing-Boeing* at the Apollo Theatre (to 1965) (2,035 performances)

1963 Theatre Workshop, Stratford East *Oh What a Lovely War!*
A Funny Thing Happened on the way to the Forum (to 1965)
Laurence Olivier appointed director of the National Theatre
National Theatre Company established at the Old Vic (to 1976)
Mayfair Theatre opened
Metropolitan, Edgware Road demolished

1964 Joe Orton *Entertaining Mr. Sloane*
John Osborne *Inadmissible Evidence*
Edward Albee *Who's Afraid of Virginia Woolf?*

1965 Harold Pinter *The Homecoming*
Finsbury Park Empire demolished

1966 Unicorn Theatre for Children takes over the Arts Theatre
Joe Orton *Loot*
Noel Coward's last stage appearance in his *Suite in Three Keys* at the Queen's Theatre

1967 Peter Nichols *A Day in the Death of Joe Egg*
Tom Stoppard *Rosencrantz and Guildenstern are Dead*
Fiddler on the Roof at Her Majesty's (2,030 performances)
Margaret Rutherford appointed DBE

1968 Abolition of theatrical censorship
Hair opens at the Shaftesbury Theatre (1,997 performances)
Trevor Nunn becomes artistic director of the RSC (to 1989)
Tom Stoppard *The Real Inspector Hound*
Alan Bennett *Forty Years On* at the Apollo Theatre
The Secretary Bird at the Savoy Theatre
English National Opera (then Sadler's Wells Opera) moves to the Coliseum

1969 Bernard Miles knighted
Peter Nichols *The National Health*
There's A Girl in My Soup transfers from the Globe Theatre to the Comedy Theatre (2,547 performances)
Pyjama Tops at the Whitehall Theatre (to 1975, 2,298 performances)

1970 Noel Coward knighted
Sir Laurence Olivier appointed a Life Peer
Sam Wanamaker establishes the Globe Playhouse Trust
Young Vic Theatre Company established
Peter Brook's production of *A Midsummer Night's Dream*
Anthony Shaffer *Sleuth* at the St. Martin's Theatre (to 1973)
Christopher Hampton *The Philanthropist* (to 1973)

1971 Anthony Marriott and Alistair Fort *No Sex Please, We're British* (to 1987)
Trevor Nunn becomes director of the RSC
Living Theatre at the Roundhouse

1972 Bush Theatre founded
The Actors' Company founded
Lyric, Hammersmith demolished
Tom Stoppard *Jumpers*
Tim Rice and Andrew Lloyd Webber *Jesus Christ Superstar* opened at the Palace Theatre (to 1980)
Peter Brook *The Empty Space*

1973 Peter Shaffer *Equus*
Richard O'Brien *The Rocky Horror Show*
New Theatre renamed The Albery
New London Theatre opened
Ceiling of Shaftesbury Theatre collapses

1974 Joint Stock Theatre Group established
The Coliseum becomes the home of English

National Opera
Tom Stoppard *Travesties*
The Mousetrap transfers to the St. Martin's Theatre
Oh Calcutta! opens at the Duchess Theatre (to 1980, 3,918 performances)

1975 Alan Ayckbourn *The Norman Conquests* at the Apollo Theatre
Henry Fonda makes only West End stage appearance in solo play *Clarence Darrow*

1976 National Theatre opened
Terence Rattigan knighted

1977 Peter Hall knighted

1977-81 RSC at the Donmar Warehouse

1978 Tim Rice and Andrew Lloyd Webber *Evita* (to 1986)
Charles Strauss *Annie* (to 1982)

1979 Gate Theatre, Notting Hill founded
Lyric, Hammersmith reopened
Peter Shaffer *Amadeus*

1980 Ronald Harwood *The Dresser*
Howard Brenton *The Romans in Britain*
David Edgar/RSC *The Life and Adventures of Nicholas Nickleby*
New Victoria Cinema becomes the Apollo Victoria

1981 Andrew Lloyd Webber and Trevor Nunn *Cats*
Nell Dunn *Steaming*

1982 Barbican Centre opens
RSC moves to the Barbican
Ray Cooney *Run for your Wife* at the Criterion Theatre (to 1989)
Michael Frayn *Noises Off* at the Savoy (to 1986)

1983 Michael Hordern knighted
Andrew Lloyd Webber *Starlight Express* at the Apollo Victoria
Andrew Lloyd Webber's Really Useful Theatre Company buys Palace Theatre

1984 Theatre of Comedy Company buys the Shaftesbury Theatre
Anthony Sher plays Richard III for the RSC
National Theatre presents *Guys and Dolls*

1985 Anthony Quayle knighted

1985-94 *Me and My Girl* at the Adelphi

1986 Jonathan Miller *Subsequent Performances*
Phantom of the Opera opened at Her Majesty's Theatre
Les Miserables opened at the Palace Theatre (to 2005)

1987 Theatre Museum opened in Covent Garden
Jonathan Miller appointed Artistic Director of the Old Vic

1988 Judi Dench appointed DBE
National Theatre redesignated as Royal National Theatre

1989 Site of Globe Theatre rediscovered
Buddy (to 2002 5,140 performances)
Miss Saigon at Drury Lane ((4,263 performances)

1990 Almeida Theatre opened
Keith Waterhouse *Jeffrey Bernard Is Unwell*
Peter Ustinov knighted
Sam Mendes appointed Artistic Director of Donmar Warehouse
RSC at the Barbican closed by £4,000,000 deficit

1991 Ian McKellen knighted

1992 Dustin Hoffman plays Shylock at the Phoenix

1993 Anthony Hopkins knighted
Restoration of Art Deco features at the Adelphi

1994 Globe Theatre, Shaftesbury Avenue renamed the Gielgud
Oliver! at the Palladium (1,385 performances)
Derek Jacobi knighted

1996 The Reduced Shakespeare Company *The Complete Works of Shakespeare (abridged)*

1997 Trevor Nunn becomes director of the Royal National Theatre
Oficial opening of the Globe Theatre, Bankside

1998 Ian Holm and Michael Gambon knighted
Sixth Sadler's Wells opened

1999 Nigel Hawthorne knighted
The Lion King at The Lyceum

2000 Anthony Sher, Tom Courtenay and Peter Shaffer knighted
Paul Scofield appointed Companion of Honour
The Arts Theatre reopened
Really Useful Theatre Group purchases Stoll Moss Theatres Ltd

2001 *The Woman in Black* passes 5,000 performances at The Fortune

2002 *Starlight Express* closes after eighteen years
Cats closes after 21 years
RSC leaves the Barbican
Chitty Chitty Bang Bang opened at the Palladium

2003 Alan Bates knighted
Andrew Lloyd Webber *Bombay Dreams* at the Apollo Victoria
Hackney Empire restored
Nicholas Hytner takes over from Trevor Nunn at the National Theatre

2004 Prince of Wales theatre reopens after refurbishment
Alan Bennett *The History Boys*

2006 *Evita* revived at The Adelphi
Samuel Beckett Centenary season
Closure of the Theatre Museum announced by the V & A.

Further Reading

Richard Anthony Baker - *British Music Halls : An Illustrated History* (Sutton Publishing 2005)

Martin Banham (ed) - *The Cambridge Guide to Theatre* (Cambridge University Press 1992)

Ronald Bergan - *The Great Theatres of London* (Revised edition Andre Deutsch 2004)

Michael Billington - *Stage and Screen Lives* (Oxford University Press 2002)

Noel Coward - *Autobiography* (Methuen 1987)

Jonathan Croall - *Gielgud : A Theatrical Life* (Methuen 2001)

Jim De Young and John Miller - *London Theatre Walks* (2nd edition Applause 2003)

Andrew Gurr - *Playgoing in Shakespeare's London* (Cambridge University Press 1987)

Phyllis Hartnoll (ed) - *The Oxford Companion to the Theatre* (4th edition Oxford University Press 1983)

Ronald Harwood - *All the World's a Stage* (Methuen 1984)

Robert D. Hume (ed.) - *The London Theatre World 1660-1800* (Southern Illinois University Press 1980)

Hugh Hunt, Kenneth Richards, John Russell Taylor - *The Revels History of Drama in English Volume VII 1880 to the Present Day* (Methuen 1978)

Alan Kendall - *David Garrick : A Biography* (St. Martin's Press 1985)

Dennis Kennedy (ed.) - *The Oxford Encyclopaedia of Theatre and Performance* (Oxford University Press 2003)

William Kent - *London for Shakespeare Lovers* (Methuen 1934)

Raymond Mander and Joe Mitchenson - *The Theatres of London* (New English Library 1975)

James Shapiro - *1599 : A Year in the Life of William Shakespeare* (Faber and Faber 2006)

Elizabeth Sharland - *From Shakespeare to Coward : A Guide to Historic Theatrical London and the World Beyond* (Barbican Press 1997)

Dominic Shellard - *British Theatre Since the War* (Yale University Press 1999)

Simon Shepperd and Peter Womack - *English Drama : A Cultural History* (Blackwell 1996)

J.C. Trewin - *The Gay Twenties : A Decade of the Theatre* (Macdonald 1958)

J.C. Trewin - *The Turbulent Thirties : A Further Decade of the Theatre* (Macdonald 1960)

Simon Trussler - *Cambridge Illustrated History of British Theatre* (Cambridge University Press 1994)

Gavin Weightman - *Bright Lights, Big City : London Entertained 1830-1950* (Collins and Brown 1992)

Jean Wilson - *The Shakespeare Legacy : The Material Legacy of Shakespeare's Theatre* (Bramley Books 1995)

INDEX

An asterisk denotes an illustration or caption.